110 CBT TIPS and TOOLS

Proven Cognitive Behavioral Therapy Strategies for Working through Anxiety, Depression, Perfectionism, Anger, Regret, Stress, and More

Judith A. Belmont, MS
Bestselling author of the TIPS Series

110 CBT TIPS AND TOOLS
Copyright © 2025 by Judith A. Belmont

Published by
PESI Publishing, Inc.
3839 White Ave
Eau Claire, WI 54703

Cover and interior design by Amy Rubenzer
Editing by Chelsea Thompson

ISBN 9781683737933 (print)
ISBN 9781683737940 (ePUB)
ISBN 9781683737957 (ePDF)

All rights reserved.
Printed in the United States of America.

TABLE OF CONTENTS

Introduction ix

1. **Recovering from Low Self-Esteem: Kicking the Habit of Self-Criticism and Self-Doubt** 1
   - *TIP #1:* Treat Yourself Like Your Best Friend, Not Your Worst Enemy 3
   - *TIP #2:* Challenging Distorted Self-Talk 5
   - *TIP #3:* Challenging Your Negative Core Beliefs 8
   - *TIP #4:* Your Worth Never Changes 11
   - *TIP #5:* Goodbye to the Old Notion of Self-Esteem and Hello to Self-Compassion 13
   - *TIP #6:* Choose a Growth Mindset Over a Fixed Mindset 15
   - *TIP #7:* Use Affirmations to Change Self-Talk from Negative to Positive 17
   - *TIP #8:* Affirmation Practice 20
   - *TIP #9:* Tips to Cultivate an Attitude of Gratitude 22
   - *TIP #10:* Journaling Prompts for Self-Esteem 25
   - *TIP #11:* Self-Test to Embrace Your Greatness and Overcome Self-Doubt 27

2. **Challenge Depressive Thinking: Changing Thoughts to Change Your Life** 31
   - *TIP #12:* Learning and Recording Your Psychological ABCs 32
   - *TIP #13:* Recognizing Unhelpful Thinking with a Cognitive Distortion Log 34
   - *TIP #14:* Keeping a CBT Thought Log 38
   - *TIP #15:* Reframe Your Negative Thoughts from Permanent to Temporary 41
   - *TIP #16:* Be a Fact Checker: Get Rid of ANTs and Crack NUTs 43
   - *TIP #17:* Getting Down to Your Core Beliefs 45
   - *TIP #18:* Observe Your Thoughts with an Observing Head 48
   - *TIP #19:* Use Coping Cards for Any Occasion 50
   - *TIP #20:* Behavioral Activation and Activity Scheduling 54
   - *TIP #21:* A Menu of Activities to Improve Your Mood and Get Connected 59
   - *TIP #22:* Self-Test to Challenge and Eliminate Depressive Thinking 62

3. **Accepting Imperfections: Making Peace with Mistakes and Shortcomings** 65
   - *TIP #23:* Strive for Authenticity, Not Perfection 67
   - *TIP #24:* Strategies to Eradicate the "Shoulds" 69

- *TIP #25:* From Self-Criticism to Self-Compassion ... 71
- *TIP #26:* Thinking in Temporary, Not Permanent, Ways ... 73
- *TIP #27:* Lessons Learned from Successful Failures ... 75
- *TIP #28:* Inspiring Quotes from Successful Failures ... 77
- *TIP #29:* How Mistakes Can Change the World for the Better ... 79
- *TIP #30:* Trade in Your Perfectionistic Words ... 81
- *TIP #31:* Overcoming the Cognitive Distortions Resulting in Procrastination ... 83
- *TIP #32:* Practical Strategies to Get Yourself Going and Avoid Procrastination ... 87
- *TIP #33:* Self-Test to Accept Imperfections ... 90

4. **Coping with Anxiety and Worry: Calming Your Emotions by Calming Your Mind** ... 93
   - *TIP #34:* Using a Cognitive Distortion Diary to Manage Anxiety ... 95
   - *TIP #35:* Restructuring Your Cognitive Distortions ... 98
   - *TIP #36:* Coping with Anxiety Using Positive Reframing ... 101
   - *TIP #37:* Dialing Down Your Anxiety ... 103
   - *TIP #38:* Cope with Anxiety with Coping Cards ... 106
   - *TIP #39:* Be a Mindful Spectator of Your Thoughts ... 109
   - *TIP #40:* Eliminate the ANTs and Crack the NUTs ... 111
   - *TIP #41:* Exposure Techniques to Confront Anxiety ... 114
   - *TIP #42:* CBT Problem-Solving Using IDEAS ... 118
   - *TIP #43:* Using Quotes and Positive Affirmations to Quell Anxiety ... 122
   - *TIP #44:* Self-Test to Cope with Anxiety and Calm Your Mind ... 125

5. **Overcoming Guilt and Regret: Finding Ways to Forgive Yourself and Stop Ruminating and Reworking the Past** ... 129
   - *TIP #45:* Using the Double Standard Technique ... 131
   - *TIP #46:* Challenge Cognitive Distortions by Cognitive Restructuring of Regrets ... 133
   - *TIP #47:* Even More Techniques for Cognitive Restructuring ... 135
   - *TIP #48:* Using Positive Reframing for a Fresh Take on Regret ... 138
   - *TIP #49:* How to Stop Reading Old News Like It Belongs on the Front Page ... 140
   - *TIP #50:* Embrace the Three Basic Components of Self-Compassion ... 142
   - *TIP #51:* Write a Compassionate Letter to Yourself ... 145
   - *TIP #52:* Self-Reflect on Guilt and Regret ... 147
   - *TIP #53:* Self-Forgiveness Check-In ... 150
   - *TIP #54:* Use Self-Forgiveness Affirmations ... 152
   - *TIP #55:* Self-Test to Overcome Guilt and Regret ... 154

6. Managing and Growing from Stress: Learning to Be a Stress Manager and Not a Stress Carrier .. 157

- **TIP #56:** Make Stress Your Friend 159
- **TIP #57:** The 7 Cs of Stress Resilience 161
- **TIP #58:** Accept That Life Is Like Swiss Cheese 164
- **TIP #59:** Keep a Stress Diary 166
- **TIP #60:** Humor Check-In 169
- **TIP #61:** Triggers, Triggers . . . and More Triggers 171
- **TIP #62:** Moving from Posttraumatic Stress to Posttraumatic Growth 175
- **TIP #63:** Ten Ways to Move Forward No Matter What 179
- **TIP #64:** Fifteen Tips for Emotional Resilience 182
- **TIP #65:** Have Goals That Are Bigger-Than-Self 185
- **TIP #66:** Self-Test for Managing and Growing from Stress 188

7. Managing Anger: Control Your Anger So You Won't Lose Control 191

- **TIP #67:** The Benefits of Separating Thoughts and Feelings 193
- **TIP #68:** Learning Communication Skills to Express Anger Assertively 195
- **TIP #69:** No One Makes You Feel Angry—You Own Your Feelings! 197
- **TIP #70:** Avoid Put-Downs Disguised as Questions 200
- **TIP #71:** Anger Is Not Aggression! 201
- **TIP #72:** Anger-Producing Cognitive Distortions 203
- **TIP #73:** Strategies for Keeping Anger in Check 205
- **TIP #74:** Keeping an Anger Log 209
- **TIP #75:** Writing a Letter to Move Past Anger and Toward Forgiveness 211
- **TIP #76:** Quiz: How Forgiving Are You? 213
- **TIP #77:** Self-Test to Manage Your Anger 215

8. Improving Interpersonal Relationships: Increasing Empathy and Improving Assertive Communication Skills 219

- **TIP #78:** Recognizing Styles of Communication 220
- **TIP #79:** Using "I" Messages and Avoiding "You" Messages 224
- **TIP #80:** Assertive Rights and Responsibilities 226
- **TIP #81:** Be NICE 228
- **TIP #82:** Communication Pitfalls to Avoid 230
- **TIP #83:** The Underlying Reasons for Aggressive and Non-Assertive Behavior 233
- **TIP #84:** How to Listen—and Not Just Hear! 235
- **TIP #85:** Handy Guide to Effective Communication 237

- TIP #86: Comparing Effective Communication and Ineffective Communication ... 241
- TIP #87: Forgiveness Check-In ... 244
- TIP #88: Self-Test for Improving Interpersonal Relationships ... 246

9. Staying Mindful: Learning to Be Present with Nonjudgmental Awareness ... 249

- TIP #89: Take a Mindful Moment ... 250
- TIP #90: Develop a Beginner's Mind ... 252
- TIP #91: Be an Observer of Your Thoughts ... 254
- TIP #92: Use Cognitive Defusion Visualizations ... 256
- TIP #93: The Gift of Radical Acceptance ... 257
- TIP #94: Using Visualizations for Radical Acceptance ... 259
- TIP #95: Mindfulness-Based Relaxation and Calming Practices ... 261
- TIP #96: Gratitude Prompts and Putting Gratitude into Action ... 264
- TIP #97: Mindful Conversation ... 267
- TIP #98: Mindful Self-Compassion ... 269
- TIP #99: Self-Test on Staying Mindful ... 271

10. Wellness Tips for a Happier You: Going from Surviving to Thriving ... 275

- TIP #100: Develop Happiness Traits ... 276
- TIP #101: Emotional Wellness Inventory ... 279
- TIP #102: Using a Metaphorical Toolkit for Personal Growth and Resilience ... 281
- TIP #103: Mindset Matters: Shift from a Fixed Mindset to a Growth Mindset ... 283
- TIP #104: How Grateful Are You? Take This Attitude of Gratitude Quiz ... 286
- TIP #105: Set a Positive Intention Each Day ... 288
- TIP #106: Using Quotes for Growth and Empowerment ... 290
- TIP #107: Prioritize Self-Care Strategies with a Self-Care Inventory ... 293
- TIP #108: Practical Goal-Setting Strategies ... 298
- TIP #109: Review, Reflect, and Renew ... 300
- TIP #110: Self-Test for a Happier You ... 302

Concluding Remarks ... 305
References ... 306
About the Author ... 307

INTRODUCTION

Welcome! Thank you for your interest in learning how cognitive behavioral therapy (CBT) can improve your own life as well as the lives of others. Whether you are a mental health professional looking for resources for your clients, are a therapy client yourself, or are seeking skills for self-help, you'll find practical, easy-to-understand tips and resources for incorporating CBT strategies into your work and life. Just as a real-life toolbox provides hobbyists and professionals an array of tools to fix things, the tips in this book are designed to be figurative tools for fixing common issues that affect our mood and sense of well-being.

This book is a natural outgrowth of my four-book *TIPS and Tools for the Therapeutic Toolbox* series, as well as my other self-help books and therapeutic card decks. It makes an ideal companion book for clients working on lessons that their therapist has drawn from any of the *Therapeutic Toolbox* titles, particularly the two group therapy books in the series. It builds on my previous work to crystallize the most important topics and resources for common problems that lead people to seek therapy.

About CBT

The focus of CBT is in the name itself: *cognitive behavioral therapy*. "Cognitive" points to the importance of understanding our cognitions, or thoughts, to change unhealthy patterns of thinking that lead to common problems, such as anxiety, depression, and low self-esteem. CBT recognizes that many of our disturbing emotions are caused by problems in the way we *think*, so focusing on identifying, disputing, and changing these thoughts can help us *feel* different. It is much easier to identify toxic thought patterns and learn skills to combat disturbing thoughts than to focus on altering feelings, which cannot be changed directly. For example, trying to talk ourselves or a client out of feeling a certain way would be pointless as well as inappropriate and dismissive. Conversely, identifying and then challenging our upsetting thoughts helps us gain power over unhelpful and disturbing emotions.

What's more, our behavior results from the thoughts and feelings we have, which means CBT helps us shift not only how we feel but what we *do*, including how we engage with the world and people around us. CBT is an active approach; practicing skills and putting thoughts into action is the key to bringing emotional relief. This type of therapy stresses the importance of new ways of thinking. After all, your old way of thinking will not give you new solutions. You can literally change your life by changing your thoughts!

The following diagram, often referred to as the "cognitive triangle," summarizes the crux of CBT. When we distinguish between our thoughts, feelings, and behaviors and see how they affect one another, we can clarify how our thoughts that are triggered by events affect our feelings and cause us to act a certain way. Generally speaking, situations themselves don't make us feel a certain way. For example, you might say your critical boss stresses you out, but the stress results from what you are thinking about your boss's words or actions. Or perhaps you're feeling stressed after seeing snow predicted in the weather report. Outside events such as snow do not really have the power to stress you out directly—it is what you tell yourself about the situation that will cause you to have feelings of annoyance or anxiety. Someone who loves to ski might be excited about the forecast, while someone who is not fond of shoveling will interpret the prospect of a snowfall differently.

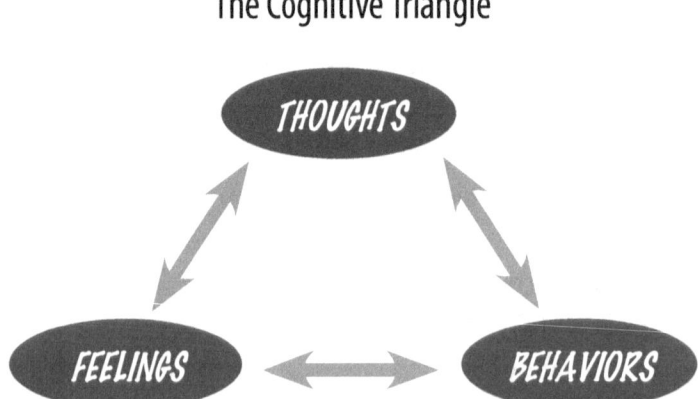

CBT is the world's most widely used treatment for common mental health issues such as anxiety, depression, and low self-esteem. The beauty of CBT is that it can be applied to just about any challenging situation due to its focus on life skills training—you certainly do not need to have a clinical disorder to benefit from learning CBT skills. We all face challenges in daily living, and CBT provides the framework and tools to help us manage our thoughts in order to better manage life.

How to Use This Book

The book comprises 10 chapters focusing on common emotional and mental health problems or relevant CBT topics. Each chapter features a brief overview of the importance of the topic, including an inspirational quote, followed by 11 topic-specific experiential tips—or TIPs, as I style them, which stands for **t**heory, **i**mplementation, and **p**rocessing. Each TIP concludes with an affirmation to serve as an encouraging reminder to retain and practice what you've learned. The last TIP of each chapter includes a self-test meant to summarize, crystallize, and reinforce the topics and takeaways of that chapter.

Here is a closer look at how the TIPs are broken down to make their lessons clear and concise:

- **Theory:** Introduction of the importance and relevance of the skill
- **Implementing skills:** Behavioral interventions such as worksheets, handouts, guided imagery exercises, activities, and self-tests that build skills for solving common mental health problems
- **Processing the activity:** Brief summary and reflections on the importance of the skill for strengthening mental health and wellness

Each TIP is self-contained so you can easily skip to the lessons you need most by perusing the table of contents. The resources in the book are all reproducible; I suggest filling out the activities on a copied page so you always have a clean version to revisit personally or with clients.

I recommend that you frequently revisit the TIPs that you found helpful and do the activities again and again. CBT skill building is not meant to be a one-and-done practice. Just as a physical exercise regimen requires regular repetition to really make changes in our level of physical fitness, the CBT skills in this book need to be repeated and practiced often to improve your habits of thinking. To further the analogy, starting an exercise or CBT routine might be very difficult at first, but repetition and practice makes the exercises easier and less challenging with time.

In a literal toolbox, not all the tools are useful to solve every need. A screwdriver cannot do the job of a hammer. Likewise, some activities in this book will be useful to you for certain challenges you or your clients face, while others might not be immediately relevant. It should also be noted that while CBT is very helpful for facilitating new coping skills, if you as an individual find that your symptoms and mental distress do not improve with learning various skills in this book, it's recommended that you seek the help of a mental health professional. No matter how many tools you have at your disposal, human beings need support from others to build a road to well-being, and at times this effort might require a trusted professional. In addition, there are times that medication or other interventions will be important parts of an effective treatment plan.

My wish is that the 110 TIPs and tools in this book will become valuable resources that lead to personal and professional growth. Thank you for allowing me to be your guide in improving your thoughts to improve your life!

CHAPTER 1

Recovering from Low Self-Esteem: Kicking the Habit of Self-Criticism and Self-Doubt

Low self-esteem is the breeding ground of many mental health disorders, such as anxiety, depression, eating disorders, and substance abuse. It results from a nagging, critical voice in your head telling you that you are damaged, inferior, not good enough, or just plain unworthy. Those with low self-esteem tend to compare themselves to others unfavorably and are more likely to find ways to beat themselves up rather than boost themselves up. This tendency in turn leads to isolation, avoidant behaviors, and self-protectiveness, which ironically only serve to make the internal hurt more persistent.

Low self-esteem is not just an inside job—all too often it affects our relationships with others negatively and leads to difficulties in school and work. Fear of disapproval and anxiety over potential rejection can lead to distancing, neediness, or both. Those with low self-esteem look to others for approval and validation of their worth instead of finding it within. Unfortunately, unless there is a sense of inner confidence, self-love, and unconditional self-acceptance, there will always be a neediness for approval and worries about what others think. No amount of outward success will ever quell the inner critic or fill the void inside.

While insight alone will not help you shed your self-critical habits, considering how you got there might offer some useful information. Maybe you have had experiences in the past that resulted in a judgmental and critical self-view and inner voice. If you have low self-esteem, it is safe to guess that most people from your past who contributed to it likely had low self-esteem themselves. Often, well-meaning caregivers who set the stage for low self-esteem were doing their best to teach and nurture but might have been reeling from their own set of unresolved trauma and mental health issues. After all, people cannot give others what they don't have to give in the first place.

When most people think of self-esteem, they think of it as resulting from defining themselves as having better-than-average characteristics, such as being smart, successful, attractive, or popular . . . or all of the above! The problem with that notion is that it makes self-esteem conditional—to have it, you need to excel in most (or at least some) areas of your life. Where does that leave everyone else? Are all "below-average" people doomed to low self-esteem? The answer is *Of course not!* Many people who are smart and accomplished, who seemingly "have it all," are not happy people, while others who are not as accomplished, wealthy, or popular are content with their lot.

That does not mean we should not try to excel or improve ourselves. The problem arises when we define our worth by those measures. Self-worth comes in all shapes and sizes to people with all shapes and sizes and abilities. You don't have to be the most attractive or the wealthiest person in your social group, or have the smartest children or the best house on the street, to have a strong sense of self-worth.

In this chapter we will explore how to cultivate true self-esteem, not the conditional kind. You will learn how to quell your nagging self-doubt and how you can love yourself without strings attached.

Regardless of where low self-esteem, nagging self-doubts, and a negative inner voice originate, CBT focuses on building skills and empowering yourself. It does not focus on blaming others for how you got there. Instead, it helps you move from being a *victim* to being a *victor*. CBT gives 100 percent of the control to the individual to move forward by unlearning unhealthy patterns and embracing a healthier self-view. CBT teaches skills that help turn the inner critic into an inner cheerleader.

"You yourself, as much as anybody in the entire universe, deserve your love and affection."

–Buddha

Treat Yourself Like Your Best Friend, Not Your Worst Enemy

Theory

If you have low self-esteem, you likely talk to yourself in ways you would never use when talking to anyone else. When you reserve the rudest, most critical comments for yourself, how can you see yourself as a good friend? After all, the longest and closest relationship you will ever have in your life is your relationship with yourself. Use this as a wakeup call to treat yourself better than ever!

Implementing Skills

Reflect on these questions:

How do you speak to yourself? Do you speak to yourself in self-downing ways, saying things that you would never even think of saying to anyone else? If so, how?

_____
_____
_____

Do you listen more often to your inner nurturer or your inner bully?

_____
_____
_____

What do you say to yourself that continues to beat you up and keep you down?

_____
_____
_____

Are you haunted by certain things that you have done in the past, perceived flaws that you have, or missteps you made that you just cannot forgive? If so, what are they?

_____
_____
_____

If you have problems with self-esteem, chances are that you answered these questions in a self-deprecatory way. There's a strong likelihood that you are unforgiving toward yourself and treat yourself worse than you would anyone else. You might even think you deserve this harsh treatment, considering how many times you've failed, screwed up, or "blown it." If you just can't seem to stop treating yourself so unkindly, try the following visualization.

Reflect for a moment on a person in your life that you truly love and admire. Who is it? What is it about them that you admire and respect? Now, imagine this person that you love confides in you that they say the same things to themselves as you have written on the preceding lines. How would you respond? Chances are you would be supportive and reassuring, instead of critical and unforgiving. Imagine what you would say to that person. How would you be supportive of this person you so admire? How would you try to soothe and nurture them?

_____
_____
_____

Now imagine that person becomes you. Can you see yourself in the same way as someone you most admire, flaws and all? If not, why not? If you can, how does it feel? How does it feel to be soft, compassionate, and forgiving to yourself? How does it feel to treat yourself like a dear friend?

_____
_____
_____

Keep in mind that loving yourself is an important step to being able to love others in a healthy way. How about reminding yourself why you are so lovable?

_____
_____
_____

Processing the Activity

Reflecting on the questions in this TIP will help you gently shift your perspective of yourself to one of a compassionate friend. You are the only person who will be with you throughout your whole life, from start to finish. Don't you deserve to build yourself up rather than tear yourself down?

"My relationship with myself is the longest relationship I will ever have, and I will treat it with more care moving forward."

Challenging Distorted Self-Talk

Theory

CBT is known for *thought disputing*, which is the act of replacing negative and distorted thinking habits with more factual, positive thoughts. Low self-esteem is so often based on distorted and negative self-talk, and the following exercise will help you start to turn around negative self-downing talk and instead cultivate self-talk that is healthier and more rational. This TIP will show the importance of being a "thought detective." It will help you notice when your thoughts are off track so you can shift your perspective to look at the same problem in a more solution-oriented way. (In TIP #13 we will take this important concept of CBT a step further in focusing on identifying the common cognitive distortions that twist our thinking.)

Implementing Skills

In the following table, distorted and negative self-talk—the kind of thinking that leads to low self-esteem—is replaced by healthier alternatives. Since thoughts so often precede our emotions, also in this table are the emotions that are likely to result from changing those thoughts into healthier alternatives.

Challenging Distorted Self-Talk

Distorted Self-Talk	Resulting Feelings	Healthier Self-Talk	Resulting Feelings
I am defective	Depressed, sad, hopeless	I have had setbacks but I have the power to make my life better now	Hopeful, optimistic
I am unlikable	Depressed, inferior	I have many good qualities and I am working to like myself	Confident, positive
I should have known	Regretful, guilty	I forgive myself for my mistakes and will learn from them	Positive, empowered

Distorted Self-Talk	Resulting Feelings	Healthier Self-Talk	Resulting Feelings
I can't handle stress	Overwhelmed, stressed	I can handle what is challenging and I will grow from the challenges	Motivated, resilient
My childhood will always affect me	Hopeless, depressed	I have more clarity and can change	Optimistic, hopeful
I cannot change how I react	Stuck, defeated	I can react differently now with the new tools I am learning	Empowered, energized
I am not smart enough	Down, depressed	I am smart and capable in many ways	Self-loving, motivated

Now It's Your Turn

Using the template on the next page, write down examples of your own negative self-talk that undermines your self-esteem and the resulting feelings, and then replace the negative irrational thoughts with healthier alternatives and note the resulting feelings.

For more help in rethinking your negative and irrational thoughts, use the technique of *relabeling*. Take a sheet of adhesive-backed labels and on each one write a negative thought that you tell yourself about yourself. Let's take the first example in the previous table: "I am defective." Write that label on a piece of paper. Then take another label and write the healthier self-talk: "I have had setbacks but I have the power to make my life better now." Put that label over the initial label. This will be a great practice for relabeling your thoughts!

Processing the Activity

This TIP is an introduction to how thought disputing can help you change your thoughts to change your life. Notice how the distorted self-talk reveals a lot of dramatic, all-or-nothing thoughts that are not grounded in fact, whereas the healthier self-talk is more specific and factual.

"I will reframe and relabel my self-sabotaging self-talk
so that I can reclaim my sense of self-worth."

Challenging My Distorted Self-Talk

Distorted Self-Talk	Resulting Feelings	Healthier Self-Talk	Resulting Feelings

Challenging Your Negative Core Beliefs

Theory

The concept of *core beliefs* is central to the CBT framework. Core beliefs are fundamental self-statements and interpretations about ourselves, others, and the world that underlie how we interpret events in our lives. For example, those with low self-esteem often hold on to a core belief that they are unlovable, unlikable, pathetic, damaged, or inferior. Those core beliefs in turn cultivate negative interpretations of everyday events, leading to fear of speaking up, fear of rejection, and self-consciousness in social situations. These anxiety-provoking situations further lead to a never-ending cycle of negative, self-sabotaging thoughts and behaviors.

All too often, people get stuck in focusing on how they learned these self-sabotaging messages in the first place: critical parents and caregivers, bullies in school, being teased by siblings, having been socially and romantically rejected, and so on. Sure, there are some fundamental reasons for how we learned to not trust ourselves and our worth, and how we got the idea that we were not likable or good enough, but making those connections does not change those erroneous core beliefs altogether. Hurts from the past are to be learned from, not to be relived again and again.

That is the beauty of CBT. CBT honors trauma and the hurt we feel from learning harmful core beliefs, but it focuses on giving us the tools to change our core beliefs now.

Implementing Skills

Think of an onion that has many layers to peel to get to the inner core. Our core beliefs are like the core of the onion, and our negative thoughts are the layers.

This analogy shows how one negative core belief will taint your reactions to multiple situations in everyday life. It also shows the power of how challenging and replacing that negative core belief will help you love and accept yourself and your place in the world. If you get distracted by anxiety about everyday life issues, such as worrying about what you say, how you say it, and how people react to you, you won't get to the root of those anxious thoughts—an overall underlying sense that you are flawed and not good enough. By digging deep into your underlying self-talk, you can tackle the symptoms of low self-esteem and manage your reactions in a healthier way.

The good news is that core beliefs are learned—so they can be unlearned.

The Low Self-Esteem Cycle

Triggering Situation	Core Belief	Resulting Negative Beliefs	Emotions	Behaviors
Going to a party where I will not know many people	I'm unlikable	I'm not one of the "beautiful people" here	Anxious	Do not make eye contact
	I'm inferior	No one is attracted to me	Depressed	Sit in a corner isolated
	I'm not an interesting person	It's too painful to be rejected; people are probably pitying me	Dejected	Leave abruptly; binge drink/eat when I get home

Here are some examples of how we can tackle those core beliefs with more rational self-talk, leading to the positive self-esteem cycle shown in the next table.

Challenging Self-Talk

- "Some people like me—there are always people that will and will not like me. That does not define my worth as a person."
- "I need to work on liking myself and the rest will fall into place."
- "What others think of me is much less important than how I view myself, and I will work to chip away at my irrational thoughts. I have control over this."
- "I know I have some issues to work on, but I am a good person with good values."
- "I tend to get anxious when I go to parties alone. It makes me feel more isolated and exaggerates by low self-worth."
- "I am just as worthy as anyone else, even if I am less confident. I am not inferior to anyone."
- "I have identified my low self-confidence issues and will make small attempts to overcome my limitations."
- "I will learn from this situation and get the social support I am seeking."

The Positive Self-Esteem Cycle

Triggering Situation	Core Belief	Resulting Positive Beliefs	Emotions	Behaviors
Going to a party where I will not know many people	I'm likable	I will make an effort to meet others	Confident	Make eye contact
		I will initiate conversation with others to meet new people	Excited	Initiate conversation; talk and laugh with others
		I will work to improve my social skills	Hopeful	Try new skills to "break the ice"
	I'm valuable	I have a lot to offer others	Motivated	Smile at people
		I am just as good as others	Confident	Go up to new people and initiate conversation; ask for someone's number to make social plans

Processing the Activity

You can see that a negative core belief underlies a multitude of negative thoughts, negative feelings, and maladaptive behaviors. This can result in a never-ending cycle unless the core beliefs are examined and challenged. Core beliefs need to be unlearned, challenged, and defeated. As a result, the behaviors also change for the better.

Our perceptions shape our sense of reality and our view of ourselves. In the CBT model, if you accept your unhealthy core beliefs without question, your perceptions will be muddy and unclear. You will continue to see yourself and the world through figuratively smudgy glasses.

In many cases, the greatest change you can make in your life is changing your mind. Challenging your negative core beliefs will stop hundreds of offshoot negative interpretations of everyday life. In TIP #16, we will go further into how to uncover and get to the bottom of your core negative beliefs using the "downward arrow" technique.

"I will work to identify the negative core beliefs that I have learned which are faulty. I deserve better."

Your Worth Never Changes

Theory

No one questions the worthiness of a newborn child. As we grow older, mistakes are inevitably made and imperfections can become quite pronounced, yet it is important to note that inner worth never varies. We are just as valuable and worthy as the day we were born. However, those with low self-esteem compare themselves to others and to their own expectations of themselves that did not materialize. This judgmental nonacceptance of themselves brings them further and further away from realizing their own intrinsic value, flaws and all.

Implementing Skills

Here are some visualizations and demonstrations to remind us of our intrinsic worth.

The Dollar Bill Demonstration

This exercise is one of my tried-and-true favorites for demonstrating that we all are just as worthy as the day we were born, despite how much we might feel crushed, crumpled, and worn down by life. Take a bill of any denomination that you have in your purse or wallet. Without actually tearing up the bill, give it some wear and tear by creasing it, crushing it, stepping on it, or tossing it around. When you are finished, flatten out the bill. Despite having more folds, wrinkles, and creases, note that the bill is still worth the same amount. This is a great analogy when applied to our own self-worth. No matter how stepped on and crumpled we feel in life, our worth never really changes.

Visualize Yourself as a Newborn Baby

When we see a newborn baby, we tend to see them as beautiful and worthy human beings, and do not judge them against other newborns in the nursery. Each of us is still the same beautiful person who came into this world so innocent and full of promise, no matter how much we may have gone astray since then. For this exercise, visualize yourself as a newborn or actually look at a picture of yourself as a very young child. Ask yourself, *What makes me less worthy now than this beautiful young child?* When we see a newborn or young child, we don't expect that beautiful being to live a flawless life. Why don't we give ourselves the same leeway now to be seen as beautiful, flaws and all?

We All Have a Gem Inside of Us

A polished stone or gem bought from a craft store will provide a great visual reminder of your intrinsic worth. Keep this gem with you as a touchstone throughout the day, reminding you that you are worthy. Every time you touch this stone, think of one positive thing about yourself to remind yourself that you are special and worthy. This activity will help to balance out the negative self-talk that robs you of the chance to embrace your greatness.

Processing the Activity

These visualizations will be helpful in quieting the inner critic and learning to believe in yourself and your worth once again. Since negative self-talk and nagging self-doubt can be very persistent, practice these visualizations often to counteract that judgmental voice inside of you. Appreciate the beauty within you that has never really left.

"No matter how imperfect I am or how worn I feel, I will not lose sight
that I am a beautiful person who deserves love and goodness in my life."

Goodbye to the Old Notion of Self-Esteem and Hello to Self-Compassion

Theory

Many people see self-esteem as a result of being successful, "above average," better than others at some things. However, we all know people who are quite successful and still feel low about themselves. I think about the very famous, wealthy, and talented actor Robin Williams, who died by suicide after being extremely depressed. His overwhelming sense of guilt and regret was evident in his interviews. All the fame, money, and accolades in the world could not change his low self-view.

This TIP will focus on the real way people get self-esteem, which is to be *self-compassionate*. Those who are accepting of themselves, who try their best but don't measure their worth through their successes and achievements, will find greater happiness in life. Teaching children self-compassion offers them a tremendous start in navigating life in growing up, and you can teach yourself self-compassion at any age.

Implementing Skills

There are many ways to increase your focus on self-compassion in your life. The following are ways to practice kindness to yourself as you increase self-acceptance and self-forgiveness.

Keep a Journal

Consider keeping a self-compassion journal where you write at least one thing you love about yourself each day, regardless of your successes and failures. For example, if you failed to get that promotion you wanted, you might say to yourself, "I am proud of myself for trying" and "I am still just as worthy, whether I'm promoted or not." That would be a healthier alternative to low self-esteem self-talk such as "I should have tried harder" our "I'll never be good enough."

Write a Letter to Yourself Showing Self-Compassion

Kristin Neff, author of *Self-Compassion: The Proven Power of Being Kind to Yourself* (2015), suggests writing a letter of self-compassion to yourself. In this letter you might explain how to forgive yourself for regrettable behavior from the past that still haunts you. You could acknowledge the trauma and pain you have experienced that has led to being so hard on yourself. Writing a letter to yourself showing self-forgiveness, self-love, and nonjudgmental acceptance can be quite powerful.

Loving Kindness Meditation

On her website (https://self-compassion.org), Kristin Neff has many free downloadable exercises and guided imagery on the topic of self-compassion, including guided meditations. Whether you listen to one of those exercises or do your own version of a loving kindness meditation, the idea is to be nonjudgmental, loving, and kind to yourself. She suggests touching your heart and rubbing it with your hands together, saying very soothing and loving words to yourself.

Assemble a Self-Compassion Toolkit

Metaphorical toolkits are one of my most integral techniques for keeping important life skill concepts in mind. Creating such a toolkit can be a powerful way to reinforce lessons of self-compassion. You can use a bag, box, bowl, or other container to hold various objects and written reminders to increase your self-love. For example, Hershey's Kisses or Hugs candies can remind us to be kind to ourselves and others and give literal hugs and kisses freely. Other helpful items might include coping cards with affirmations and positive self-statements, scented oils or lotions to calm and treat yourself, and cards from your loved ones or pictures of them. What would you add to your self-compassion toolkit?

Processing the Activity

The one common theme among all the suggested activities is to remind yourself that you are worthy no matter what, and that self-esteem springs more from unconditional self-love than any judgmental measures you or others impose. When you are self-compassionate, the inner critic does not have room to coexist.

"I deserve to be kind and loving to myself despite my shortcomings and mistakes made in the past."

Choose a Growth Mindset Over a Fixed Mindset

Theory

The field of positive psychology includes new areas of research about self-esteem and mental health that fit well into the CBT orientation. In her book *Mindset: The New Psychology of Success* (2007), psychologist Carol Dweck emphasizes that the smartest and most accomplished people are not generally the happiest or most resilient. Rather, her research has shown that the main determinant of happiness and self-satisfaction is having a *growth mindset* over a *fixed mindset*.

Those with a *growth mindset* focus on effort, learning, and determination and do not judge their worth based on their past success or failures. Passion and perseverance are more valued than measurements of success. Those with a *fixed mindset*, on the other hand, define themselves by what they have done or by their innate abilities, so they would be more likely to feel defeated after failure or setbacks. It follows that those with a growth mindset tend to like themselves more and do not beat themselves up when times get tough.

Mindset psychologist Angela Duckworth further expands on the importance of having a growth mindset with the notion of "grit." In her book *Grit: The Power of Passion and Perseverance* (2016), she explains that people are happier and more resilient when they have passion and perseverance for their work and interests, as opposed to people who are innately more talented.

The important lesson from both Dweck and Duckworth is that growth and success are possible for anyone regardless of their level of skill and innate talent.

Implementing Skills

The following chart differentiates a fixed mindset from a growth mindset.

Fixed Mindset	Growth Mindset
• Natural ability and intelligence are considered most important	• Effort and perseverance are considered most important
• Believes abilities are fixed (can't be altered)	• Believes abilities can be developed
• Believes aptitude matters more than determination	• Believes determination matters more than innate ability
• Focus is on successful outcomes	• Focus is on commitment and learning
• Tends to be an inflexible thinker	• Tends to be a flexible thinker
• Believes innate ability is the most important factor in success	• Believes grit is the most important factor in success
• Defeated by failure	• Perseveres after failure

Now It's Your Turn

Looking at the two columns, which one fits you more? Do you tend to have a growth mindset or a fixed mindset? It is never too late to develop the skills to shift your mindset, change your perceptions, and pursue a meaningful life.

In the table that follows, write down characteristics of yourself that reflect either a fixed mindset or a growth mindset. Change any fixed mindset self-statements to reflect a growth mindset. Some examples are provided for you first.

My Thoughts About Myself Reflecting a Fixed Mindset	My Thoughts About Myself Reflecting a Growth Mindset
I am not good at my job anymore.	Some of my coworkers do have better skills in some areas, but I also contribute to the team and I value my efforts.
I used to be one of the smartest people on the team but now I am being outshone.	I still have the passion and interest for my work and will keep learning and growing.

Processing the Activity

How did it feel to change your negative self-talk to a growth mindset? Can you appreciate the difference it will make in your life? The idea behind this distinction is not to avoid succeeding. Quite the contrary—a growth mindset, including grit, enthusiasm, and perseverance, will help you stay motivated.

"I value my ability to commit myself to my pursuits and passions and find meaning and value in my efforts."

Use Affirmations to Change Self-Talk from Negative to Positive

Theory

Affirmations are positive self-statements that reassure us of our worth and help us overcome our negative self-talk. Affirmations help us stay motivated and empowered. Using affirmations helps to counteract low self-esteem with words of encouragement and belief in yourself. Regular use of affirmations, such as daily or even many times a day, will help you challenge self-critical and self-downing self-talk. Make sure your affirmations do not have strings attached. For example, "I will do great at my presentation" puts too much pressure on the outcome. Better to rephrase it as "I am proud of how I prepared."

Implementing Skills

Here are some examples of affirmations, with room for you to fill in your own. There is no limit to the number of affirmations you can tell yourself regularly so that you can stay positive, grounded, and proud!

Positive Affirmations

- I am proud of my efforts and my commitment to doing the best I can.
- I am just as important as anyone else.
- I am a worthy person.
- I am lovable and deserve to love and be loved.
- I will choose to live each day in the present.
- I will learn from my mistakes and keep on improving.
- I deserve to be happy.
- I don't need another person to complete me.
- I am enough.
- I will accept my feelings and honor them, not belittle them.
- I deserve to forgive myself for my missteps of the past.
- I am doing the best I can.
- I am a beautiful person, flaws and all.
- My mistakes are opportunities to learn.

- I am done with judging myself or others—I will focus on loving, not judging.
- My needs are as important as everyone else's.
- I value my opinions.
- What I have to say is just as important as what others have to say.
- I am not inferior to the people around me.
- I forgive my younger self for being hurt and not making good choices.
- Today I will embrace my greatness.

Now It's Your Turn

Write some of your own affirmations that are meaningful to you.

_____
_____
_____
_____
_____
_____
_____

Reflection

Which affirmations did you read or write that resonated with you? Why?

_____
_____
_____

How would your life be different if you believed 100 percent in these affirmations?

_____
_____
_____
_____

If you still have a lot of self-doubt and self-criticism, what affirmations could help you avoid buying into those self-critical thoughts?

_____
_____
_____
_____

What thoughts are getting in the way of your believing this list of affirmations for yourself?

_____
_____
_____
_____

Do you think others deserve these affirmations more than you?

_____
_____
_____
_____

Processing the Activity

If you are dealing with self-doubt and low self-esteem, using affirmations often will be very helpful in overcoming your negative and self-sabotaging self-talk. Affirmations will help you believe in your abilities and your value.

In the next TIP we will focus on how to use affirmation practices in your daily routine.

> "I deserve to feel good about myself, and affirmations help remind me of my worth, beauty, and specialness."

Affirmation Practice

Theory

This TIP is a follow-up to the previous one, which introduced you to the importance of affirmations. If you are struggling with low self-esteem, having a variety of affirmation practices at your fingertips will support you in embracing your self-worth.

It is helpful to choose a regular time when you can spend a few minutes with an affirmation practice. Doing it in the morning when you wake up can help set a positive tone for the day. If the morning is too rushed, choose a time that works better for you to take a few moments to yourself for self-care.

Implementing Skills

Read Your Affirmations Out Loud Daily

Having a regular habit of saying affirmations helps keep positive thoughts about yourself at the forefront of your mind. Having an affirmation ritual, such as saying an affirmation in the mirror when you wake up or go to sleep, will start or end your day on a positive note. It is best to practice your affirmations at least once or twice per day, and saying them out loud can have more of an impact than just reading or thinking about them.

Write Your Affirmations on Coping Cards

Put your affirmations on note cards, sticky notes, or notes on your phone or computer. There are also apps available that allow you to choose from a list of affirmations or add your own and have notifications sent to you at regular intervals. A good activity would be to write one new affirmation each day, whatever suits your mood at the time. At the end of each day, you can read this affirmation over and consider how you were able to stay focused on that thought throughout the day.

Put Your Affirmations in a Jar or Box

At the end of each day, write out your affirmations for that day on cards or slips of paper, put them into a box or jar, and periodically review them. An alternative activity is to pick one card each day out of the container to serve as your mantra for the day. Just think—if you had even one affirmation each day for a year, how many positive thoughts you would have! You might just need to get a larger container!

Put Your Affirmations into Action

Find one action each day to put your affirmation into practice. For example, if your affirmation for the day is "What I have to say is just as important as what others have to say," make it a point to express yourself during the day to someone at work, at school, or in your personal life even if you are worried about their disapproval. This will help your affirmation come alive through developing assertive skills.

Keep an Affirmation Journal

Record your daily affirmations in a journal, and each day process how it went. How did you feel working on accepting that affirmation? Did it help you? Did you try any positive actions based on that affirmation? How did that feel?

Make an Affirmation Picture or Poster

You do not need to be artistic to use drawing, painting, or other forms of art to make a decorative sign of your favorite affirmation. Frame it on the wall or use a plexiglass stand so that you can change it regularly. This is a great activity to do with friends and family. What a great message to give to the young people in your life—that affirmations can be powerful, creative, and fun!

Affirmation Checklist

The checklist below has examples of affirmations that you can use each day to remind yourself to stay positive about yourself.

- ❑ I am strong.
- ❑ I have strength.
- ❑ I am determined and successful.
- ❑ I am a good and worthwhile person.
- ❑ I am a unique and special person.
- ❑ I have inner strength and resources.
- ❑ I am confident and competent.
- ❑ I hold my head up high.
- ❑ I deserve to be happy and have a good life.

Add your own:

_____

_____

Processing the Activity

Affirmations can be very powerful. Incorporating affirmations into your life can happen in many forms. Being liberal and creative with affirmations can also be a family activity. The important thing is to have a regular practice using affirmations as a cornerstone of how you think about yourself and your life. It will be a way of spreading positivity about yourself, others, and the world!

"I am a beautiful person and deserve to love and be loved."

 # Tips to Cultivate an Attitude of Gratitude

Theory

This TIP offers some ideas of how to improve your *attitude of gratitude*. When we are grateful, we are happier with ourselves and the world. Gratitude is such an important aspect of self-esteem that I have included more gratitude TIPs in other chapters of this book as well, as it lays the foundation of so many areas of mental health and wellness. Focusing on gratitude can help boost self-esteem and self-love. After all, you can't be positive with a negative mind!

Implementing Skills

Here are some ways to welcome an attitude of gratitude in your life.

Look for Gratitude in Everything You Do

Even in the midst of unpleasant situations or tasks, we can often find a silver lining. Consider these examples:

Often Regarded as Unpleasant	Finding the Gratitude
Paying taxes for your home	Having a home
Cleaning toilets	Indoor plumbing
Stuck in traffic	Having a car
Your crying baby	You love your child
Doing the laundry	Clean clothes to wear
Having a job you don't like	Paycheck
Interpersonal conflict	Opportunity to improve your assertive skills
Getting sick	You are alive
Making mistakes or failing	Getting the chance to try again wiser
When things don't go well	Getting a fresh start

What do you tend to perceive as uncomfortable or irritating in your own life? Can you identify anything within these unpleasant experiences that you are grateful for?

Have a Gratitude Ritual

How about simply starting the day with a big "thank you?" You might find it helpful to think of three things (or choose any number) that you are grateful for each day and make it a ritual. The things you are grateful for can be anything—what you have, what others did, what you did. You might find it helpful to be specific. For example, instead of "I am grateful for my kids," choose something that happened in the last day that you appreciate, such as "I am grateful to have taken a nice walk with my daughter; I enjoyed talking and laughing with her."

Keep a Gratitude Diary or Journal

Keep a separate book or notebook for a gratitude diary or journal. There are many you can buy with prompts, or you can use your own prompts such as those listed below. Prompts can help you be more specific about what you are grateful for, and they will help you be a keener observer about what you appreciate in your life. The more specific, the more it will stick.

Ideas for Prompts

- I am grateful for something I did today . . .
- I am grateful for the actions or words of others . . .
- Things I especially enjoyed today . . .
- I am grateful for this quote or affirmation that helped me today . . .
- I am grateful to try to improve upon my day tomorrow by . . .
- I felt fortunate today when . . .
- Using my five senses, this is what I heard, saw, smelled, felt, or tasted today that I appreciate . . .
- Ways I showed my kindness today to others . . .
- Ways I showed my kindness today to myself . . .
- This was the best part of my day . . .
- Who I am most grateful for today . . .
- How I expressed my gratitude to others today . . .
- My attitude of gratitude was challenged today by my thoughts, my choices, or the behaviors of others . . .
- How I could better handle attitude of gratitude challenges in the future . . .

Have a Gratitude Box or Jar

Every day, write down things that you are grateful for on note cards or slips of paper and put them into a box, jar, or other container. When you need a gratitude boost, take the cards from the container and read them.

A gratitude box or jar is a great activity for the whole family. Keeping the container in your kitchen or living space helps everyone keep in mind all the things in life to appreciate. You can use the preceding prompts to structure how to be specific in sharing what you are grateful for. Consider having a daily ritual of putting one more thing into the jar. Again, identifying specific things you are grateful for will help you and your family get into the gratitude habit. Periodically, review the notes of gratitude as an individual or family activity, which will offer positive reminders of gratitude that you can share yet again.

Create a Metaphorical Gratitude Toolkit

Using a box, jar, or other container, assemble items to remind you of your attitude of gratitude. For example, a thank-you note will remind you to be grateful, a small glass heart or polished gem will remind you of your lovability and the importance of giving love to others, and a smiley sticker will remind you of the importance of staying positive and looking for the good in life. It can be fun to find small objects around your home, at a thrift or dollar store, or in nature that represent love, gratitude, and appreciation.

Processing the Activity

Hopefully these ideas will help you welcome more positivity and gratitude into your life. However, you want to make sure it is not forced. If you have low self-esteem or are anxious and depressed, it might be hard to feel grateful for anything. Recognize that if you are struggling, gratitude is not on your top list of skills. Recognizing the importance of gratitude is not meant to trigger you to beat yourself up for not being grateful enough. Allow yourself to be "gratitude challenged" while working on resolving the issues that make it hard to let gratitude into your life. As you keep trying these ideas for gratitude, be sure to show yourself patience and kindness in your attitude of gratitude journey.

"An attitude of gratitude can help me look for the good in myself and what I appreciate rather than what is missing."

Journaling Prompts for Self-Esteem

Theory

Journaling is a great tool for self-reflection. It is an effective way to reinforce positive learning and replace erroneous habits of thinking that cut you down rather than build you up. It can help you gain insight and process your reactions to situations.

Journaling for self-esteem can reinforce the lessons in this chapter, such as challenging negative core beliefs, using affirmations, choosing a growth mindset over a fixed mindset, and developing an attitude of gratitude. Or you might choose to journal without any structure and simply pour out your thoughts and feelings, so you can express yourself and clarify your thoughts and feelings honestly and nonjudgmentally.

For those who want more support and guided prompts, there are a variety of self-help journals available for purchase. Prompts can be especially helpful for those whose negative core beliefs are so strong that without some structure, they might just end up reinforcing their own negative self-worth. In this exercise, I offer a set of prompts to structure a journal so that the writing will not devolve into negative self-bashing but rather provide a vehicle for self-empowerment and self-esteem management.

Implementing Skills

The following are some prompts for journaling for self-esteem. You might choose at least one prompt a day, writing a few lines or a paragraph in response. Or commit five to ten minutes a day (or more), perhaps with the help of a timer, to journaling for self-esteem.

- How does my self-esteem need improvement?
- What are my core beliefs about myself? Are they negative or positive? Are they true or exaggerations?
- What messages do I tell myself that are not productive or healthy for me?
- How do I describe myself? Is it different from how people who love me describe me?
- What are my core beliefs about myself? Do they need to be challenged to become more positive?
- Where did I learn messages that undermine my self-esteem? How can I unlearn them now?
- What feelings have resulted from low self-esteem?
- What behaviors have resulted in low self-esteem?
- What choices can I make now to boost my self-esteem?
- What are some affirmations to remind myself of my worth?
- What support from others do I need to improve my self-esteem?

- What specifically can I do to open up or ask others for help?
- What are some things I admire about myself?
- What am I proud of?
- What values do I have that I would like to pursue more and how can I do so?
- How can I be kinder and more compassionate to myself?
- How can I be more forgiving to myself?
- What makes me special?
- Who are my role models? What have I learned from them?
- What situations have I gone through that have made me a deeper person?
- What do I like about myself?
- What would I like to be more accepting of myself about?
- How can I describe myself in a highly positive and loving way?
- What would I say to my younger self?
- What would I say to my future self?
- What are some of my favorite things about myself?

Processing the Activity

If you struggle with low self-esteem, consider taking time every day to journal for self-esteem. Even five minutes a day will help you keep focused on accepting and loving yourself. Using prompts can help you uncover erroneous core beliefs while acknowledging and processing your feelings and reactions, empowering you to replace those faulty beliefs with healthier alternatives. It is worth the investment of time, since self-esteem is the foundation of how you see yourself, others, and the world.

"Journaling with prompts will help me boost my
self-esteem and live my best life."

Self-Test to Embrace Your Greatness and Overcome Self-Doubt

Theory

At the end of each chapter in this book, there will be a self-test to help you determine how well you have incorporated the previous TIPs. In this first section, I have crystalized the main points on the topic of self-esteem, and this eleventh TIP offers you a quick self-check on how you are doing in this area. Consider revisiting the TIPs in the chapter periodically until you feel an increased sense of mastery. Improving self-esteem takes dedication and practice—it is not a one-and-done effort. Unlearning old messages and replacing them with healthier ones takes persistent practice. But with this practice, you can in essence rewire your thoughts and your reactions.

Use this self-test to remind you of important skills to work on and to monitor your progress. Using this checklist periodically to remove self-doubt and kick the habit of self-criticism will provide the foundation of self-love and self-acceptance. Don't you deserve to live your best life with the best version of yourself?

Implementing Skills

In the self-test that follows, rate how true each statement is for you, from 1 to 10, to assess which areas you are doing well in and which areas need some improvement. The higher the score in each item, the higher your mastery in that area. The test is not designed to give you a one-and-done score. Your self-help journey is a continual one, and the important thing is to work to keep improving on yesterday. Making several copies of this self-test will allow you to keep retaking it to monitor your progress.

At the end of this self-test you will be prompted to calculate a total score and an average score. To get the average score, divide your total score by the number of items you responded to. For any items that are not applicable to you, just write "N/A" and subtract those items from the number you divide by when calculating your average score. As you continue taking the self-tests throughout this book, compare your average scores across the different topics. This will give you a snapshot of which areas need the most attention and which areas are the strongest.

Keep this test handy whenever you want some support and reminders on what tools you can use to work on the areas covered in this chapter.

Self-Test to Embrace Your Greatness and Overcome Self-Doubt

Using a scale from 1 to 10, with 1 being "not true" and 10 being "very true," rate how true these statements are for you.

Not true   **Very true**

1   2   3   4   5   6   7   8   9   10

____ I treat myself like a best friend and talk kindly to myself.

____ I feel I am enough and as worthy as anyone else.

____ I am self-compassionate.

____ I do not beat myself up over mistakes; I forgive myself for not knowing then what I know now.

____ I am focused more on my effort and commitment in important things rather than on my achievements.

____ I use positive self-statements such as affirmations to improve my self-esteem and draw courage and strength from them.

____ I refuse to be steeped in negative thinking about myself and my past missteps. Instead, I look toward using what I have learned to be the best I can be *now*.

____ I tend to be more grateful than bitter and focus on what I have in my life rather than what I lack.

____ I tend to have an attitude of gratitude and show my gratitude to myself and others with words of appreciation and kindness.

____ I have identified and challenged my negative core beliefs about myself and have turned my thoughts into more positive and accepting ones.

____ I use journaling as a way to keep my self-esteem and self-appreciation at the forefront of my efforts. I am worth it!

Total score: _____

Average score (*total score ÷ 11 or items answered*): _____

In the space below, process and explain your answers.

_____
_____
_____
_____
_____

If you would like further structure to process your answers to the self-test and your reactions to the chapter, here are some prompts to guide you.

My thoughts: _____
_____

My feelings: _____
_____

My self-talk: _____
_____

What I have learned: _____
_____

Additional thoughts and strategies: _____
_____
_____
_____

Processing the Activity

The purpose of this self-test is not to have a fixed score, as each time you take it the score will reflect where you are on that day. Rather, it is meant to be used as a tool for identifying areas to improve upon in your self-esteem journey at a given time. The higher your scores, the more you are able to embrace yourself no matter what. Periodically retaking this self-test will allow you to track your progress, with the goal of improving your scores on each item. Comparing your average score from this test with your average scores from the other chapter self-tests will help you identify which areas you would like to focus on improving in your CBT journey.

"I am choosing to prioritize my relationship to myself, as it is the foundation of all my relationships with others."

CHAPTER 2

Challenge Depressive Thinking: Changing Thoughts to Change Your Life

CBT offers various techniques that help to identify and change negative thinking habits that lead to depression. In this chapter we will go over some of the hallmark CBT techniques that have helped millions of individuals gain power over their depressive thought habits.

One of CBT's signature tools is identifying common thinking errors, known as *cognitive distortions*, which lead to depressive thinking and feelings. You can't expect someone who feels depressed to "snap out of it" and just feel better because they want to or think they should. Feelings cannot be changed directly by willing them to go away. However, learning ways to identify and change the unhealthy thought habits that lead to depression can help lift feelings of depression.

The worksheets and logs in this chapter can be used time and time again for various situations in which distorted thinking interferes with well-being and happiness. This will take practice—remember, mental fitness is like physical fitness. Knowing how to exercise, or even trying it once or twice, is not the same thing as following a regular exercise routine. Continued commitment is the key to real change and success. Similarly, commitment to regular practice of CBT skills will help you prevent or overcome depressive thinking and be more empowered to change your thoughts to change your life. It is also true that when you start a physical exercise regime, it might seem hard at first, but building up your muscles and fitness makes it easier over time. It is the same with developing CBT skills—it may seem awkward and time consuming at first, but regular practice will help you develop your mental fitness.

"The primary cause of unhappiness is never the situation but your thoughts about it. Be aware of the thoughts you are thinking. Separate them from the situation, which is always neutral, which always is as it is."

–Eckhart Tolle

TIP #12: Learning and Recording Your Psychological ABCs

Theory

Perhaps one of the most useful CBT models that has helped me significantly in my counseling practice is the ABCDE model. In the 1950s and 60s, cognitive psychology pioneers Albert Ellis and Aaron Beck both used models such as the one in this TIP and over half a century later, this model continues to embody an important cornerstone of CBT.

The ABCDE model helps us dissect a situation and clarify thoughts, feelings, and reactions to that situation. This has proved to be a significant tool for millions of individuals who suffer from negative and depressive thought habits. It helps to change self-sabotaging thinking habits and patterns into more positive and healthier ones. CBT trains people to recognize that the negative or depressive thoughts they accept as true are just interpretations, not facts. By learning how to recognize and dispute those upsetting interpretations, we can replace them with healthier, more positive, more accurate thoughts.

Implementing Skills

This ABCDE model is demonstrated in the following example.

A: Activating Event or Adversity	B: Beliefs About the Event (Thoughts)	C: Consequences (Feelings and Behaviors)	D: Dispute	E: Effect of Disputing
I'm at a party with people I don't know.	They are so interesting and accomplished. They are much more educated and wealthier than me. I am so inferior. I can never be as good as them.	I feel ashamed, sad, depressed, hopeless, and unconfident. I withdraw from the group.	I admire them, but they are no better than me. I am just as worthy. Comparing myself to others is not helpful or healthy.	I feel confident. I'm able to converse with others and am no longer anxious about speaking up. I'm meeting new friends. I'm having fun with them.

Now It's Your Turn

Use the following template to write your own examples of how you can change your upsetting interpretations to think and feel better.

My ABCDE Thought Diary

A: Activating Event or Adversity	B: Beliefs About the Event (Thoughts)	C: Consequences (Feelings and Behaviors)	D: Dispute	E: Effect of Disputing

Processing the Activity

This model can be used time and time again for different situations that trigger depressive thoughts. As you can see in the example, challenging negative, self-downing thoughts will change your feelings and behaviors. In stressful times, we are often not able to dissect a situation with mental clarity, and this ABCDE model will provide structure to help you do just that.

As an additional bonus, once your behaviors change, people will respond to you differently. When you think more positive and act more positive, you will get reinforced by others.

"I can change my thoughts to literally change my life."

Recognizing Unhelpful Thinking with a Cognitive Distortion Log

Theory

As we have established, the distinguishing characteristic of CBT is its focus on the importance of our perceptions in interpreting situations. In this TIP we delve a bit deeper into unhealthy thinking habits with the notion of *cognitive distortions*. Conceptualized by psychiatrist Aaron Beck in the 1960s, this is one of the most central features of CBT.

The idea underlying cognitive distortions is that thought patterns that twist or misinterpret reality result in emotional distress. By recognizing the specific type of distortion, you can then attempt to objectively change your thinking patterns. This TIP includes some of the common types of cognitive distortions that lead to depressive thinking. In this list, you will notice common thought habits that many people don't even question. Focusing on these negative habits can be a very important tool in your CBT toolbox.

Implementing Skills

The following is a list of common cognitive distortions that cause considerable emotional distress, perpetuating the downward spiral into depression and anxiety. Notice how these common distortions are extreme, absolute, and not grounded in fact. Each distortion is accompanied by examples applied to typical real-life situations. Since this chapter addresses depression, the examples show how cognitive distortions are often self-downing and applied to one's own self-view, leading to feelings of depression.

This list is by no means exhaustive, and in the activity that follows, you will write some of your own habitual distortions and examples.

Common Cognitive Distortions

- **All-or-nothing-thinking:** Viewing things in black and white, blowing things out of proportion.
    - "I can't do anything right."
    - "Nobody likes me."
    - "Nothing ever goes right for me."
- **"Should" statements:** Judgmental and unforgiving statements that are rigid and inflexible.
    - "I should have known better."
    - "I should be further along in my life by now."
    - "I should not be so sensitive."

- **Fortune telling:** Thinking you can predict the future based on the way you are thinking now.
    - "I will never get over this."
    - "I will be alone the rest of my life."
    - "I never will be able to feel truly happy."
- **Jumping to conclusions:** Assuming things are facts based on little evidence.
    - "She didn't call me back—she must not like me."
    - "He wasn't honest with me—I can never trust him again."
    - "I screwed up this relationship—I am not capable of having a healthy one."
- **Mental filtering:** Focusing on the negative aspects of something and ignoring the positive.
    - "My legs are heavy, which makes my figure unattractive."
    - "My teenager got a detention; I failed as a parent."
    - "I got a C on that assignment—I am such a bad student."
- **Discounting the positive:** Not only ignoring the positive aspects of something but actively rejecting them (similar to mental filtering but more extreme).
    - "I have some good friends at work, but the new hire didn't want to join me for lunch. I feel completely unlikable."
    - "I am a terrible actor! Even though I got praise for my performance, the reviewers were just being nice. I am sure they could tell I stammered and messed up some of my lines."
    - "I got a couple of bad evaluations, which makes all the positive ones not important."
- **Labeling:** Categorizing yourself (or others) unfairly in generalizing ways.
    - "I'm just stupid."
    - "I'm unlovable."
    - "I'm just a jerk."
- **Comparing:** Comparing yourself unfavorably with others, which lowers your sense of self-worth.
    - "My teammates are so much better at soccer than me."
    - "I feel so stupid compared to him."
    - "She seems to have it all together and it makes me realize how inferior I am."
- **Minimization:** Failing to respect your feelings and even your competence.
    - "So many people have it worse—I feel guilty for feeling this way."
    - "It should not be so important to me—I'm just a stickler."
    - "He probably is complimenting me on my work since he just likes to make people feel good even if they don't earn it."

- **Emotional reasoning:** Assuming that your feelings are evidence of the truth.
    - "I feel defective, so I must be defective."
    - "I feel awkward around him—he must not like me."
    - "I feel anxious walking here in the city, so it must be dangerous for me."
- **Blaming and personalization:** Unfairly assigning all the guilt and responsibility to others (blaming) or to yourself (personalization), when the situation really involved other factors.
    - "He makes me so mad."
    - "She ruined my life."
    - "It's all my fault that our work team is stressed out. I let them down."

Now It's Your Turn

Consider the following examples. Then, in the template on the next page, identify some of your own thinking errors and reframe each error in a less extreme, more rational way.

Irrational Thought	Type of Cognitive Distortion	Healthier Alternative Thought
I will never recover from this breakup.	All-or-nothing thinking Fortune telling Emotional reasoning	I will work on getting over the breakup although it will be tough.
I am pathetic.	Labeling All-or-nothing thinking Emotional reasoning	I am in pain right now, but I will work on developing skills to think more clearly. I am worthy.
I should be further in my life by now. I haven't accomplished anything and I blame only myself.	"Should" statements All-or-nothing thinking Minimization Discounting the positive Blaming	I have had setbacks, but I have learned from them and will be wiser moving forward.

Processing the Activity

Recognizing, reframing, and restructuring your cognitive distortions can be one of the most useful tools you have to combat depressive thinking. As you work on replacing interpretations with facts, try to notice the type of distortion that is exaggerating your negative spin on things. By being an objective observer of your thoughts, you will reap the benefits of clearer thoughts to brighten your mood.

"I will be more careful in the things I say to myself and stick to the facts rather than my self-downing interpretations."

My Cognitive Distortion Log

Irrational Thought	Type of Cognitive Distortion	Healthier Alternative Thought

Keeping a CBT Thought Log

Theory

Thought logs are central to a CBT toolbox. Having a variety of logs or diaries helps you focus on different ways of dissecting thoughts and replacing unhelpful thoughts with healthier ones. Whether you use a variety of logs at different times or find one that works best for you, the important thing is to use this type of tool to challenge unhealthy thoughts.

The sample log in this TIP examines positive and negative thoughts after a triggering event. You will identify the type of cognitive distortion along with the strength of certainty of your positive and negative thoughts. This log will help you gain more objectivity and skepticism about any negative idiosyncratic thinking. Rating the degree of certainty further helps you evaluate the accuracy of your thinking and question extreme, black-and-white thoughts. The last part of the log offers the opportunity to turn negative thoughts into proactive goals.

Implementing Skills

The sample CBT thought log on the next page demonstrates how to dissect your thoughts, emotions, and behaviors after a triggering event. Following the sample is a blank log that you can use to dissect your own response to a challenging situation. Making copies of this template can help you practice replacing negative thoughts with more helpful and accurate ones on a regular basis.

Processing the Activity

This process—identifying the types of cognitive distortions in your thinking, gauging your certainty about those thoughts, and disputing them—helps make healthier thoughts more believable. CBT logs offer opportunities to challenge your unhealthy thought habits and develop healthier ones with practice over time.

"I commit myself to learning better ways of thinking about myself and my life by practicing skills that give me a sense of self-empowerment."

CBT Thought Log: Example

1. Situation or Activating Event: Going to a friend's wedding without a plus-one

2. Negative Thoughts: I feel like a loser that I have no one to go with. I *hate* being alone. I feel pathetic. People will feel sorry for me.	**8. Disputing My Cognitive Distortions:** I am not pathetic or a loser—that is unfair to me and untrue. I will continue to look for a partner. I am as worthy as anyone else.
3. Type of Cognitive Distortions: All-or-nothing-thinking Labeling Mental filtering Fortune telling	**9. Certainty of My Disputing:** ⟵ 1 2 3 4 5 6 7 **8** 9 10 ⟶
4. Certainty of My Distortions: ⟵ 1 2 3 4 5 6 **7** 8 9 10 ⟶	**10. Positive Thoughts:** I am happy for my friend. I am looking forward to having a good time. My friends will be happy I am there.
5. Negative Emotions: Depressed Anxious Ashamed	**11. Positive Emotions:** Excited Hopeful Grateful
6. Strength of Negative Emotions: ⟵ 1 2 3 4 5 6 7 **8** 9 10 ⟶	**12. Strength of Positive Emotions:** ⟵ 1 2 3 4 5 6 7 **8** 9 10 ⟶
7. Unhealthy Behaviors: Keep to myself Socially distance myself Leave early	**13. Healthy Behaviors:** Engage with others Try to make meaningful conversation Smile and make good eye contact Try out assertive skills

14. Conclusions and Goals: I will use this wedding as an opportunity to enjoy spending time with my friends, meet new people, and enjoy dancing. I will actively work on my negative thinking so I can feel just as worthy as anyone else there, married or not.

CBT Thought Log

1. Situation or Activating Event:

2. Negative Thoughts:	**8. Disputing My Cognitive Distortions:**
3. Type of Cognitive Distortions:	**9. Certainty of My Disputing:** ← 1 2 3 4 5 6 7 8 9 10 →
4. Certainty of My Distortions: ← 1 2 3 4 5 6 7 8 9 10 →	**10. Positive Thoughts:**
5. Negative Emotions:	**11. Positive Emotions:**
6. Strength of Negative Emotions: ← 1 2 3 4 5 6 7 8 9 10 →	**12. Strength of Positive Emotions:** ← 1 2 3 4 5 6 7 8 9 10 →
7. Unhealthy Behaviors:	**13. Healthy Behaviors:**

14. Conclusions and Goals:

Reframe Your Negative Thoughts from Permanent to Temporary

Theory

Cognitive reframing is a central concept in CBT that encourages us to look at things with a different point of view. Just like a new frame on a picture changes its whole appearance, reframing our perceptions and shifting our mindset changes our attitude. One very effective way to cognitively reframe is to differentiate permanent from temporary thinking. Oftentimes, the assumption underlying our depressive thinking is that our negative thoughts and feelings will always be that way. Replacing permanent self-talk with a temporary alternative can make our problems more manageable and help us think more optimistically.

Implementing Skills

The following table shows examples of permanent thinking and how to shift them to temporary thinking.

Permanent Thinking	Temporary Thinking
I don't know how to relate to people.	I am working on developing skills to improve my confidence in social situations.
I don't trust people.	I have been disappointed by some people in my life but am finding people who I am learning to trust.
I'll never get over this.	I will learn from this.
I am way too sensitive.	Right now, I am feeling very vulnerable.
I can't express myself.	Up until now, I have had trouble expressing myself.
People ignore me.	I am not confident in myself and am building skills to be more open with people.

Now It's Your Turn

Write down some of the negative things you tell yourself that show permanent thinking, then change each thought to be more temporary. Try to replace all-or-nothing language like "always," "forever," "I am bad," or "I can't" with more realistic phrases such as "up until now," "right now," "I am learning" or "I will."

Permanent Thinking	Temporary Thinking

Processing the Activity

When we transform our self-talk from permanent thinking to temporary, we allow lightness and hope into our lives. Reframing our language in this way offers the possibility for better times ahead.

"I am a work in progress and improving every day as I learn to think in ways that are more hopeful and that allow for growth. I will focus less on the things that have not turned out in my life and will focus instead on the things that have. I have faith that as my life story unfolds, no matter how complicated the plot, it will all come together."

Be a Fact Checker: Get Rid of ANTs and Crack NUTs

Theory

In developing the CBT framework in the 1960s, psychiatrist Aaron Beck emphasized the importance of examining *automatic negative thoughts*, or ANTs, in developing healthier thought habits. The premise is that in depressive thinking, we often we accept our ANTs as true and do not realize we are telling ourselves stories rather than sticking to the facts. David Burns expounded on this acronym in his popular book *Feeling Good* (1999), where he focuses on disputing ANTs, while Elisha Goldstein, in *Uncovering Happiness* (2015), addressed *negative unconscious thoughts*, or NUTs. Both acronyms remind us to look at the automatic, unconscious self-sabotaging thoughts we have in response to triggers in our everyday life. These self-sabotaging thoughts lead to depressive feelings, lack of motivation, and sadness.

Implementing Skills

The two acronyms will help you remember to stop to examine the self-downing thinking caused by believing your automatic, unconscious, "go-to" cognitive distortions. Check your facts; dispute your interpretations. Time to get rid of the ANTs that will drive you NUTs!

The following are some examples of ANTs and NUTs and ideas of how to challenge them.

Automatic Negative Thoughts/ Negative Unconscious Thoughts	Challenging the ANTs and NUTs
"I can't do anything right."	"I actually do many things well—that is just an exaggeration because I am depressed right now."
"I failed in my marriage."	"I am only partly responsible for the marriage not working out. I tried my best and learned many things that I will use moving forward in other relationships."
"I wasted my life."	"Life is always full of chances and opportunities. It's never too late to build on yesterday."

Now It's Your Turn

In the chart that follows, list some of your recurring self-downing thoughts, then challenge them!

Automatic Negative Thoughts/ Negative Unconscious Thoughts	Challenging the ANTs and NUTs

Processing the Activity

Acronyms such as ANTs and NUTs can be a catchy way to increase your awareness of your irrational patterns of thinking. Picturing those unconscious negative thoughts as pesky bugs or tough nuts to crack can put a little humor into your CBT practice—as well as serving as a great visual reminder to get rid of your ANTs and stop believing the NUTs once and for all!

> "I will challenge my ANTs so I won't go NUTs!"

Getting Down to Your Core Beliefs

Theory

Another major cornerstone of CBT is the unearthing and discovery of your *core beliefs* from which a variety of negative beliefs originate. Core beliefs are the fundamental assumptions we have about our self and our worth; in the case of depression, these beliefs are faulty ones.

Imagine looking around you right now while wearing smudgy glasses. It would be hard to see clearly. Likewise, if you look at yourself and the world through faulty core beliefs, you will not see things clearly and will have distorted perceptions. It is hard to have positive thoughts when core beliefs set the stage for negativity and distorted thinking.

There are a lot of manifestations of faulty core beliefs, such as anxiety about speaking up in social situations; fear of rejection, disapproval, or criticism; and poor lifestyle habits such as substance abuse. The manifestations are many, but the core beliefs can usually be crystallized to just a few root beliefs. The *downward arrow technique*, popularized by psychiatrist David Burns, helps people get to the bottom of their faulty core beliefs.

Implementing Skills

The following example uses the downward arrow technique to demonstrate how the core belief of being a "pathetic loser" underlies depression, anxiety, and a host of negative self-talk.

The Downward Arrow Technique

Presenting problem: I am afraid to ask that person to go out with me in case they say no.
Ask yourself: If that were true, what would that mean?

Your answer: That would mean I am unattractive and not good enough for them.
Ask yourself: If that were true, what would that mean?

Your answer: It would mean that I likely will never attract people I am attracted to.
Ask yourself: If that were true, what would that mean?

Your answer: It would mean that I will probably be alone the rest of my life.
Ask yourself: If that were true, what would that mean?

Your answer: It would mean I am just unlikable.
Ask yourself: If that were true, what would that mean?

⬇

Your answer: It would mean I am a pathetic loser.
CORE BELIEF: I am a pathetic loser.

Now It's Your Turn

Try using the downward arrow technique with a challenge you are facing. Continue asking yourself "If that were true, what would that mean?" as many times as it takes to reach a core belief.

Presenting problem: _____
_____

⬇

If that were true, what would that mean? _____
_____

⬇

If that were true, what would that mean? _____
_____

⬇

If that were true, what would that mean? _____
_____

⬇

If that were true, what would that mean? _____
_____

⬇

CORE BELIEF: _____
_____

Processing the Activity

Once you get to your core belief, you can then use a CBT thought log to challenge it. Or you might draw a new diagram with upward arrows, starting with the negative core belief at the bottom and working your way upward by challenging the distorted thoughts and challenging the accuracy of the statements, leading to healthier thoughts and more positive feelings. Using self-compassion will be helpful in moving upward to challenge the negative thoughts stemming from a faulty core belief.

Since we generally hold just a few basic core beliefs, but the manifestations that stem from those core beliefs are plentiful, this technique can be used over and over again to work through various life issues.

"I will make a conscious decision to get to the core of my beliefs that limit me and choose healthier ways of interpreting situations in my life."

Observe Your Thoughts with an Observing Head

Theory

Acceptance and commitment therapy (ACT), originated by Stephen Hayes, combines CBT with mindfulness strategies. One of Hayes's (2005) central techniques to handle depressive and irrational thoughts is to use the process of *cognitive defusion*. Techniques of cognitive defusion are used to distance yourself from an upsetting thought so you are looking *at* it, not *from* it. I liken this technique to developing an *observing head*. This means watching your thoughts, often using imagery, from a distance. You note the thoughts but do not react to them or take them personally. In essence, you distance yourself from depressive thinking,

Implementing Skills

In ACT there is a focus on using metaphors and visualizations to help people heal from disturbed thinking and feeling. As you distance yourself from your thought, you might find it helpful to say, "I am having the thought that . . ." rather than just thinking that thought. For example, the thought that *I am invisible to people* can be replaced with *There I go again—I am having the thought that I am invisible and unimportant*. Simply noting a thought versus accepting it without a doubt can make the difference between a depressed feeling and a calm and even happy feeling.

The following are some cognitive defusion visualizations to help you distance yourself from your negative thoughts.

- **Watch your thoughts on a screen:** Imagine you are in a movie theater and watching your disturbing thoughts on the screen. Imagine sitting in the front row, then move back a few rows, and end the imagery with sitting in the back of the theater. As you watch your thoughts on the screen, you are merely observing, not reacting to them.

- **Describe without judgment:** All too often, our judgments and opinions creep into our observations of the world around us, which is not helpful if these thoughts are persistently self-downing. We might think we are describing something in an impartial way, but judgments are deep-seated. To improve mindfulness and your observing head, look at something about yourself, another person, or your surroundings in a nonjudgmental way. For example, look in a mirror or on your smartphone camera. Describe what you see. If you are looking impartially with an observing head, you might say, "I have two eyes, a nose, dark hair, and some freckles." If you are looking judgmentally, you might say, "My hair looks frizzy. Boy, do I look tired. My nose is too large, and I have too many wrinkles."

- **Leaves in a stream:** One of Hayes's best known cognitive defusion visualizations is imagining that you are putting your thoughts on leaves in a stream and watching them float away and eventually disappear. This is a great example of looking *at* your thoughts instead of *from* them.

- **Thoughts on a cloud:** In this visualization, imagine looking at the clouds and seeing your thoughts on the clouds. Seeing them in the sky helps you keep a great deal of distance from them. Watching them from afar helps to take away the emotionality of your disturbing thoughts so that you can just note them without getting attached to them as they float away.

- **Thoughts on a train:** Imagine yourself looking over a bridge and watching a train go by, with each car on the train having a thought written on it. Watch your thoughts as they go by under the bridge and disappear down the tracks.

Now It's Your Turn

Using any of these visualizations, think of some of your negative and disturbing thoughts and practice looking at them rather than from them. Or draw leaves, clouds, or a train and write your thoughts on it.

Processing the Activity

How did this visualization help you distance yourself from your negative thoughts? What negative thoughts did you choose? If you found this exercise helpful, spend a few mindful moments each day doing this exercise to practice using your observing head. Remember, the goal is to look *at* your thoughts rather than *from* them.

"When I distance myself from my negative thinking, I am able to feel more at peace with myself and am more self-accepting."

Use Coping Cards for Any Occasion

Theory

Coping cards are perhaps one of the most valuable and useful tools in the CBT toolbox. Coping cards are generally made with note cards, but they can be made on other things such as sticky notes, a document on your computer, or an app on your smartphone. Coping cards help you use CBT strategies in everyday life to manage your thoughts during times of negative thinking and emotional upset. They are reminders to help ground you so that you can think more clearly when emotions cloud your sense of reason. They are reminders of your worth and your ability to work through whatever difficulties you are facing. They can serve as your positive inner voice when your inner critic gets the better of you.

Implementing Skills

There are many types of coping cards. They can be affirmations for encouragement, reminders of rational thoughts that you want to keep at the front of your mind, or behavioral reminders such as "do a visualization" or "breathe deeply and slowly." They can be two-sided, with one of your persistent cognitive distortions on one side and the more rational alternative on the other side. They can be positive quotes or thoughts to help brighten your mood. There is no limit to what type of coping cards can be meaningful to you. Coping cards can keep changing along with your needs. They are also easy to create and portable to be bring with you wherever you go.

The following are some examples of prompts you could use for coping cards.

Affirmations

- I am a beautiful person.
- I am resilient and can get through this.
- I can forgive myself for not knowing *then* what I know *now*.
- I deserve to be happy.

Situational Coping Statements

- When I am in the meeting, I will try to say at least one thing to not give in to the fear of saying something stupid.
- I will count to ten and use my mindful breathing exercise when I find myself in a situation at work when I compare myself unfavorably with my coworkers.

Disputing Negative Thoughts and Beliefs (Two-Sided Cards)

- I have wasted my life and I can't get the time back. I am overwhelmed by my poor choices. ➜ I have learned a lot from my life experiences, both good and bad, and will build on my experience and wisdom to make better choices now.
- I'll never have confidence speaking up at meetings. ➜ I will keep on working on skills to improve my assertiveness and self-confidence, work on my fear of saying something stupid, and have faith in myself that what I have to say is important.
- I am way too sensitive—there is something wrong with me. ➜ My sensitivity is a gift and allows me to be a more empathetic and deeper person. I deserve to be proud of myself.

Turning Complaints into Goals (Two-Sided Cards)

- I don't have many friends. ➜ I am practicing assertive skills so I can take risks and engage more with people.
- I feel a lack of meaning in my life. ➜ I will take some time to look into what is missing and what I can do to pursue more meaning and sense of purpose.

Reminders to Use CBT Skills

- When I am upset and feeling down on myself, I can:
    - Read a page in my self-help book
    - Read a few affirmations
    - Take a walk
    - Fill out my CBT log
    - Reach out to someone I trust
    - Write down my irrational negative thought and dispute it
- When I am depressed or upset in a situation, I will use my psychological ABCs to recognize my irrational beliefs and change them to more rational thoughts:
    - **A**ctivating event
    - **B**elief
    - **C**onsequence
    - **D**isputing irrational belief
    - **E**ffect of healthier thinking on my mood and behavior

Self-Coaching Statements

- Even when my palms are sweaty, my heart races, and I feel like I am going to have a panic attack, it does not mean I will. And even if I do, I won't get hurt or die from panic.

- When I feel triggered, it does not mean I will spiral out of control. I will use all my CBT tools to guide me and strengthen my confidence in combating my strong feelings. Instead, I will keep working on controlling my reactions to my triggers and have mastery over them.

Inspiring Quotes

- "Regret doesn't remind us that we did badly. It reminds us that we know we can do better." –Kathryn Shultz
- "Self-compassion is simply giving the same kindness to ourselves that we would give to others." –Christopher Germer

Now It's Your Turn

Write some coping cards that you would find beneficial for your own unique situation. You can make copies of the template on the next page and fill them in, get note cards, or make notes on your computer or smartphone so you can have them wherever you go! Consider putting your coping cards in a box, reviewing them from time to time, and carrying the ones that resonate with you around with you.

Processing the Activity

Some people find it helpful to laminate their coping cards, decorate them, or use a slip ring to hold them together. One of the best things I have ever received from a client was a set of laminated coping cards she made with index cards, held together with a ring. She had duplicated her set for me, with the rationale that since she found them so helpful, maybe my other clients might find them helpful also!

"With my tools for coping, I will strengthen my belief in myself and my trust that I can get through anything."

My Coping Cards

Behavioral Activation and Activity Scheduling

Theory

Thus far in this chapter, we have focused mostly on thoughts and feelings. In this TIP we will focus on the behavioral aspect of CBT. The B in the ABCDE model stands for belief, so the focus on behavior actually goes under the letter C for consequence, which includes feelings and behaviors.

As we have seen in virtually all the TIPs, thoughts, feelings, and behaviors all interact with one another. Especially in the case of depression, if people wait to feel motivated to take action, they may never do so, as depression often leads to inactivity (and vice versa). *Behavioral activation* focuses on taking action despite a low level of motivation. The idea is that activity helps improve mood. Increasing our activity level—such as doing daily tasks and having an outlet for exercise—can lead to a sense of engagement and mastery. Even if we are not motivated at first, choosing to be active ends up building on itself and helps us feel better.

Behavioral activation can also be helpful for specific situations. For example, if you are fearful of speaking up in a group, the feeling would be anxiety, and the thought that causes anxiety may be *I don't want to say something stupid* or *I have nothing worthwhile to add*. The subsequent behaviors would be staying silent, or speaking up but having your voice quiver, or even skipping the meeting to avoid potential embarrassment. You may even use substances or emotional eating to try to cope with the anxiety, depression, and loneliness, which can bring on a whole host of other physical and mental problems.

Using behavioral activation, you might identify certain behaviors that will help you stop this negative cycle, such as practicing in front of a mirror what you can say in the group meeting, creating coping cards to review before the meeting, and making a commitment to say at least one thing in the meeting.

Because choosing healthy behaviors is so important for our mental health, this TIP offers ideas of how to develop new habits to replace less helpful ones, such as avoidant or self-destructive habits. Through behavioral activation, you will adopt new behaviors to accompany and encourage healthy thinking skills, resulting in improved mood.

Implementing Skills

Activity Monitoring

To employ behavioral activation strategies, it is helpful to start with activity monitoring. This means monitoring your behaviors in a given day or week and noticing how you schedule your time. The following example shows one non-working or non-school day, but you might find it helpful to monitor your whole week and observe your activities and your mood associations. Looking at your log, you can observe what is working for you and what is not.

Time	Activity	Feelings
7:30–8:00 a.m.	Wake up, take a shower, and brush teeth	Low mood
8:00–9:00 a.m.	Eat breakfast and watch TV	Low mood
9:00–10:00 a.m.	Watch more TV	Worse mood
11:00 a.m.–12:00 p.m.	Check email and go for a half-hour walk	Better mood
12:00–2:00 p.m.	Meet a friend for lunch	Engaged and happy
2:00–4:00 p.m.	Go back home and take a nap, then go on Facebook	Low mood
4:00–6:00 p.m.	Watch old movies	Worse mood
6:00–7:00 p.m.	Have dinner while reading my self-help book	Better mood
7:00–8:00 p.m.	Go to the grocery store and drugstore	Better mood
8:00–9:00 p.m.	Play video games	Low mood
9:00–10:00 p.m.	Message friends to make plans	Better mood
10:00–10:30 p.m.	Get ready for bed and read my affirmation book	Better mood

In this example, you'll note that the higher moods were associated with being active and socializing (or planning to socialize) with others, while watching TV was not contributing to a better mood. The best this person felt was when they were engaged with another person and not isolated. The person's goal, then, would likely be to increase opportunities for engaging with others.

Now It's Your Turn

Over the next week, monitor your activities and mood to identify your own patterns and goals. You can make copies of the following template or create your own log.

My Activity Log

Time	Activity	Feelings
5:00–6:00 a.m.		
6:00–7:00 a.m.		
7:00–8:00 a.m.		
8:00–9:00 a.m.		
9:00–10:00 a.m.		
10:00–11:00 a.m.		
11:00 a.m.–12:00 p.m.		
12:00–1:00 p.m.		
1:00–2:00 p.m.		
2:00–3:00 p.m.		
3:00–4:00 p.m.		
4:00–5:00 p.m.		
5:00–6:00 p.m.		
6:00–7:00 p.m.		
7:00–8:00 p.m.		
8:00–9:00 p.m.		
9:00–10:00 p.m.		
10:00–11:00 p.m.		
11:00 p.m.–12:00 a.m.		

Activity Scheduling

After you have identified your goals for engagement, fitness, involvement, and socialization, the next step is to do what is called *activity scheduling*. This tool helps you increase the behaviors that help you feel better and, by extension, decrease the time you spend on activities that are associated with low moods. Activity scheduling can help you stay focused on achieving your behavioral goals by specifying some manageable steps you can take over the course of the week. Having these goals written out can serve as a reminder and motivator.

Here are some examples of activities you might schedule:

- Taking a 30-minute walk five times per week
- Going to an exercise class in person or online
- Working in your garden
- Cleaning out a room or closet for a half hour
- Researching groups and meetups in your community where you could meet others with similar interests
- Signing up for an art class
- Calling two friends
- Making a lunch date

You might also include reinforcement for completing your goals if you think you need help with motivation. Doing things that you enjoy and find value in will ensure you are engaged in meaningful activities, which can alleviate feelings of depression.

Now It's Your Turn

In the activity scheduling log that follows, write down your desired activities for the week ahead. These should be steps that will bring you closer to your behavioral goals. Check off the days that you work on your various goals. At the end of the week, use the final column to review how you did and how these activities made you feel.

Processing the Activity

Behavioral activation techniques such as activity monitoring and scheduling help you develop an action plan as part of your self-help toolbox. The ideas given here are just a couple of ways to increase your activity level to create more meaning and engagement in your life. There is no right or wrong way to get yourself motivated. Whatever strategies you use, remember—the more you can clarify your goals, commit to them, and give yourself some framework to be active in your physical and mental health, the more empowered you will be. Being action-oriented is one of the most important ways to think better and feel better.

"When I am actively engaged in my life, and feel productive and see meaning in my activities, I feel happier."

My Weekly Goals and Desired Activities

Goal	Sun	Mon	Tues	Wed	Thur	Fri	Sat	Sun	Notes and Mood Check

A Menu of Activities to Improve Your Mood and Get Connected

Theory

This TIP offers various behavioral activities and CBT techniques and strategies to activate more positivity in your life. The more active you are in your personal growth, the more you will be able to lighten your mood and get out of your head and into your life, while getting yourself moving!

Implementing Skills

The following are evidence-based ways to alleviate feelings of depression, and some of these areas are in fact fields of training for therapists (e.g., art therapy, movement therapy, and music therapy). Use this list to commit to finding pleasure and healing through activities you enjoy.

Music

Listening to music can be a great source of pleasure for people and can be especially healing if certain songs evoke emotions to help heal. Most people find that certain songs resonate with the mood they have at the time and can provide comfort and inspiration. Learning which songs evoke meaningful emotions for you can be an important tool to improve your mood. Singing along to a song can also be emotionally healing and help you feel more engaged with life. Ironically, when you feel sad, sad songs can make you feel happier because they resonate in a way that assures you that you are not the only one who feels this way and binds you to the sense of a shared common humanity.

What songs work for you? How can you incorporate music—whether through listening, singing, or both—into your everyday life? Playing or learning an instrument can be especially healing and engaging, as well as singing. If you find singing especially healing, how about looking into local choirs or choruses to join, or participating in karaoke? If you enjoy playing an instrument, how about finding others who share your same interest to make music together? When you share your interests with others, you get an added benefit of social connection around a shared love for an activity. Consider making a playlist of songs that can improve your mood.

_____
_____

Exercise

The benefits of exercise are well researched and accepted by mental health and health professionals alike. The Mayo Clinic recommends engaging in at least 30 minutes of exercise three to five days per week to lessen feelings of depression. Consider noting your mood before and after exercise. Often people feel better after moderate exercise, which makes them feel good about themselves. Exercise in itself is good for the mind and body, but it also has the added benefits of potentially providing a social connection, such as by walking or playing sports with others. You might consider playing a group sport such as basketball, volleyball, tennis, or pickleball. Even working out at the gym gets you out among others.

What form of exercise works for you? What type of exercise do you enjoy? Are there groups or teams you can join to share your love of an activity with others? Think of at least one type of exercise you can commit to this week for a half hour at least three times over the week, and note how your mood is affected.

_____
_____

Art

The act of being creative through various art media can be healing. You don't have to be an experienced artist to make a beautiful creation. Enjoying the process of creating is what can lighten your mood and help you feel engaged and positive. All too often, people limit themselves by the mindset that they are not "creative" or "artistic." However, we all have creativity within us. Explore a creative outlet that you enjoy. It doesn't have to be something you consider "fine art"—knitting, resin art, fused glass, writing, mosaics, painting, and ceramics are all great creative outlets. Take a class, find a tutorial on YouTube, try a craft kit. Giving yourself the gift of an artistic outlet can also help to connect you with others who share the same interest; that social connection is in itself healing.

Are there creative art forms that you would like to pursue? Are there opportunities to learn in your community or join with others for a supportive experience of a craft or art?

_____
_____

Movement

Movement is an antidote to depression, and movement practices can be a pleasant way to release negativity and stress. Practices such as tae kwon do, tai chi, and yoga have mind-body benefits, and joining a class will put you in company with others who have similar interests. Dancing is another form of fun and exercise, whether it be social dancing or classes.

Are there practices you can incorporate that will be pleasurable and also bring you in contact with others who share similar interests? If this interests you, what are some practical ideas for how you can incorporate more movement in your life?

_____
_____

Bibliotherapy

Reading can provide a great sense of pleasure, comfort, and stimulation. Reading self-help books can directly help you with alleviating depression, but reading fiction also can improve your mood and get you involved in a new world of ideas to get fresh perspectives on life. Joining a book club has the added benefit of social connection. Consider listening to audiobooks when you walk or drive or work around the house, which can also engage you and offer new perspectives to help your personal growth.

Are there certain types of books that you enjoy and that improve your mood? Are there ideas you have that could help you to incorporate reading or listening to audiobooks into your life more? Are there self-help books that can structure your journey to love yourself more fully and positively? Consider taking time each day to work on your CBT self-help skills using various workbooks and resources available in print or online.

_____
_____

Cinematherapy

Watching movies that inspire you or resonate with your issues are often helpful in lessening the isolation of depression. It can help provide insight and will often reach you on an emotional level. Inspirational clips from various movies can be found on YouTube, such as the speech Sylvester Stallone's character gives to his son in *Rocky* or the speech Al Pacino's character makes to the football players in *Any Given Sunday*. Searching the internet for inspirational movie clips or scenes can help elevate your mood.

_____
_____

Processing the Activity

Which behaviors would you like to do more of? Which ideas appeal to you, and how can you incorporate these ideas into your everyday life? Getting involved in ways that are appealing to you will be an important way to improve your mood by feeling involved and energized. Make a plan to incorporate at least one behavioral activity every day for at least 15 minutes to get you started.

"As I become more proactive, I use each opportunity to show
confidence and motivation for my continued growth and self-love."

Self-Test to Challenge and Eliminate Depressive Thinking

Theory

This self-test will crystallize the 11 TIPs in this chapter to challenge and eliminate depressive thinking. As in all the other chapters, I encourage you to revisit the TIPs in this chapter and repeatedly do the activities that you find helpful until you have lessened the grip of negative, depressive thinking. This will take a lot of practice; this self-test will help you identify where you need to focus your attention.

Implementing Skills

In the self-test that follows, rate how true each statement is for you, from 1 to 10, to assess which areas you are doing well in and which areas need some improvement. The higher the score in each item, the higher your mastery in that area. The test is not designed to give you a one-and-done score. Your self-help journey is a continual one, and the important thing is to work to keep improving on yesterday. Making several copies of this self-test will allow you to keep retaking it to monitor your progress.

At the end of this self-test you will be prompted to calculate a total score and an average score. To get the average score, divide your total score by the number of items you responded to. For any items that are not applicable to you, just write "N/A" and subtract those items from the number you divide by when calculating your average score. As you continue taking the self-tests throughout this book, compare your average scores across the different topics. This will give you a snapshot of which areas need the most attention and which areas are the strongest.

Keep this test handy whenever you want some support and reminders on what tools you can use to work on the areas covered in this chapter.

Self-Test to Challenge and Eliminate Depressive Thinking

Using a scale from 1 to 10, with 1 being "not true" and 10 being "very true," rate how true these statements are for you.

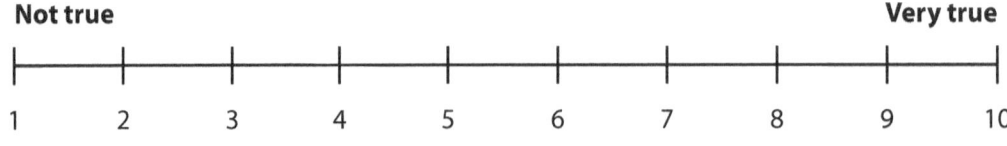

____ I am able to identity my thoughts and feelings in response to a situation.

____ I actively dispute my thoughts that lead to depressive feelings.

____ I am not focused on blaming and take responsibility for my feelings.

____ I am aware of my cognitive distortions that explain my negative thinking.

____ I am using the cognitive distortions log to work on eliminating my distorted thinking.

____ I have used the CBT thought log to work on changing my negative thinking to more factual and accurate interpretations.

____ I am focusing on reframing my thoughts from permanent to temporary thinking.

____ I am identifying my ANTs and NUTs and challenging them.

____ I have discovered my core beliefs and am using the downward arrow technique to change them.

____ I am using an observing head and techniques for cognitive defusion in managing my disturbing thoughts.

____ I have made some coping cards relevant to me and am using them daily.

____ I have made a log for activity monitoring and/or behavioral activation to become more behaviorally and physically active in my recovery from my low moods.

____ I have identified some action-oriented and sensory ways to cope with depression, such as listening to music, creative outlets, movement, inspirational movies, and reading.

____ I have a regular routine for exercise to benefit my mind and body.

____ I am focused on my behavioral goals, making lists, and scheduling things to do to be more proactive.

Total score: _____

Average score (*total score ÷ 15 or items answered*): _____

In the space below, process and explain your answers.

_____
_____
_____
_____
_____
_____

If you would like further structure to process your answers to the self-test and your reactions to the chapter, here are some prompts to guide you.

My thoughts: _____
_____

My feelings: _____
_____

My self-talk: _____
_____

What I have learned: _____
_____

Additional thoughts and strategies: _____
_____
_____
_____

Processing the Activity

The purpose of this self-test is not to have a fixed score, as each time you take it the score will reflect where you are on that day. Check in with yourself intermittently to see how your score changes over time, especially if you are actively working on defeating depressive thinking. Higher scores reflect that you are feeling happier. The goal is to keep tackling negative thinking habits that cause depression. Comparing your average score from this test with your average scores from the other chapter self-tests will help you identify which areas you would like to focus on improving in your CBT journey.

"I commit myself to challenging my negative thinking habits and using behavioral strategies to master my moods and my life."

CHAPTER 3

Accepting Imperfections: Making Peace with Mistakes and Shortcomings

Perfectionism is one of the greatest self-esteem robbers, and it leads to a vicious cycle. The more perfectionistic you are, the more you are bound to fall short, and thus your self-esteem is bound to suffer because you are not the way you think you "should" be. As a result, you end up becoming even more perfectionistic so as not to make further mistakes. When people are perfectionistic, they seek to make themselves feel worthy by setting external, impossible-to-achieve benchmarks for themselves; when they inevitably fail to reach these benchmarks, they feel inadequate. Perfectionism involves too much focus on what is on the outside, measured by success and results, rather than inner benchmarks such as self-acceptance, self-compassion, self-love, and effort.

Perfectionism is a result of shame-based thinking—thinking you are not good enough the way you are, needing to prove your worth, trying to please others to feel good about yourself. Perfectionism is all based on judgment and preconditions to worthiness. This is a setup for failure, or at least feeling like one. This mindset naturally leads to depression and anxiety because you never feel "good enough." Being so hard on yourself takes a toll emotionally and even physically. Obsessive-compulsive disorder, body dysmorphia, substance abuse, and psychosomatic illnesses are also natural outgrowths of perfectionism.

In this chapter we will focus on how to shift from needing to be perfect to loving and embracing yourself without meeting any criteria for worthiness. Self-love and self-acceptance are a given—they do not need to be earned. How about shifting your focus from being perfect to becoming perfectly you? After all, it took trillions of combinations of cell possibilities to form you; why would you want to be someone else? Doesn't that amazing coincidence count for something?

If you find yourself striving for perfection, remember that missteps, failures, and wrong turns can sometimes bring you to the right place! Moving forward in life does not mean taking a straight path forward. When we are perfectionistic, we do not allow ourselves to veer off our path enough to have what could become our greatest learning experiences—experiences that might even propel us forward. Being kind to yourself and accepting twists and turns as unavoidable for a complete and full life will help you overcome your fear of failure while helping you make peace with your imperfections.

"Perfectionism is a twenty-ton shield we lug around thinking it will protect us when, in fact, it's the thing that's really preventing us from taking flight."

–Brené Brown

Strive for Authenticity, Not Perfection

Theory

Perfectionistic people often have one word that keeps on popping up in their self-talk: SHOULD. We learned in TIP #13 that "should" statements are a type of cognitive distortion that warp our thinking, leading to anxious, depressive thoughts. Although there are other cognitive distortions underlying perfectionism, "should" statements lead the pack. "Should" statements can rule your life even when they lack any evidence of truth and are guided more by emotional reasoning, which is another common cognitive distortion in perfectionism. In this TIP we will replace demanding self-talk with more flexible and self-loving self-talk. The goal is to strive for authenticity instead of perfection. To quote cognitive therapy pioneer Albert Ellis, "Stop shoulding on yourself."

Implementing Skills

In the following list are some common "shoulds" in perfectionistic self-talk, along with examples of alternative self-talk that seeks authenticity instead of perfectionism. Notice the rigid, inflexible, harsh messages of perfectionistic thinking as opposed to the kinder, more gentle and flexible messages of authenticity. Use this as a template to change your own "shoulds" to kinder, gentler messages.

Perfectionistic Versus Authentic Self-Talk

Perfectionistic Self-Talk	Authentically *You* Self-Talk
I should be better off by now.	I am working to improve my life.
I should not be so sensitive.	I am sensitive and it makes me who I am.
I should be thinner.	I am working on loving myself at any size.
I should have handled things differently.	I am learning skills now to handle things better.
I should have known better.	I wish I knew better then but I am learning now.

Now It's Your Turn

Change your perfectionistic thoughts to more authentic ones.

Perfectionistic Self-Talk	➡	Authentically *You* Self-Talk
	➡	
	➡	
	➡	
	➡	
	➡	
	➡	

Processing the Activity

Being a "should" buster and challenging perfectionistic thoughts takes practice and patience. After all, many unrealistic and judgmental messages are deep-seated and take a lot of focus to overturn. The important thing is not to focus on blaming others or yourself for how you got these messages, because that will get you stuck in places in the past over which you have no control. The important thing is to move forward with wisdom and insight to become authentically *you*.

"I will strive not for perfection but for authenticity."

Strategies to Eradicate the "Shoulds"

Theory

In working on eradicating the "shoulds," there are no one-size-fits-all techniques that work for everyone all the time. At different times, different practices work the best. This TIP offers some additional "should"-busting techniques to build on the previous TIP. There are seven techniques—I recommend trying one each day for a week to see what works best for you as you work on becoming a "should"-buster.

Implementing Skills

The following are some helpful techniques for busting your "shoulds."

- **Make coping cards:** Write your "should" statement on one side and your "authentically you" statement on the other.

- **Make a "should" jar:** Create a "should" jar or box where you place your "should" statements as you print or write them down on slips of paper (or use your coping cards). This will help remind you that your "should" statements need to get out of your head and into the jar!

- **Write your argument down:** If you are plagued by persistent "shoulds," write out why you deserve not to hold on to them, and why they are not really true. Identify where they came from, question the validity of the people or experiences that gave you these unhealthy messages, and let go of what you do not agree with.

- **Repeat a mantra or affirmation:** Think of affirmations or mantras that challenge your judgmental "shoulds." Write them on coping cards, put up sticky notes by your computer, or put them in a jar to pull out each morning. They can contain any words of wisdom that will help you bust your "should" messages. For example, "I love myself the way I am with no preconditions."

- **Use quotes for inspiration:** Find some quotes that provide reassurance and comfort to eliminate your "shoulds" once and for all. Quotes have a special way of making us feel validated and can help motivate us to put self-critical thinking to rest. Find quotes that relate to your own situation. For example, if your "should" is that you should have been a better person, using this quote from Maya Angelou might help you find more compassion for yourself: "Do the best you can until you know better. Then when you know better, do better."

- **Change your "should" to a preference:** Change your language to reflect a wish rather than a demand. For example, "I should have known better" can become "I wish I knew better" or "It would have been preferable if I handled things differently, but I did not have the skills at the time."

- **How about a hug?** When we are hard on ourselves, we keep re-traumatizing ourselves with our criticisms. How about writing out or even saying your "should" out loud and, after each phrase, give yourself a hug to comfort yourself and remind yourself that you are still lovable despite the missteps.

Processing the Activity

These practices can offer you a menu to choose from as you work to quell that critical voice in your head and embrace who you truly are. Don't you deserve it?

"I will work on eradicating my 'shoulds' once and for all."

From Self-Criticism to Self-Compassion

Theory

Perfectionism can be viewed as a trauma response. We scold ourselves in the same way we might have been scolded or critiqued when we were young, continuing to make ourselves feel flawed and inferior unless we are perfect. This is not to focus blame on parents, family members, teachers, peers, or others. Most people do what they think is right at the time, or else are acting out their own trauma—in either case, they simply did not have the mental clarity to act any better. Regardless of where the need for perfection comes from, it is our responsibility to take care of ourselves going forward. Self-compassion offers the key to putting critical self-talk to rest.

Implementing Skills

The following list shows how self-critical self-talk can be changed to self-compassionate self-talk.

Self-Criticism	Self-Compassion
I'm defective.	I am beautiful and only feel defective because I am still building up my self-compassion and self-esteem.
I should be better by now.	May I be kind to myself and not hard on myself.
I wasted so much time.	No time is wasted—my circuitous path led me to where I am today.
I should have known better.	I forgive myself for not having the ability to know better back then.
I need to earn the respect of others.	I have nothing to prove—I am a good person and I love and respect myself.

Now It's Your Turn

In the chart that follows, write down your own self-critical thoughts and practice turning them into self-compassion.

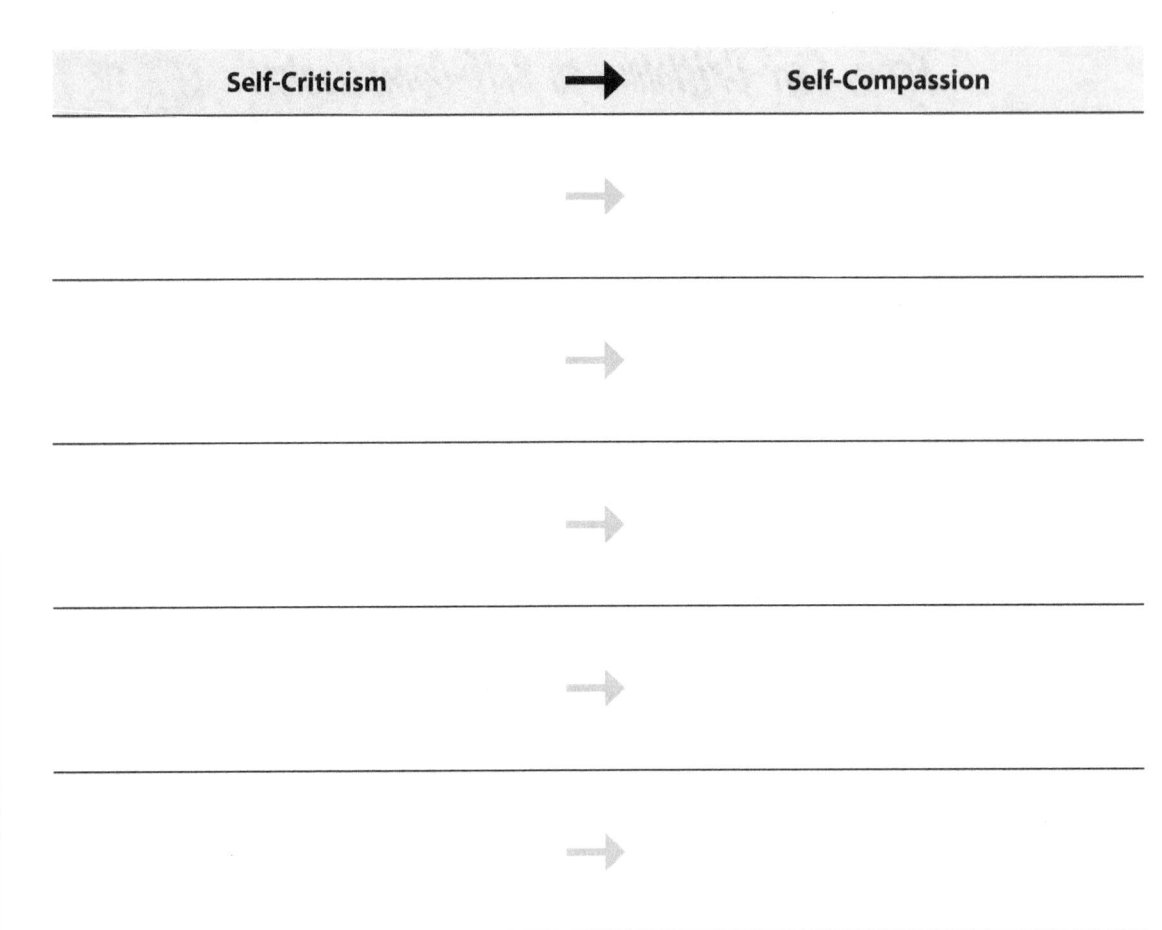

The Tranquility Prayer

A take on the Serenity Prayer, this Tranquility Prayer is for self-acceptance and self-compassion:

*Please grant me the inner peace to love and accept myself unconditionally,
while honoring the need to change and improve for my own sake as well as for others,
and having the wisdom to know the difference.*

Processing the Activity

Self-compassion is the new self-esteem. It is non-evaluative and self-accepting. People who are more compassionate to themselves tend to be happier and more resilient. No matter how little or much we have received love from others, we can always shower ourselves with self-love and compassion.

*"I do not deserve to be so hard on myself.
I deserve only love and self-compassion."*

Thinking in Temporary, Not Permanent, Ways

Theory

As we discussed in TIP #15, one self-sabotaging cognitive habit is thinking in permanent ways rather than temporary ways. All too often we think that our thoughts and feelings will *always* be that way. Permanent thinking like this lies at the root of perfectionism, anxiety, and depression. Here are some more practical tools for moving from permanent to temporary thinking habits.

Implementing Skills

Here are some phrases you can use to change your self-talk from permanent thinking to temporary thinking:

- Up until now . . .
- Previously I . . .
- I am learning now that . . .
- At this point in time . . .
- At this point in my life . . .
- Right now . . .
- Currently I . . .
- Moving forward, I . . .
- I learned that . . .
- Before I did _____, but now I do _____.

The following are some examples of permanent self-talk phrases. Examine how it's possible to change them to more temporary self-talk, which is less rigid, more flexible, and more accurate.

Permanent Self-Talk ➡	Temporary Self-Talk
I fail at every relationship I have.	Up until now I have had difficulties with relationships, but I have learned many things along the way.
I'm bad at starting conversations.	I have had a lot of trouble starting conversations, but at this point I am learning better skills.
I lack confidence.	Moving forward, I am learning to be easier on myself and develop my confidence with healthier thinking habits.
I have made so many mistakes—I can't afford one more.	I have forgiven myself for my missteps in the past and am moving forward with self-compassion and insight.

Now It's Your Turn

Think of some of your permanent self-talk and, using the phrases provided previously, change them to temporary thinking.

Permanent Self-Talk	➡	Temporary Self-Talk
_____	→	_____
_____	→	_____
_____	→	_____
_____	→	_____
_____	→	_____

Processing the Activity

How did it feel to replace permanent thoughts with temporary thoughts? When you free yourself from perfectionistic and rigid self-talk, you are honoring your growth and your ability to rise above adversity and old messages that might have held you down. Don't you deserve it?

"I will no longer exaggerate my flaws and shortcomings. I commit myself to looking at myself in a way that honors my ability to grow and change."

Lessons Learned from Successful Failures

Theory

There is no shortage of examples of famous people, both currently and in history, that became wildly successful after at least one major failure or, more often, a string of failures. These examples show how important resilience and fortitude are, regardless of how many mistakes were made. These people who became outwardly successful after failure refused to be defined by their failures. In fact, they were motivated by them. Seeing this list of notable people who experienced failure provides a helpful perspective for defeating the notion that perfectionism makes you better. In reality, perfectionism makes you stuck. Having a resilient mindset is what leads to success after failure. Having passion, loving what you do, and persevering with lessons learned can lead to great success despite missteps and even failures, just as they have for people throughout history.

Implementing Skills

The following are some examples of successful failures. (I could have included dozens more.) Can you imagine if they had allowed their failures to make them doubt themselves and stop trying? Their stories make it seem like failure is almost necessary for success.

Learning from Successful Failures

- At age 30, Steve Jobs was removed from Apple, the company that he founded. In his famous Stanford commencement speech, Jobs said that experiencing humiliating public failure turned out to be the best thing that happened to him, as he was able to reinvent himself and pursue what he still loved. He went on to develop Pixar Animation, the iPad, and the iPhone, along with other innovations. He also met his wife and started a family during this period of "failure."

- Henry Ford's first automobile company went into bankruptcy after 18 months, yet he went on to found the successful Ford Motor Company.

- Steven Spielberg was rejected from USC's film school.

- Dr. Seuss sent his first book, *And to Think That I Saw It on Mulberry Street*, to 27 publishers who all rejected it before he found a publisher.

- Walt Disney reportedly was told he did not have enough imagination and was fired from his job at a newspaper.

- Albert Einstein is said to have been late in talking and labeled "mentally slow" on his school record.

- Early in her career, Oprah Winfrey was demoted from her job as a news anchor and later moved to hosting a talk show—the medium through which she became a household name.
- After his sole performance at the Grand Ole Opry, Elvis was allegedly told by the talent coordinator to go back to driving a truck.
- Michael Jordan was cut from his high school varsity basketball team as a sophomore.
- Abraham Lincoln suffered a nervous breakdown and several political setbacks before becoming one of the most revered presidents in history.
- Sir James Dyson wanted to invent a bagless vacuum design. It took him 15 years and 5,000 prototypes to finally create the Dyson vacuum as we know it today.
- J. K. Rowling's first Harry Potter book was rejected by 12 publishers. When she wrote it, she was a single mother on welfare. She started writing her ideas for the book on a napkin at a coffee shop.

Processing the Activity

This short sample list of successful failures provides a great perspective on perfectionism. What all these successful failures have in common is that they loved what they did, believed in what they did, and were not deterred by their setbacks. The lesson is that failures and mistakes are just part of the journey to success and that passion, resilience, and motivation are the key to success, regardless of how many times your efforts turn into failures. How about you? Are there failures you have experienced that could help you pave the way for your own successes, small or large?

"Just because I might have taken the wrong turn doesn't mean I won't end up in the right place."

Inspiring Quotes from Successful Failures

TIP #28

Theory

The examples of famous successful people are so inspiring that in this TIP, I am including inspiring quotes from well-known successful failures. Quotes have a way of normalizing failure and resonating with us in ways that make an impression. Quotes normalize our struggles and allow us to be comforted by being part of the human condition, which helps us feel not so alone. Quotes also have a way of making truths digestible and relevant, and they help us look at things from a different perspective. In short, the use of quotes is a perfect fit for helping us apply CBT concepts to our lives—quotes can comfort us, improve how we think and feel, and lift our mood by helping to comfort us and change our perspective.

Implementing Skills

Consider the following inspirational quotes from famous successful failures:

- "You don't learn to walk by following rules; you learn by doing and by falling over." –Richard Branson

- "My great concern is not whether you have failed, but whether you are content with your failure." –attributed to Abraham Lincoln

- "Success is not final, failure is not fatal: it is the courage to continue that counts." –attributed to Winston Churchill

- "Do not judge me by my successes; judge me by how many times I fell down and got back up again." –Nelson Mandela

- "Failure is only the opportunity to begin again, this time more intelligently. There is no disgrace in honest failure; there is disgrace in fearing to fail." –Henry Ford

- "It's important to be willing to make mistakes. The worst thing that can happen is you make them memorable." –attributed to Sara Blakely

- "It's fine to celebrate success, but it is more important to heed the lessons of failure." –attributed to Bill Gates

- "I have gotten a lot of results! I know several thousand things that won't work." –Thomas Alva Edison

- "Failure is a detour, not a dead-end street." –Zig Ziglar

- "It is impossible to live without failing at something, unless you live so cautiously that you might as well not have lived at all. In which case you have failed by default." –J. K. Rowling

- "Think like a queen. A queen is not afraid to fail. Failure is another stepping stone to greatness." –Oprah Winfrey

- "Success isn't about the end result, it's about what you learn along the way." –attributed to Vera Wang
- "You always pass failure on your way to success." –attributed to Mickey Rooney
- "The secret of life is to fall seven times and to get up eight times." –Paulo Coelho
- "Most great people have attained their greatest success just one step beyond their greatest failure." –Napoleon Hill
- "Everybody goes through disappointments; it's how you overcome those disappointments." –Michael Jordan

Processing the Activity

If you found these quotes helpful, consider making them into coping cards or putting them in a quote jar to inspire you. You can continue to add your own favorite quotes on a regular basis. Searching for inspirational quotes is a positive activity in itself. As a creative twist, how about writing some of your own inspirational words of the truths you have learned from setbacks, failures, and opportunities?

"Failure is a way of learning that makes an impact and gives me valuable information for my road to success."

How Mistakes Can Change the World for the Better

Theory

Do you know what Scotchgard™, Post-it® Notes, and the Nobel Prize have in common? They all came to fruition in the aftermath of mistakes that were made. This TIP builds on the previous two TIPs to show that even unfortunate mistakes can end up leading to astonishing success. That should be convincing enough to help you realize that perfectionism is very overrated! In this TIP you will be prompted to review how some of your own mistakes may have turned into some of the best things that happened to you.

Implementing Skills

Half a century ago, researchers at 3M were trying to develop stronger, tougher adhesives. In the process, one of the scientists, Spencer Silver, discovered a form of adhesive that was only lightly sticky—a failure for that experiment. However, some years later, his colleague Art Fry was growing frustrated with paper bookmarks, which kept falling out of his hymnal as he practiced with his church choir. Recalling the failed adhesive experiment, he partnered with Silver and they developed what became the widely used 3M Post-it Note.*

Around the same time, and also at 3M, a research team led by Patsy Sherman was trying to develop a new type of rubber for airplane fuel lines. By accident, a beaker of rubber was dropped onto the floor and the liquid splashed onto Sherman's canvas shoes. While the experimental mixture didn't change how the shoes looked or felt, it wouldn't wash out. Sherman and fellow chemist Sam Smith realized it could be used to protect fabrics from fluids—a mistake had led to the discovery of Scotchgard.**

Alfred Nobel was a nineteenth-century Swedish chemist who invented dynamite. Accidental explosions sometimes occurred in his factories, including one that killed Nobel's younger brother Emil. This is not to mention the destructive uses that dynamite was put to, including as a weapon of war, and it's possible that Nobel regretted his invention. To further cause guilt, years later when another of his brothers, Ludvig, passed away in Cannes, the French newspapers confused him with Alfred—one paper's headline was "The merchant of death is dead." Perhaps it was this glimpse at how the world would remember him that inspired him to leave the better part of his fortune to establish the Nobel Prizes.***

---

* Post-it.com. (n.d.). *History timeline: Post-it® Notes*. https://www.post-it.com/3M/en_US/post-it/contact-us/about-us

** Smithsonian National Museum of American History. (2014, May 12). *Patsy Sherman: Scotchgard™ inventor*. https://invention.si.edu/node/1145/p/430-patsy-sherman-scotchgard-inventor

*** Encyclopaedia Britannica. (n.d.). *Alfred Nobel*. https://www.britannica.com/biography/Alfred-Nobel

Now It's Your Turn

Use the following prompts to reflect on how your own failures might have led to success.

What are some mistakes you have made that turned into something positive? If we look hard enough, there are often blessings in unexpected places!

_____
_____

Can you think of changing your mistakes (or fears of making mistakes) into goals like Alfred Nobel did? After all, mistakes can be great motivators to redirect our lives.

_____
_____

Things of beauty can also be the result of mistakes. Think of a beautiful vase that is broken. Although the vase will never be whole again, it can be made into a beautiful mosaic. Mosaics offer a beautiful image of broken pieces making something that is even more beautiful. How can that apply to your life? Are there broken dreams or regretful mistakes that you can integrate with your life to make you see yourself and your life as even more enriched, meaningful, and beautiful?

_____
_____

Another great visualization is to think of some of your failed dreams and mistakes as stepping stones toward something meaningful based on the lessons learned. Have there been setbacks for you that have turned into stepping stones?

_____
_____

Processing the Activity

Hopefully this TIP has resonated with you and helped you realize that mistakes are often necessary precursors to success. Giving up the fear of making mistakes and the need to be perfect will free you to be more creative and go to "plan B." Sometimes the best gifts we get in life are not ones that we arrange for ourselves, but ones that arise without our direct intervention.

"Instead of trying to be perfect, I will work on
being perfectly happy with myself."

Trade in Your Perfectionistic Words

Theory

In this TIP we will focus on the type of self-talk that leads to perfectionism. Of course, in life-and-death situations such as delicate surgeries and complicated flying missions, perfection or near perfection is required. However, most perfectionists are not dealing with life-and-death situations. Even when safety is not an issue, people who are perfectionistic give themselves a figurative narrow tightrope to walk on, rather than a large plank where mistakes and missteps can be allowed. After all, in most of life, as in sports, sometimes we lose even when we play well.

People who are perfectionistic talk to themselves in rigid and extreme ways that reflect cognitive distortions. I will never forget a client who said to me many years ago, "I have had so many failures, I can't afford one more" as a way of justifying her perfectionistic tendencies. Interestingly enough, she could only cite two such "failures," but they loomed larger than life and resulted in excessive anxiety and low self-esteem.

When we talk to ourselves in rigid, inflexible ways, there is no room for error, growth, or learning. This TIP will help you learn to trade in your harsh self-talk for words that are more flexible and kind to yourself. Chances are that if we are perfectionistic toward ourselves, we will also be that way with our loved ones and others around us, which gives us even more reason to trade in our words for something more compassionate and wiser.

Implementing Skills

In the table that follows, the perfectionistic words are changed into more flexible, healthier self-talk. In bold are the key words to trade in with more flexible, compassionate words. I offer examples of both perfectionistic self-talk and perfectionistic words toward others, since if you are hard on yourself, you will likely be hard on others too.

Perfectionistic Words	→	Flexible, Compassionate Words
I **can't** stand making mistakes.	→	I **try** to avoid mistakes.
I **should** not be so careless.	→	I **would like** to be more careful.
It's **terrible** that I did that.	→	I **will** learn from my mistake.
I **must** stop screwing up.	→	It's **unfortunate** that I did that.
You **should** have known better.	→	I **wish** you had known that.
You **never** listen, do you?	→	I **often** wonder if I get my point across.

What inflexible words do you use that you can trade in? Write some of your negative self-talk or negative thoughts about others and circle the rigid words and then trade them in for healthier alternatives. Notice that perfectionistic words show either the cognitive distortions of all-or-nothing thinking or "should" statements.

Perfectionistic Words →	**Flexible, Compassionate Words**
→	
→	
→	
→	
→	

Processing the Activity

When you trade in your words from rigid to flexible, you are allowing kindness and flexibility into your world. Being critical only leads to decreased esteem for yourself and others and does not teach the lessons you hope to teach. When you trade in your words, everybody wins.

"I will use flexible words to show care and compassion to myself and others."

Overcoming the Cognitive Distortions Resulting in Procrastination

Theory

Procrastination seems to go hand in hand with perfectionism. Underneath both is the fear of making a mistake, which can cause emotional paralysis and inaction. Sometimes it seems safer not to make a choice at all—but ironically, not making a choice is making a choice by default! In the case of perfectionism, when people are hard on themselves already, they often fear making choices they may later regret, which would cause them to be even more down on themselves.

Even putting off healthy choices like exercising more or quitting smoking can be a result of perfectionistic thinking. Those who have trouble accepting their imperfections tend to think in *all-or-nothing* ways, believing that they must be "all in" to achieve their goal and that anything less is a failure. In their determination to avoid failure, people often keep putting off taking small steps to change their habits. However, there is a middle ground between succeeding and failing. Making minor changes in our daily habits can lead to sustained change over time.

In this TIP we will explore ways to remove the thought blocks of procrastination by identifying and challenging distorted thinking habits. Afterward, continue on to the next TIP to learn some practical steps you can take to change your behavior and ultimately change your life!

Implementing Skills

Consider the following examples of distorted thinking and how these thoughts could be challenged. For each type of distortion, after reading the example provided, add your own example. Write down the distorted thought you have and then challenge it.

All-or-nothing thinking: You think in black-and-white terms and are afraid of failing, so you don't even start.

Distorted Thought	➝	Challenge
I need to lose 20 pounds, but I don't have willpower and always fail, so why even try?	➝	This is black-and-white thinking. Even if I lose a few pounds, I will feel better. I do not have to reach a number to be successful—I can feel successful along the way.
	➝	

"Should" statements: "Shoulds" produce feelings of guilt that paralyze you from taking action.

Distorted Thought	➡	Challenge
I should have more willpower. Every time I fall off my diet plan, it makes me even more down on myself, which makes me feel more depressed and unmotivated.	➡	Success is not only in the destination; it's also in the journey. I will try to make little steps toward my goal.
	➡	

Fortune telling: Thinking you can predict the future and then feeling hopeless based on your own prediction.

Distorted Thought	➡	Challenge
I have always been heavy since having children and will always be heavy, so why bother even trying?	➡	I will not always be that way if I commit myself to a healthier diet and exercise. I can be more fit and feel more proud of myself.
	➡	

Mental filtering: You focus on the negative aspect of something and discount the possibility of positives arising from imperfect actions and choices.

Distorted Thought	➡	Challenge
Even if I lose weight, I still will look heavy and unattractive since I have a stocky frame.	➡	I will feel proud of myself for making progress and I can be proud of the way I look.
	➡	

Labeling: You label yourself (or others) unfairly in all-or-nothing ways that prevent you from pursuing your goals.

Distorted Thought	➡	Challenge
I'm just inept.	➡	It is unfair to label myself this way. I am not lazy—I am afraid to fail, but I am working on making peace with not being perfect.
	➡	

Emotional reasoning: You feel a certain way and make assumptions based on those feelings that your feelings are evidence of the truth.

Distorted Thought	➡	Challenge
I feel inadequate, so I am inadequate.	➡	I am not inadequate. I just feel that way now. I am working to stick to the facts, not my interpretations, which will allow me to keep on trying to feel successful.
	➡	

Comparing: You compare yourself unfavorably with others, which lowers your sense of self-worth and leads to fear of making mistakes.

Distorted Thought	➡	Challenge
I will never be as fit and thin as my girlfriends, so I feel unmotivated to even try to improve my health. Instead, I'll comfort myself with food.	➡	It is not healthy or relevant to compare myself with others. I will only compare myself to myself and how I am improving on yesterday.
	➡	

Blaming and personalization: You unfairly assign all the guilt and responsibility to others (blaming) or to yourself (personalization), when the situation really involved other factors.

Distorted Thought	Challenge
I blame myself for not being a good role model for my children—it will be my fault if they struggle with their weight when they get older.	I cannot blame myself for choices my children will make when they are older. I am doing my best now to make sure they eat sensibly and nutritiously.

Processing the Activity

What are some things you procrastinate about? Can you identify the irrational thoughts and cognitive distortions that are holding you back? After looking at the preceding examples and writing down your own examples, consider revisiting your thoughts daily and challenge them with healthier ways of thinking in order to get going!

> "I will combat my irrational thoughts that lead to my being stuck and will take steps each day to move toward the life I want and deserve."

Practical Strategies to Get Yourself Going and Avoid Procrastination

Theory

Now that you have explored the cognitive distortions that keep you from taking action, you are ready to develop behavioral strategies to get going. In this TIP we will explore various practices to overcome procrastination so you can make progress toward achieving your goals. The important thread throughout these TIPs is to not measure your success in reaching the destination, but rather to focus on the journey and the mini successes along the way. Goals are important to strive toward, but they are not the only guarantor of success. I will continue to use the example of procrastinating on developing exercise and diet strategies with the goal of losing weight.

Implementing Skills

The following are some practical strategies to get yourself going and avoid procrastination.

Focus on the Process, Not the Results or Goal

When you focus on the future and expect yourself to be happy when you reach your goals, the future might never come the way you expect. Never put off your happiness for some future goal.

- **Perfectionistic thought:** "I will be happy when I lose 20 pounds."
- **Healthier thought:** "I can be happy going toward my goal of loving myself and making myself the healthiest I can be."

Replace Perfectionism with the Pursuit of Excellence

David Burns offers a two-column technique that he refers to as "Perfectionism vs. the Healthy Pursuit of Excellence" (*The Feeling Good Handbook*, 1999, p. 176). Through the use of this technique, irrational fears related to perfectionism are answered in healthier and more positive ways, just as cognitive distortions are answered with more rational alternatives.

- **Perfectionistic thought:** "I am motivated by fear of failing to lose weight."
- **Pursuit of excellence:** "I am motivated by enthusiasm to try my best to improve my health."

Weigh the Pros and Cons of Procrastinating

The cost/benefit analysis is a mainstay of CBT. Write out the pros and cons for procrastination versus taking action. This practice can help us organize our thinking and look at the benefits and drawbacks in a rational, objective way.

The Cons of Procrastination	The Pros of Overcoming Procrastination
I will not improve my health.	I will get healthier through a healthier diet and exercise.
I will stay overweight.	I will feel better and look better if I lose some weight and build muscle.
I will continue to be unhappy with my level of fitness and lack of muscle tone.	I will be motivated and feel more in control of my body and proud of myself if I take steps to make myself healthier and more fit.

Practice Response Prevention

Response prevention is a behavioral technique to reduce unwanted bad habits by removing the availability of the things that are hard to avoid.

Example: Go through your pantry and refrigerator and remove tempting foods that do not fit your nutrition goals, and replace those foods with a variety of healthier options.

Use a Behavioral Chart

Make yourself a behavioral chart for each day of the week, state a goal, and give yourself checks for each day that you accomplish the goal.

Example: Make a chart to manage your food and increase your exercise. Put your goals (such as eating only healthy snacks between meals, exercising at least 30 minutes four times a week, eating fruit instead of candy, etc.) on one end of the chart. Then give yourself a check mark for each day you accomplish your goal. Seeing the checks is often reinforcement enough, but you might also want to save enough checks to reward yourself with a non-food award, such as going to a movie or treating yourself to a new pair of shoes or an online movie.

Choose Proactive Self-Talk, Not Reactive Self-Talk

Rephrasing your reactive thoughts into proactive thoughts can be empowering and motivating. Reactive self-talk leads to procrastination; proactive self-talk leads to taking control of your life.

Reactive Self-Talk	Proactive Self-Talk
I *should* lose weight.	I *want to* lose weight.
I *have to* exercise and live healthier.	I *want to* exercise and live healthier.
I *don't* have willpower.	I *do* have willpower even though it is challenging.
I *can't* do this.	I *can* do this with strategies.

Break Your Large Goal into Small Mini-Goals

Instead of focusing on the big overriding goals, break each goal into small mini steps that are more manageable, and pick one of these smaller goals to tackle each day or week.

Here are some examples of mini-goals:

- Start a food/mood diary
- Start an exercise log
- Choose fruit over candy for one day or week
- Take the stairs instead of the elevator

Use Coping Cards for Inspiration

Write words of motivation on note cards or on your computer. They can include affirmations, inspirational quotes, or personal reminders.

Here are some examples:

- I can do this!
- I am worth it.
- I will enjoy the journey of empowering myself.
- "Just believe in yourself. Even if you don't, pretend that you do and, at some point, you will." –Venus Williams

Processing the Activity

Can you think of your own situation that you would like to be more proactive about? Write down how you can apply each of the ideas in this TIP to your own situation. The array of practices to choose from can help you figure out what practices will work best for you. In starting out, choose one practice each day for a week or two, then continue with the most effective practice for the following weeks. You do not need to tackle too much at one time. As the saying goes, "slow and steady wins the race," meaning that consistent efforts are more effective than bursts of intense effort. Seeing this as a journey and being patient with yourself can help you relax and enjoy the positive direction you are going in, without judgment as to how fast you should be getting there.

> "I will try out a variety of specific strategies, both by challenging thought blocks and by putting my efforts into action, to empower myself to reach my goals. After all, life is not what happens to me but what I happen to do about it!"

Self-Test to Accept Imperfections

Theory

In this chapter we have focused on how to stand up to perfectionistic thinking and dispute and change irrational thoughts blocks that can lead to inaction and avoidance. We also focused on how to change your behavior to literally change your life. As with all the other chapter self-tests, this test serves as a review of some of the major ideas of the chapter. Keep on revisiting the TIPs in this chapter, filling out the worksheet in this TIP with your own examples, so you can improve your ability to be clear-thinking, motivated, and proactive.

Implementing Skills

In the self-test that follows, rate how true each statement is for you, from 1 to 10, to assess which areas you are doing well in and which areas need some improvement. The higher the score in each item, the higher your mastery in that area. The test is not designed to give you a one-and-done score. Your self-help journey is a continual one, and the important thing is to work to keep improving on yesterday. Making several copies of this self-test will allow you to keep retaking it to monitor your progress.

At the end of this self-test you will be prompted to calculate a total score and an average score. To get the average score, divide your total score by the number of items you responded to. For any items that are not applicable to you, just write "N/A" and subtract those items from the number you divide by when calculating your average score. As you continue taking the self-tests throughout this book, compare your average scores across the different topics. This will give you a snapshot of which areas need the most attention and which areas are the strongest.

Keep this test handy whenever you want some support and reminders on what tools you can use to work on the areas covered in this chapter.

Self-Test for Accepting Imperfections

Using a scale from 1 to 10, with 1 being "not true" and 10 being "very true," rate how true these statements are for you.

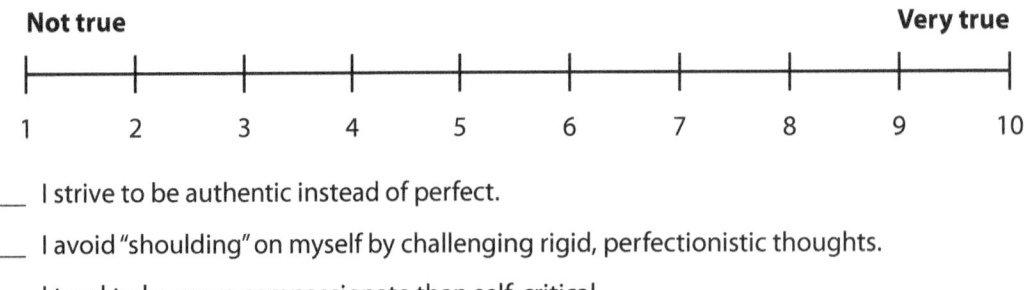

____ I strive to be authentic instead of perfect.

____ I avoid "shoulding" on myself by challenging rigid, perfectionistic thoughts.

____ I tend to be more compassionate than self-critical.

____ I am not hard on myself—I treat myself like a friend.

____ I tend to think in temporary instead of permanent ways.

____ I am not afraid of failure, as failures can be stepping stones to success.

____ I replace perfectionistic self-talk with more self-compassionate self-talk.

____ I try to communicate in a way that is nonjudgmental and accepting to myself and others.

____ I show compassion and empathy to others.

____ I am inspired by people who manage to move on after setbacks and even failures.

____ I am inspired by the fact that mistakes can lead to amazing success, and I do not let fear of mistakes hold me back.

____ I have become aware of and can challenge my cognitive distortions that lead to procrastination.

____ I have identified and put into practice active strategies to pursue my goals and avoid procrastination.

Total score: _____

Average score (*total score ÷ 13 or items answered*): _____

In the space below, process and explain your answers.

_____
_____
_____
_____
_____
_____

If you would like further structure to process your answers to the self-test and your reactions to the chapter, here are some prompts to guide you.

My thoughts: _____
_____

My feelings: _____
_____

My self-talk: _____
_____

What I have learned: _____

_____

Additional thoughts and strategies: _____

_____

_____

_____

Processing the Activity

Use this checklist periodically to assess your progress and continue improving your ability to overcome perfectionism while increasing self-acceptance and self-compassion. Look at the items that were the highest and lowest on your list to identify areas that are easier for you and areas that need attention. Comparing your average scores with the other chapters will allow you to see the chapter topics in which you have more mastery and which ones need more attention. How does your ability to defeat perfectionism compare?

Your general overall score will vary over time. It is helpful to keep a record of your scores to see if you are improving in your ability to let go of perfectionism.

"With enough focus on my negative and inflexible self-talk, and commitment to positive action, I will confidently move forward in my life."

CHAPTER 4

Coping with Anxiety and Worry: Calming Your Emotions by Calming Your Mind

We all have anxiety. It is not only a fact of life but an adaptive one at that. Anxiety can be likened to a low-fuel warning light on your car's dashboard. Just as the gas light warns you that you are running close to empty and need to refuel, anxiety alerts you to issues that need attention so that you can achieve insights and emotionally refuel.

We need some amount of anxiety to be safe. For example, if we did not have some anxiety about getting into a car accident, we would not take proper precautions to obey traffic rules, drive defensively, and proceed with caution.

The problem arises when anxiety gets out of control. Anxiety can help us stay safe, but when anxiety immobilizes us and becomes unmanageable, it can significantly negatively impact our lives and sense of well-being. Anxiety disorders are a result of out-of-control, exaggerated thinking where even realistic fears spiral into unrealistic ones. Anxiety disorders, and in particular generalized anxiety disorder, are often regarded as the most common type of mental health disorder diagnosed in the US, and anxiety is the number one symptom prompting people to seek psychological treatment. It is estimated that a third of the US population will experience significant anxiety symptoms that interfere with personal well-being at some point in their lifetime.

CBT is widely regarded as the most effective psychological treatment for anxiety, since the various types of anxiety disorders all center around illogical, exaggerated thoughts. Although medications are commonly prescribed to quell anxiety, the underlying issues causing anxiety are best addressed by CBT. CBT offers people the tools to identify, challenge, and replace unhealthy patterns of thinking with more positive, factual, and realistic thinking habits.

This chapter offers the most effective CBT tools to challenge and replace the cognitive distortions that cause anxiety, helping to quell and manage anxious thinking. The key to improvement is to practice these techniques often. It takes repetition and constantly revisiting issues to restructure your way of thinking. After all, it took many years of "practice" to develop unwanted symptoms of anxiety, so it is unrealistic to think that anxiety can be cured without much effort. But if used often and repeatedly, the techniques in this chapter offer a blueprint for success in changing your thoughts to calm your mind, which will in turn calm your emotions, making anxiety adaptive and manageable.

Aside from CBT strategies to change the way we think, relaxation and mindfulness strategies are also key to dealing with extreme anxiety. Excessive anxiety affects the body as well as the mind in acute physical reactions such as shortness of breath, irregular heartbeat, churning stomach, and sweating. Sometimes anxiety and panic might be so debilitating that we need help to calm our bodily sensations at the same time as our minds, so mindfulness and thought strategies make a good team. We will focus on these mind-body techniques in subsequent chapters, since mindfulness and relaxation strategies are crucial to so many areas of mental health and wellness.

"Today I escaped anxiety. Or no, I discarded it, because it was within me, in my own perceptions—not outside."

–attributed to Marcus Aurelius

Using a Cognitive Distortion Diary to Manage Anxiety

Theory

You may recall TIP #13, where we listed some of the cognitive distortions that lead to depression. The concept of underlying cognitive distortions is central to CBT; here, we will explore more examples relating to anxiety. Without identifying cognitive distortions that underlie anxious thinking, anxiety has little chance of dissipating. Using a diary to identify your own anxiety-inducing distortions will help chip away at the thinking patterns that result in anxiety.

Combating the irrational thoughts will take a lot of practice and persistence. This TIP will remind you of the major distortions so you can learn to identify your cognitive errors that are leading to anxious thoughts. I have used a common scenario and filled in examples of the anxious thoughts that characterize each distortion so it will be easier to fill out your own examples in the blank template. By uncovering your distortions, you gain power over your anxious thoughts.

Implementing Skills

Example Cognitive Distortion Diary to Manage Anxiety

Anxiety-producing situation: A person with low self-esteem is feeling inferior to others at a party and fearful of speaking up and engaging socially.

Type of Distortion	My Distorted Thoughts
All-or-nothing-thinking: Viewing things in black and white, blowing things out of proportion.	"I am never relaxed while talking to people." "It would be terrible if I were to say something stupid."
"Should" statements: Judgmental and unforgiving statements that are rigid and inflexible.	"I should be better in social situations." "I should not say something stupid."
Fortune telling: Thinking you can predict the future based on the way you are thinking now.	"I will never meet anyone and will always be alone." "I will always be anxious around others."
Jumping to conclusions: Assuming things are facts based on little evidence.	"They must find me very boring." "No one here wants to get stuck talking to me."

Type of Distortion	My Distorted Thoughts
Mental filtering: Focusing on the negative aspects of something and ignoring the positive.	"I am a total zero when it comes to communication." "I don't have anything interesting to say."
Labeling: Categorizing yourself (or others) unfairly in generalizing ways.	"I am unlikable." "I'm a loser."
Comparing: Comparing yourself unfavorably with others, which lowers your sense of self-worth.	"They seem all so confident and better than me." "I wish I could be popular like him."
Minimization: Failing to respect your feelings and even your competence.	"I should not be so anxious—others have it worse than me." "I can't do anything right."
Personalization: Taking all the responsibility for unfortunate outcomes over which you had little to no control.	"I can't attract people." "If I had a better personality or were more attractive, people would like me more."
Emotional reasoning: Feeling a certain way and assuming that your feelings are evidence of the truth.	"I feel hopeless, so I must *be* hopeless." "I feel pathetic, so I *am* pathetic."

Now It's Your Turn

Use the blank cognitive distortion diary on the next page to fill in your own examples.

Processing the Activity

Identifying distortions and recognizing their irrational basis is a cornerstone of CBT practice and essential in eliminating self-sabotaging thoughts that lead to anxiety. By sticking to the facts and identifying faulty ways of thinking, the mind becomes calmer and settles our emotions. Although anxiety-reducing medication can help symptomatically, the underlying cause of anxiety needs to be addressed to make fundamental changes in our baseline mental health.

"I pledge myself to stick to the facts and not my interpretations."

My Cognitive Distortion Diary

Type of Distortion	My Distorted Thoughts

 # Restructuring Your Cognitive Distortions

Theory

We have introduced in previous TIPs the importance of identifying cognitive distortions in tackling unhealthy thinking habits. That step is necessary to change irrational thoughts, but the work does not end there. After identifying patterns of distorted thinking, the next step is to challenge and restructure that distortion. *Cognitive restructuring* is a CBT technique used to reinterpret erroneous ways of thinking. It helps us interpret negative life events in a healthier way. By assigning a different meaning to your thoughts, anxiety can be reduced and even eliminated.

Implementing Skills

The following questions are examples of the *Socratic method*, a very important technique used in CBT to improve critical thinking skills and challenge faulty thinking patterns. Think of a persistent anxiety-producing thought you have and apply the Socratic method to uproot that way of thinking.

Self-Examination Questioning to Challenge Faulty Thinking

- Where is the evidence to support my thought?
- Is that an interpretation or a fact?
- How can I change that interpretation to something more grounded and more accurate?
- Are there any other ways to see this situation?
- What are alternative explanations?
- Am I biased against myself? Would I think the same thing of others that I admire if they were in this situation?
- Am I holding to unrealistic expectations of myself?
- Am I looking at things in black or white? If so, how can I change to shades of gray?
- Where did these thinking habits come from? How can I change them now?

Can you think of other questions that can help you tackle your exaggerated beliefs? Write your answers to these questions for your own personal situation.

_____
_____
_____
_____
_____

After using the Socratic method for cognitive restructuring, using what is known as a *thought log* can be very effective for recognizing the automatic negative thoughts that underlie anxiety. It helps us break the never-ending spiral of negative thinking and allows us to use our anxiety more like the gas light in a car. You can regard anxiety as useful, like that symbol on your car dashboard lighting up when the gas level is low. It provides useful information—and if you do not heed it, you will run out of gas!

You might find the "3 Cs" useful to remind yourself of the process of restructuring your thinking. The three Cs are as follows: **catch** the automatic anxiety-producing negative thoughts, **check** and question the validity of those assumptions, and then **change** those erroneous thoughts by replacing them with rational thoughts based in fact, not fiction.

The following is a sample CBT thought log. After this example, use your own situation and fill in your own log. If you do this daily for a consistent period of time, you will become better and better at catching those automatic negative thought habits that underlie anxiety.

Example CBT Thought Log

Anxiety-Producing Thought	Negative Emotion	Type of Distortion	Socratic Questioning and Restructured Thought	Healthier Emotion	Improved Behaviors
It would be awful if I said something stupid at the meeting.	Anxious Nervous Panicky	All-or-nothing thinking	Who says it would be so awful? My thoughts are as important as anyone else's.	Confident	Speak up
People will see how nervous I am.	Embarrassed Self-conscious	Mind reading Jumping to conclusions	So what if they see? Others might be nervous, too, and in any case might not be focusing on me.	Relaxed Calm	Speak up or do not but refrain from self-criticism

Processing the Activity

Using the Socratic method to challenge your erroneous thoughts is a very effective CBT technique. Using this CBT thought log, or even just writing your answers down in a journal, can help you gain objectivity and perspective over your anxious thoughts. Notice how healthier emotions and behaviors follow more rational and truthful ways of thinking.

"By challenging my erroneous thoughts and identifying my cognitive errors, I am making steps toward loving myself."

My CBT Thought Log

Anxiety-Producing Thought	Negative Emotion	Type of Distortion	Socratic Questioning and Restructured Thought	Healthier Emotion	Improved Behaviors

Coping with Anxiety Using Positive Reframing

Theory

In his book *Feeling Great* (2020), CBT pioneer David Burns takes his groundbreaking TEAM-CBT treatment approach a step beyond cognitive restructuring (that is, challenging and replacing erroneous thoughts) with a technique called *positive reframing*. In positive reframing, you focus on what your thoughts reveal about what's *right* with you, as opposed to what you perceive is wrong with you. Rather than pointing to something faulty about you or your thinking, your anxieties in fact say something wonderfully positive about you and your core beliefs.

Implementing Skills

Using this chart will help you identify what positive things your anxieties tell you about yourself and your core values.

Example Positive Reframing Log

Anxious Thought	Positive Reframing
I screwed up my chance at marriage.	I take responsibility for my shortcomings. Commitment is important to me—I just need to find the right person.
I feel lonely and am afraid I will be alone always.	I value relationships and will work hard to make them work. I learned from my shortcomings and will move forward with more wisdom and compassion.
I feel guilty about the mistakes I made as a spouse and parent.	I care very deeply about being a good person. I have a moral compass and do not put blame on others but rather have empathy for any hurt I caused.

Using your own situation, reframe your anxious thoughts into something positive they say about you and your core values.

Positive Reframing Log

Anxious Thought	Positive Reframing

Processing the Activity

You can see from the examples of positive reframing that anxiety does not have to define you by your worst moments but can instead reveal the wonderful things about you as a person and your core values. Making this attitudinal shift will help you change your perspective from negative to positive about you and your life.

"I will work to admire aspects of myself that have been hard to accept and focus on my goodness rather than my shortcomings."

Dialing Down Your Anxiety

Theory

In David Burns's TEAM-CBT approach, there are a couple other very useful concepts that help reduce anxiety and negative thoughts: the "magic button" and the "magic dial." Burns would ask clients struggling with anxious and negative persistent thoughts if they would like to use a magic button to make their anxious thoughts magically disappear. Virtually everyone answers that they would use a magic button to do that. However, after using the positive reframing technique as outlined in the previous TIP, many decide that they would not want to get rid of their anxieties and negative thoughts completely, as there are so many positives they have found that resulted from those thoughts. Rather, they would prefer taking up Dr. Burns's offer to use a magic dial to tone down the *intensity* of their anxieties. This concept makes their negative thoughts more manageable while retaining the positive things those anxieties say about them and their values. Dialing down anxiety allows you to maintain what is positive about you and retain your sense of empathy and depth from what you have experienced in life.

Implementing Skills

Here is how Burns uses the technique of the magic dial. After he does positive reframing with his clients, he asks them how much they want to dial their persistent negative thoughts down while still keeping in mind the awesome things that their negative persistent thoughts reveal about them and their core values. Dialing down the intensity of persistent thoughts becomes the goal of treatment, rather than eradicating those thoughts completely.

Using this concept by Burns, let's envision a big dial that you can adjust from 0 percent to 100 percent.

- First, write down the compelling anxious thought that you would like to make less intense.
- Then mark on the dial the percentage of anxiety this negative thought gives you at present.
- Consider what your anxious thought says about you that reflects what is positive and awesome about your basic values.
- Now mark where you would like the intensity of that negative thought to be.
- In between the two percentages, write down some positive reframing examples that can help you dial it down.

The following is an example of how to dial down your anxious thoughts.

Anxious thought: *I blame myself for my child's addiction.*

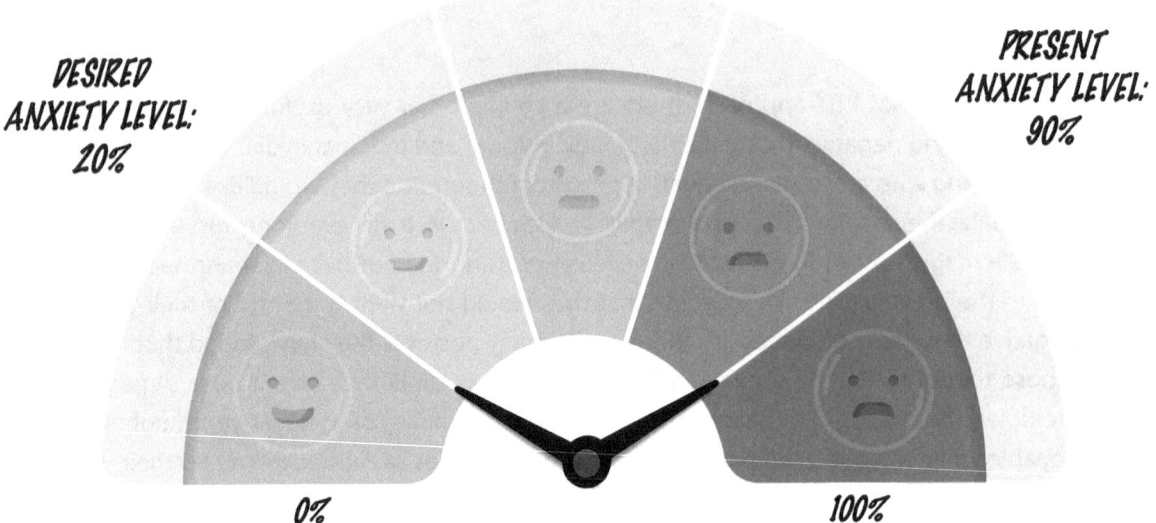

What my anxious thought says about me and my core values that I admire and want to retain:

- My desire to be a good parent is unquestionable.
- I have supported my child through his addiction and am presently part of his recovery.
- I have tried my best with the skills I have, and as I learn throughout his recovery, I am learning more and more how to handle my anxieties.
- I take my responsibilities as a parent seriously and have always done the best I could at the time.
- I am always trying to refrain from blame or anger and strive to be supportive and accepting toward him.

Now It's Your Turn

First, above the dial that follows, write down an anxious thought that you often experience.

Mark the percentage of anxiety you feel about this thought on the dial. Then mark the percentage of anxiety you would like to feel about this thought on the dial.

Finally, consider what your anxious thought shows about you that is positive. These are examples of positive reframing. Beneath the dial, write down your positive reframing examples that help you dial your anxiety down.

My anxious thought: _____
_____

DESIRED ANXIETY LEVEL: ___%

PRESENT ANXIETY LEVEL: ___%

0%   100%

What my anxious thought says about me and my core values that I admire and want to retain:
_____
_____
_____
_____
_____

Processing the Activity

This TIP helps quell the all-or-nothing thinking that people often experience when seeking to rid themselves of anxiety-producing thoughts. Instead of completely eradicating our persistent anxious thoughts, positive reframing makes the anxiety more manageable and shows positive things about ourselves and our core values. Using the tool of positive reframing to dial our anxiety down can be a powerful technique for subduing long-standing anxiety and rumination.

"I am learning to embrace what my anxious thoughts reveal about me that is positive and beautiful, and this approach allows my anxiety to be more manageable."

Cope with Anxiety with Coping Cards

Theory

In TIP #19, we introduced the notion of coping cards for dealing with depression. In this TIP I will expand on the importance of using coping cards to help manage and alleviate anxiety. In times of strong emotion, when our feelings can become upsetting and even overwhelming, coping cards can remind us of important lessons that help to calm us and keep us focused on healthy thinking.

Implementing Skills

Coping cards are visual reminders that can be made in a variety of ways, including electronically. Whether you use good old-fashioned note cards, make a series of visual reminders cut from magazines pasted on note cards, or create them in the form of alerts on your computer or phone, coping cards can be one of the most effective tools to manage all levels of anxiety. The following are a few examples of prompts you could use for coping cards that are specific to anxiety.

Combat Cognitive Distortions

- I will not do mind reading and imagine what others are thinking; I will focus on what *I* think.
- I will not jump to conclusions and assume if someone does not smile at me that they do not like me.

Self-Compassion Reminders

- I am worthy the way I am—I deserve my total unconditional love.
- If I get anxious, I will be gentle and loving to myself and will help myself get through it!

Calming Self-Statements

- I am safe and loved.
- I can handle anything that comes my way.

Calming Visualizations

- Imagine a stream on a beautiful day and release my fears into the water.
- Imagine watching a candle flicker in the dark.

Anxiety-Reducing Quotes

- "It has been well said that our anxiety does not empty tomorrow of its sorrows, but only empties today of its strength." –Charles Spurgeon
- "Rule number one is don't sweat the small stuff. Rule number two is it's all small stuff." –Robert S. Eliot

Behavioral Reminders

- I will speak up with confidence.
- I will ask for help if I need it.
- I will not allow myself to let my anxiety stop me from doing and getting what I want.
- If I panic, I will slow my breathing and use a mindful visualization.

Now It's Your Turn

Write some anxiety coping cards to help you deal with your own unique situation, using the categories listed above and any other categories that you would find beneficial. The next page contains a template that you can copy and fill in, or you can create your cards another way.

Processing the Activity

Using coping cards regularly will help to increase your awareness of your anxiety-producing thoughts while offering alternative ways of thinking and coping. In times of heightened anxiety, when thoughts and feelings become cloudy, coping cards offer strategies to stay grounded and rational. Finding the types of coping cards that work best for you will be important in the effectiveness of this strategy. The suggested topics on these coping cards are just a start. The most important thing is figuring out what types of coping cards work for you.

Consider laminating your favorite cards and putting them on a notebook ring for easy reference. You can also make coping cards for a family member or friend as a thoughtful gift for someone going through a hard time who could use helpful reminders!

"I will empower myself with coping skills that will keep me grounded in times of anxiety and stress."

My Anxiety Coping Cards

Be a Mindful Spectator of Your Thoughts

Theory

Mindfulness is widely accepted as a practice to reduce anxiety, with strategies that offer effective tools to quell a mind churning with thoughts of "What if?" so you can focus instead on the here and now. Since anxiety so often focuses on worries about what might happen in the future, learning to be calm with a present-centered focus can be quite effective. Practicing mindfulness slows down the escalation of a rapidly beating heart, sweaty palms, shortness of breath, and other bodily sensations that often accompany anxiety, helping us stop these mental and physical symptoms from precipitating full-blown panic.

Implementing Skills

In this mindfulness strategy, learning to be a *spectator of your thoughts* will help calm racing anxious thoughts and physical sensations.

1. Find a quiet space where you can relax and focus. It can be helpful to play relaxing music in the background.

2. Sit or lie down and consciously slow your breathing. Focus on breathing deeply from your diaphragm instead of breathing shallowly from your chest. To make sure you are breathing more deeply, you might put one hand on your stomach and one hand on your chest, and make sure with each inhale that the stomach rises instead of the chest.

    - Some people find it helpful to breathe through their nose with their mouth closed, and exhale though the mouth. This makes you more attentive to your breathing.
    - It might be helpful to visualize a balloon inflating in your stomach with each breath and deflating with each breath.
    - You could also visualize your breath as a color that goes into your body on each inhale, moving through to your extremities, and leaving your body with each exhale.

3. Now visualize a blackboard in front of you and write your anxious thoughts on the board. Be a spectator observing the board as you get your anxious thoughts out of your head and onto the board.

4. Imagine that blackboard is placed on a float in a parade. You are a spectator on the sidewalk, watching as the float passes. You observe your thoughts, not identifying with them. Let the float pass without reacting to it.

5. You might want to visualize the thoughts being even farther away. Here are some more images you might prefer to use:
   - Imagine that each anxious thought is written on the clouds above you and then watch those thoughts drift away.
   - Visualize your thoughts on a train going under a bridge while you stand above.
   - Put unwanted thoughts on leaves on a stream and watch them float away.
6. It can be helpful to use self-affirming phrases, such as "I am so happy I noticed these thoughts that were upsetting me" or "I will be kind to myself and stop believing in these upsetting thoughts."

Using these distancing practices regularly will help you watch your upsetting and unwanted thoughts with objectivity rather than being immersed in them.

Processing the Activity

Reflect on how it felt to distance yourself from your anxious thoughts while calming your body. Did your anxious thoughts and worries about the future seem less overpowering? Relaxing the body and keeping present focused while distancing yourself from the what-ifs of the future can be very helpful in making anxiety more manageable.

"I will distance myself from my anxious thoughts and observe them rather than identify with them."

Eliminate the ANTs and Crack the NUTs

Theory

ANTs (automatic negative thoughts) and NUTs (negative unconscious thoughts) are both memorable visualizations of negative thoughts that are so ingrained in our heads that we are often unaware that they are not actually true. We first learned about these acronyms in TIP #16, where we challenged negative thoughts to combat depression. This practice is quite effective for anxiety as well. By cracking the NUTs and eliminating the ANTs in our lives, we can better manage our anxiety.

Implementing Skills

What are some negative repetitive thoughts about yourself, others, and the world that keep going through your mind—day after day, week after week, month after month, year after year?

Examples might be: *I am pathetic. People don't like me. I'm not a good person. I wasted my youth. I will never find someone to love. The world is a mess.*

Are thoughts like these true or are they just NUTs and ANTs? Consider why these ANTs should be exterminated and these NUTs deserve to be cracked open.

Now It's Your Turn

In the first column of the table that follows, write down some ANTs and NUTs that relate to you and your situation. Then, for each example that you wrote, identify the cognitive distortions that lead to your self-talk. (For a list of cognitive distortions, revisit TIP #13.) Finally, in the third column, challenge your ANTs and NUTs. A few examples are provided first to help you get started.

My ANTs and NUTs	Type of Cognitive Distortions	Challenging Self-Talk
I am pathetic.	Labeling, all-or-nothing thinking, minimization, emotional reasoning	I am not pathetic—I am a beautiful and worthy person who deserves the best in life.
People don't like me.	Jumping to conclusions, minimization, all-or-nothing thinking, emotional reasoning	It is not true that people do not like me. There are some people who like me a lot, and I am fine the way I am. Anyway, the most important thing is that I like myself!
I will never find someone to love.	All-or-nothing thinking, fortune telling, emotional reasoning	How do I know I will never find anyone? I will enjoy the process of trying to be more open to relationships and work on my social skills.

My ANTs and NUTs	Type of Cognitive Distortions	Challenging Self-Talk

Imagine how your life would be different if you stop listening to those pesky ANTs and NUTs. How would you feel differently about yourself and your life? What practices would help you stop listening to those nutty pests once and for all?

_____
_____
_____
_____
_____
_____

Self-Help Activity

Give yourself 15 minutes to write down all the ANTs and NUTs you typically have cycling in your head. Count them. How many did you find? In a few days or weeks, list them out and count them again—are the ANTs and NUTs getting out of your head? Or are they taking over even more? If so, spend more effort identifying the types of cognitive distortions you have and challenge those unhealthy thinking habits with healthier self-talk. Sometimes counting our irrational thoughts can help us become more objective and see them for what they are: just nutty pests!

Processing the Activity

Since about 90 percent of our thoughts repeat from one day to the next, the neural pathways get ingrained after a while, becoming almost automatic because they are so deeply entrenched in our heads by constant repetition. Eliminating the ANTs and cracking the NUTs once and for all will help you quell your anxiety, clear your head, and separate fact from fiction.

"I will work to eliminate my ANTs and crack open my NUTs
to expose the absurdity of my unhealthy thought habits.
I just don't need to listen to them anymore!"

Exposure Techniques to Confront Anxiety

Theory

Exposure is a behavioral intervention in CBT that can be quite effective in overcoming all types of anxiety, including phobias. It directs people to confront their fears by intentionally being exposed to those fears in a controlled and systematic way. These exposures are broken down into a hierarchy from least threatening to most threatening. By systematically visualizing or actually experiencing a low-anxiety situation and gradually leveling up to a higher anxiety situation, the fear lessens over time, making it easier to be exposed to the same situation in the future.

The goal of exposure is not to rid us of anxiety altogether but to lower anxiety enough to be more manageable. In the exposure hierarchy, it is important to start by rating your SUDs level—SUDs stands for *subjective units of distress* and refers to rating the level of anxiety you feel about a situation using a scale from 0 (no anxiety) to 100 (full-blown panic). A SUDs level of 80–100 would be pretty debilitating; being able to lower the SUDs level to a 30 or 40 would make the situation more manageable.

Implementing Skills

Let's take the all-too-common example of someone being anxious about meeting new people at a party. For shy, reticent individuals who have low social confidence, the fear of rejection or sense that people would not want to bother with them can be very paralyzing. This might cause people to avoid parties altogether or leave early due to excessive anxiety.

Here is how the situation, feelings of anxiety, negative self-talk, and subsequent exposure hierarchy might look in this particular example.

Situation: Going to a party where I know very few people and starting a conversation with someone

Feelings: Anxious, nervous, panicked about approaching anyone

Negative Self-Talk:

- I don't know how to approach people.
- Everybody seems so much cooler than me.
- I'm not good with social situations.
- I can't stand the possibility of being rejected.
- I am anxious about sounding stupid.
- I am terrible with small talk.

SUDs Level: 100!

Goal: I would like to get over my sense of anxiety since I feel isolated. I would love to meet new friends and especially someone to date.

Exposure Hierarchy:

Action or Visualization	SUDs Level Before	SUDs Level After
Go up to someone at the party and start talking	100	60
Go to the party and look for the food without talking	80	55
Enter the room and go up to the host (who is the one person I know) right away	70	40
Practice initiating a conversation with my therapist or a friend	50	32
Practice in front of a mirror going up to someone and starting a conversation	40	20
Visualize going into the room and looking for the food	30	15
Writing out some of the ways I can introduce myself	20	10
Talking to a friend or family member who knows about my anxiety and sharing my anxieties	20	5

The person in this example identified the most anxiety-producing action they wanted to build up to—initiating a conversation with someone they don't know at a party—as well as seven steps they could take to gradually work their way up to that goal. As you can see, with each behavior, the level of distress this person felt when they contemplated taking the action was higher than the level of distress they reported after actually doing it. The step-by-step exposure to increasingly difficult scenarios helped them gain confidence and lessen their anxiety.

Now It's Your Turn

Using the template provided, fill in your own example. First, describe the anxiety-producing scenario and your feelings about it using the following prompts.

Situation: _____

_____

Feelings: _____

_____

Negative Self-Talk: _____

_____

SUDs Level: _____

Goal: _____

_____

Now, using the template on the next page, create a hierarchy toward your goal, with the actions that are most anxiety-provoking (elicit the highest SUDs levels) at the top and the actions that feel most manageable (have the lowest SUDs ratings) at the bottom. Remember, you can include visualizations and practice scenarios as part of your hierarchy—these are helpful options to give you gradual exposure to your anxieties without jumping to a high-stress real-life situation right away. For example, you might visualize taking a particular action, write down what you plan to do or say, or practice an interaction with your therapist or another trusted person.

Once your hierarchy is made, choose one of the smaller steps with a lower SUDs level to try first. Record your SUDs level after doing (or visualizing) that step. Usually, people find that their SUDs level decreases—often drastically—after practicing a step. However, if you find this is not the case, you can repeat that step until your SUDs level does decrease before moving on to the next step. Continue working up your hierarchy in this way until you feel prepared and more confident about tackling your ultimate goal.

Processing the Activity

The exposure hierarchy is a popular behavioral treatment for anxiety relating to phobias, such as fear of closed spaces, elevators, flying, or going over bridges or through tunnels. These can all be tackled with an exposure hierarchy, both in visualization and then in actual behavior. Use the preceding example to choose various behavioral goals and rate them from most stressful to least stressful. Each day, practice a behavior to chip away at your anxieties, beginning with the least stressful behaviors. As Eleanor Roosevelt is said to have advised, "Do one thing every day that scares you."

"I will not allow myself to be controlled by my anxieties—rather, I am working to be in control of them by choosing behaviors that will empower me to chip away at my irrational fears."

My Exposure Hierarchy

Action or Visualization	SUDs Level Before	SUDs Level After

CBT Problem-Solving Using IDEAS

Theory

Problem-solving is a technique used in CBT to go from defining a problem to brainstorming multiple solutions, picking a solution and implementing it, and then assessing it. The following model, titled with the acronym IDEAS, shows how you can tackle a situation in your own life that makes you anxious by careful problem-solving and weighing the pros and cons.

Implementing Skills

The following example shows how to use the IDEAS model to problem-solve an anxiety-provoking situation.

Example of IDEAS Problem-Solving

Identify the issue and why it is anxiety-provoking.

The situation is that I feel bullied at work. I am having trouble with the sarcastic comments of a coworker and notice that others laugh with him when he makes fun of me—kiddingly, but I know it is not from a place of affection. It is making me feel very unlikable and I feel nervous about speaking up in meetings in fear of saying something else he will kid me about. I feel offended but am afraid to be "too serious," as they will think I am much too sensitive.

This is challenging for me because my father used to be very sarcastic and downright critical of me, and as a consequence, I have low self-confidence. It triggers in me the sense that I am inferior and defective. I compare myself to others and always come up short.

I am using the cognitive distortions of mind reading and jumping to conclusions by interpreting how my coworkers think and assuming it is all negative. I am using all-or-nothing thinking and comparing myself with others. I am also blaming them for my feelings even though I am responsible for my feelings and no one can really make me feel anything unless I allow them to.

Develop possible solutions.

1. I could talk to my boss to explain the situation and tell her I am feeling bullied.
2. I could do nothing and hope my coworker stops if I stay under the radar enough.
3. I could engage with this coworker a little as possible and basically ignore him.
4. I could talk to my coworker and use "I" statements to tell him that I am offended by his teasing.

Evaluate the pros and cons of each solution.

Possible Solution	Pros	Cons
1. I talk to my boss to explain the situation and tell her I am feeling bullied.	My boss might talk to him and put an end to it. I will feel good about speaking up.	My boss might not do anything and think I am too sensitive. I might be embarrassed that I am so sensitive.
2. I do nothing and hope my coworker stops if I stay under the radar enough.	I will not call attention to myself. It will be "playing it safe."	It takes my control away and is avoidant. I will continue to feel ashamed and anxious.
3. I could engage with this coworker a little as possible and basically ignore him.	I might be able to avoid any difficult conversations about this issue. I will not admit to others it bothers me.	I have to work with him, so it would be very awkward and I would let him intimidate me. I will stay frustrated and disempowered.
4. I talk to my coworker and use "I" statements to tell him that I am offended by his teasing.	I will practice and use assertive skills with him and identify my rights no matter what he does. I will feel good about standing up to bullying.	He might still continue and think I am making a big deal out of nothing. I leave myself open to being the butt of more ridicule.

Act on my best option.

I choose solution #4. I will practice my assertiveness skills in the mirror and with a friend in advance. I will anticipate possible reactions from my coworker and practice sticking to my assertive mission of expressing how I feel about his teasing. I will approach my coworker next Monday before our team meeting. This solution will help me not only with him but in developing confidence in taking responsibility for my feelings, expressing my needs and wants, and standing up for myself.

Self-evaluate and assess how my solution went.

I am proud of myself for choosing this option. On Monday before the meeting, I told him I am offended when he puts me down, even if it is in a joking fashion. He initially got defensive, but I stuck to my "I" statements that I had rehearsed and was careful not to be rude, and he responded well to me expressing my feelings. He told me he was sorry and would be more sensitive in the future. I think this direct way of approaching the situation, regardless of how he might respond, was a major win for me and my personal journey in respecting myself and expressing my feelings.

Now It's Your Turn

Using the acronym IDEAS, problem-solve your own situation.

Identify the issue and why it is anxiety-provoking.

_____
_____

Develop possible solutions.

_____
_____
_____
_____

Evaluate the pros and cons of each solution.

Possible Solution	Pros	Cons

Act on my best option.

_____
_____
_____
_____

Self-evaluate and assess how my solution went.

_____
_____
_____
_____

Processing the Activity

Using this problem-solving technique can give you support and structure for making positive decisions to overcome your anxiety in challenging situations. The acronym IDEAS provides a good format for coping with anxiety-provoking situations.

❝

"I will use IDEAS as a tool to problem-solve so I can choose self-empowerment over anxiety."

Using Quotes and Positive Affirmations to Quell Anxiety

Theory

Consider the quote repeated by Winston Churchill: "Everyone remembers the remark of the old man at the point of death: that his life had been full of troubles, most of which had never happened!"

This serves as a wonderful introduction to this TIP. Many of our anxieties center on what unfortunate things could happen in the future. People with phobias and panic are so immobilized by what-ifs that they rob themselves of the present. In this chapter we have largely focused on how to replace irrational thought habits with more rational ones to stop making ourselves anxious. In this TIP we will focus on the emotionally nourishing and calming influence that positive quotes and affirmations have on our mind and emotions.

Positive affirmations and quotes comfort us emotionally in a way that cognitive restructuring and reframing cannot do alone. They lower our stress by helping us feel understood. We feel comforted that we are part of a common humanity when we see how even famous figures from history have offered comforting words about just what we are experiencing. Quotes and affirmations might quell our anxiety enough to get to a place where logical thought and reason will work. And in a time of panic, soothing reassurances that you are not alone feel like a warm blanket.

Implementing Skills

Positive Affirmations to Quell Anxiety and Worry

- "I have faith in myself to handle what comes my way."
- "My anxiety is like the gas light in a car—it is telling me of something I need to deal with."
- "I am fine. I'm safe. I have nothing to worry about."
- "I can handle anything that comes my way."
- "I have support and love from my family and friends and am not alone."
- "I have been anxious before and do not need to panic—I survived."
- "The worst thing that could happen is nothing that will cause me harm; it will be a learning experience."
- "I am more in control than I feel I am."
- "I am safe."
- "I am loved."

- "I will not worry what others think—I only have control of what I think."
- "I trust myself."
- "I am capable and strong."
- "This feeling will pass and I will get stronger."

Can you think of other positive affirmations that would help you in times of heightened anxiety?

_____
_____
_____
_____

Famous Quotes to Quell Anxiety and Worry

- "Do not anticipate trouble, or worry about what may never happen. Keep in the sunlight." –Benjamin Franklin
- "It has been well said that our anxiety does not empty tomorrow of its sorrows, but only empties today of its strength." –Charles Spurgeon
- "Every tomorrow has two handles. We can take hold of it with the handle of anxiety or the handle of faith." –attributed to Henry Ward Beecher
- "The truth is that there is no actual stress or anxiety in the world; it's your thoughts that create these false beliefs. You can't package stress, touch it, or see it. There are only people engaged in stressful thinking." –Wayne Dyer
- "There is only one way to happiness and that is to cease worrying about things which are beyond the power of our will." –Epictetus
- "Anxiety happens when you think you have to figure out everything all at once. Breathe. You're strong. You got this. Take it day by day." –Karen Salmansohn
- "Rule number one is don't sweat the small stuff. Rule number two is it's all small stuff." –Robert S. Eliot
- "My anxiety doesn't come from thinking about the future but from wanting to control it." –Hugh Prather
- "Anxiety's like a rocking chair. It gives you something to do, but it doesn't get you very far." –Jodi Picoult
- "Worry often gives a small thing a big shadow." –Swedish proverb
- "Never let the future disturb you. You will meet it, if you have to, with the same weapons of reason which today arm you against the present." –Marcus Aurelius

- "Just when the caterpillar thought the world was ending, he turned into a butterfly." –attributed to Chuang Tzu
- "How much pain have cost us the evils which have never happened." –Thomas Jefferson
- "You probably wouldn't worry about what people think of you if you could know how seldom they do." –Olin Miller
- "No amount of regretting can change the past, and no amount of worrying can change the future." –Roy T. Bennett
- "If a problem is fixable, if a situation is such that you can do something about it, then there is no need to worry. If it's not fixable, then there is no help in worrying. There is no benefit in worrying whatsoever." –Dalai Lama XIV
- "Worry pretends to be necessary but serves no useful purpose." –Eckhart Tolle
- "The best use of creativity is imagination. The worst use of creativity is anxiety." –Deepak Chopra

Processing the Activity

Using affirmations and quotes regularly will help you lessen worry and anxiety. Make a habit of spending a certain time each day, perhaps when you wake up or before bed, to repeat the most relevant affirmations and quotes of the day. Use these quotes or affirmations like you would mantras in meditation. Write them in a journal, keep a box of quotes and affirmations on printed strips, or write them on note cards, and pick one or more to focus on throughout the day for support and positivity. Put your favorites on sticky notes and post them by your computer or use them as the background image on your computer or phone. Saying them out loud can offer even more of an impact, as can recording some of them and playing them back. Using inspirational quotes and positive affirmations will help you look at your life differently and help you reframe your worries.

"I will comfort myself with positive quotes and affirmations to help me manage anxiety and help me feel hopeful and understood."

Self-Test to Cope with Anxiety and Calm Your Mind

Theory

This self-test for anxiety highlights the lessons from the TIPs in this chapter. We have focused on skills to calm emotions by challenging anxious thoughts and choosing behavioral strategies to overcome anxiety. This TIP will crystallize the important points in the chapter to help you gauge where you have been successful and what areas need more work.

Implementing Skills

In the self-test that follows, rate how true each statement is for you, from 1 to 10, to assess which areas you are doing well in and which areas need some improvement. The higher the score in each item, the higher your mastery in that area. The test is not designed to give you a one-and-done score. Your self-help journey is a continual one, and the important thing is to work to keep improving on yesterday. Making several copies of this self-test will allow you to keep retaking it to monitor your progress.

At the end of this self-test you will be prompted to calculate a total score and an average score. To get the average score, divide your total score by the number of items you responded to. For any items that are not applicable to you, just write "N/A" and subtract those items from the number you divide by when calculating your average score. As you continue taking the self-tests throughout this book, compare your average scores across the different topics. This will give you a snapshot of which areas need the most attention and which areas are the strongest.

Keep this test handy whenever you want some support and reminders on what tools you can use to work on the areas covered in this chapter.

Self-Test to Cope with Anxiety and Calm Your Mind

Using a scale from 1 to 10, with 1 being "not true" and 10 being "very true," rate how true these statements are for you.

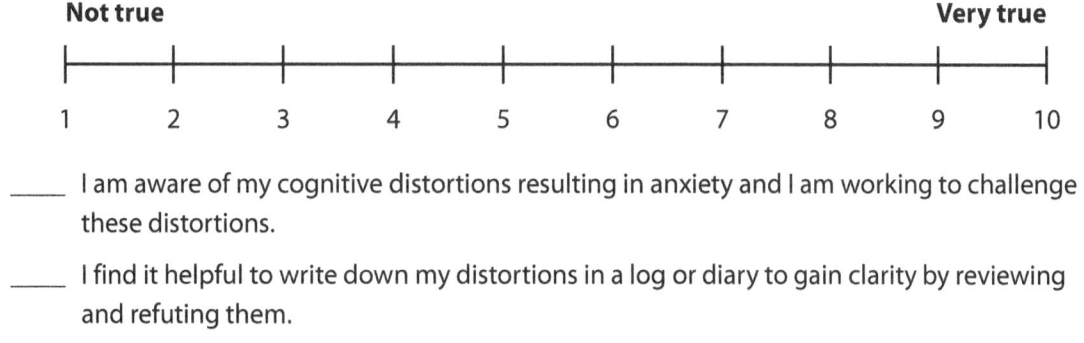

____ I am aware of my cognitive distortions resulting in anxiety and I am working to challenge these distortions.

____ I find it helpful to write down my distortions in a log or diary to gain clarity by reviewing and refuting them.

____ I challenge my distortions with cognitive restructuring.

____ I challenge my cognitive distortions with positive reframing.

____ I use strategies to dial down my anxieties.

____ I use coping cards to help support me in times of anxiety.

____ I practice distancing myself from my thoughts by being a mindful spectator.

____ I am successful at eliminating my ANTs and NUTs, which considerably lessens my anxiety.

____ I have found exposure techniques to be helpful for confronting my anxiety.

____ I use the IDEAS technique for problem-solving.

____ I find it helpful to use quotes to help me with my anxiety.

____ I use positive affirmations to help me quell my anxiety.

Total score: _____

Average score (*total score ÷ 12 or items answered*): _____

In the space below, process and explain your answers.

_____
_____
_____
_____
_____
_____

If you would like further structure to process your answers to the self-test and your reactions to the chapter, here are some prompts to guide you.

My thoughts: _____
_____

My feelings: _____
_____

My self-talk: _____
_____

What I have learned: _____
_____

Additional thoughts and strategies: _____

_____

_____

_____

Processing the Activity

CBT techniques are very effective in combating anxiety. Since anxious thoughts underlie feelings of anxiety, identifying those thoughts and accompanying cognitive distortions, as well as using self-help techniques such as coping cards and inspirational quotes and affirmations, can significantly help decrease anxiety. Building skills through practice and repetition of exercises that you find helpful will help you manage your anxiety rather than carry it!

> "I will use my anxiety as a motivator to overcome unhealthy thought habits."

CHAPTER 5

Overcoming Guilt and Regret: Finding Ways to Forgive Yourself and Stop Ruminating and Reworking the Past

To be human is to regret. Most of us can think of times when words said in the height of emotion turned quickly to regret right after the words came out of our mouths. We reproach ourselves for missed opportunities and wasted time, wish we could have known then what we know now, and rue the choices we did make that did not turn out the way we had hoped they would. Regrets are not only normal and healthy but serve as self-correctors as we learn lessons to make us act and choose more wisely going forward. Regrets are a small price to pay to avoid being the type of person who has no remorse or empathy for others, and who does not learn from lessons. These are people who end up being a danger to themselves and society. For example, the hallmark of someone with antisocial personality disorder is having no regret or remorse for wrongdoing, not caring about the feelings or even the safety of others, which makes them dangerous and unpredictable.

However, just like most things in life, too much of a good thing is not so good either. Regret that gnaws at you nonstop and clouds your worldview will lead to an endless cycle of rumination over past mistakes. When this happens, regret limits our ability to live in the present, keeping us in a mental prison which is hard to escape. We tend to live in the past rather than just learn from it.

Just think of how when we drive, we look ahead through the windshield in front of us. The rearview mirror is useful also, but it is very small in comparison to the large windshield that keeps us moving forward. When we are steeped in regret, we live life spending too much time looking back through the rearview mirror. If we drove like that, we surely would get into an accident!

In this chapter, we use the analogy of reframing our perceptions, the way you might put a new frame on a picture. Similar to TIPs #36 and #37, we will explore the concept of positively reframing your regrets to discover what is actually right (rather than wrong) about you. We will examine the crucial role of self-compassion and self-forgiveness in moving past regrets. Without self-forgiveness and self-compassion, regret leads to unrelenting depression, anxiety, and low self-esteem.

The main lesson of this chapter is not how to rid yourself of regrets, but how to reframe them and not allow your present to be stained by the past anymore. There is no turning back the clock and changing what is already done—no amount of ruminating will accomplish this. The alternative is to focus on righting any wrongs, taking responsibility for your actions and apologizing to others who were hurt in the process, and moving forward with the lessons you have learned. Regrets are valuable learning experiences that have helped shape you into who you are today. Strive to increase empathy for yourself and others, and look for the wisdom you've gained.

There is one thing we know for sure: Getting past the past is the only way you can be present in the present.

"If we have goals and dreams and we want to do our best, and if we love people and we don't want to hurt them or lose them, we should feel pain when things go wrong. The point isn't to live without any regrets; the point is to not hate ourselves for having them. . . . Regret doesn't remind us that we did badly. It reminds us that we know we can do better."

–Kathryn Schultz

Using the Double Standard Technique

Theory

The *double standard technique*, one of the most popular CBT techniques, is a perfect fit for dealing with regret. In the double standard technique, regrets and "shoulds" are seen through the lens of how we would treat a friend with the same issues.

It has always astonished me how many of us talk to ourselves in a way we would never think of talking to anyone else. When we are pulled down by regret, we berate ourselves and are critical in ways that we would never be to a dear friend. In this exercise, we take the perspective of what we would tell someone we care about if they harbored the same regrets. Would we chastise them, or would we be supportive and kind? Would we see them in a less favorable light, or would we empathize with them? Chances are you would comfort your friend and assure them that their pain of regret is a struggle of our shared humanity. If you would offer comfort to a dear friend, don't you deserve the same?

Implementing Skills

Pick a regret that is naggingly persistent in your life. What is it and what are you telling yourself about your actions? What do you think they say about you as a person? Were these actions long ago or recent? Have they helped you improve? If your regrets affected another person, have you apologized and taken responsibility? What lessons have you learned? How can you change your actions going forward?

_____
_____
_____
_____

Think about why you acted in the way you now regret. Did you have triggers from your past that coincided with your distress at that moment? Were you even aware of those triggering emotions and where they came from?

_____
_____
_____
_____

Now imagine that a dear friend confided in you that they did the same thing. How would you see the same situation if it was your friend who had taken those actions? Would you still be as critical? Or would you be more compassionate and understanding about their struggles? What would you say to that friend?

_____

_____

_____

_____

As you consider this person you care about, visualize that person fading away as you take their place. Do you think you deserve to go back to your harsh self-talk, or has your perspective shifted from criticism and judgment to compassion and forgiveness? Can you understand the circumstances that led to the mistake? Don't you deserve to be your own best friend, mistakes and all?

_____

_____

_____

_____

Processing the Activity

How did it feel to view yourself from a place of self-love rather than self-criticism? How can you manage your negative self-talk and feelings of regret going forward? Has your regret propelled you to be a better person? If so, remember that even those in our prison system get a lesser sentence for good behavior. Using that analogy, don't you deserve to be at least on parole? Using the double standard technique reminds us that we deserve to love ourselves even with our missteps, and we are worthy of compassion and forgiveness.

"I will forgive myself for not having the foresight to know what is now so obvious in hindsight."

Challenge Cognitive Distortions by Cognitive Restructuring of Regrets

Theory

CBT is known for its emphasis on changing how you think to change how you feel. Cognitive restructuring, introduced in TIP #35, is perhaps the most widely used CBT technique to change your thoughts to change your feelings. In cognitive restructuring, cognitive distortions are identified and challenged, leading to more positive ways of thinking based on fact and not fueled by negative emotion.

Implementing Skills

There are a variety of ways to use cognitive restructuring to shift your perspective on your regrets. One is to make a list of your regrets, identify the cognitive distortions involved in each one, and then restructure the regret to something that will motivate you. (The full list of cognitive distortions can be found in TIP #13.) Here are several examples of restructuring regretful self-talk, followed by a blank template for your use.

Examples of Restructuring Regrets

Regretful Self-Talk	Cognitive Distortions	Restructuring Thought
I failed in my most important relationships.	All-or-nothing thinking "Should" statements Personalization	I've had a hard time with some important relationships. I learned a lot to improve my relationships moving forward.
I ruined my daughter's life by being too strict. I was such a jerk.	All-or-nothing thinking Personalization Labeling	I understand I was reacting to my own experiences as a child and have insight into the pain that led me to be so strict. I have learned to be much more loving and accepting of my daughter and everyone else.
I regret being "just a housewife" and not having a career. I accomplished so much less than my friends.	Comparing Jumping to conclusions Mental filtering	I did the best I was able to in providing my family with love and care. Now that my children are older, I have the freedom to take classes and pursue my interests.

Now It's Your Turn

Try this method for your own regrets by completing the following chart.

Regretful Self-Talk	Cognitive Distortions	Restructuring Thought

Processing the Activity

Regrets can be debilitating, especially if you see your regrets as having impacted others in your life. There is no turning back the clock. Aside from apologizing and making amends to those in your life that were affected by your behavior, you cannot take back what has been done. Take the lesson and work hard on leaving behind both the self-berating and the tendency to look at life through the rearview mirror. In life, as in driving, it is important to look back sometimes, but most of our success will happen when we move forward with a much larger view ahead.

"I owe it to myself to recognize when I am not thinking clearly. When I am filled with cognitive distortions, I am not the best person to listen to about myself!"

Even More Techniques for Cognitive Restructuring

TIP #47

Theory

Cognitive restructuring is so helpful for dealing with regrets that this TIP offers even more strategies on the topic. If regrets are deeply ingrained, they will need to be constantly revisited with a new perspective. Having various techniques to get unstuck from regrets will help you find what works best for you. With repeated practice, you'll find that regret can actually be a helpful tool for self-improvement! Use regret as a springboard to success, looking forward instead of backward.

Implementing Skills

Use the Socratic Method

Ask yourself the following questions to examine your negative beliefs:

- Who says I am not a good person because of the mistakes I made?
- Where is the evidence?
- Am I using emotional reasoning or am I sticking to the facts?
- What other ways are there to look at this?
- Am I being way too hard on myself?
- What would I think if it was a dear friend with the same situation?
- Did my wrong steps lead me to the right places?

Using these questions (and adding your own), use this space to cross-examine your regrets.

_____
_____
_____
_____
_____

Reframe Your Regrets from Unproductive to Productive

Instead of letting your regrets churn endlessly in your head, consider how your regrets have motivated you to improve as a person. Regret can propel us forward and guide us if we let it.

People who are positive are not defined by their regrets and missteps, but instead are motivated by them.

Consider the following examples, then write down your own.

Unproductive Regret	➡	Productive Regret
I burned so many bridges with people with my anger.	→	I have apologized and taken responsibility for my actions, and in my behavior toward others now I am much more empathetic and kind.
I screwed up my chances to be with my ex-partner.	→	I learned lessons in that relationship that I will use moving forward in other relationships.
	→	
	→	

Turns Your Regrets into Goals

For every regret you have, turn it into a goal. Keep the lesson and don't hang on so tightly to what cannot be changed. It is up to us to give ourselves permission to use the pain of the past to propel us forward instead of keeping us stuck.

Consider the following examples, then write down your own.

Regret	➡	Goal
I took out my anger on others and ruined many relationships that way.	→	I am practicing mindfulness and self-awareness, which is helping me to stay regulated and treat other people with respect and kindness.
I ruined my marriage by cheating.	→	In my present relationship my goal is to be completely faithful. I am holding myself accountable.
	→	
	→	

Move from "Why" to "What's Next?"

There is a certain benefit to self-reflection and exploring the "whys" of our behaviors. However, in the case of regret, the whys can keep you trapped in obsession. "Why was I so clueless? Why wasn't I truer to myself? Why did I screw up so badly? Why didn't I hold my temper?"

Reflection can help to some degree, but once you reflect and try to understand your behavior, or your lack of action, it is healthier to move from focusing on "why?" to "what's next?"

Consider the following examples, then write down your own.

Why?		What's Next?
Why didn't I hold my temper?	→	Going forward, how can I better recognize when I am feeling overwhelmed and express my anger in healthier, kinder ways?
I loved my previous partner—why did I cheat?	→	What steps will I take to ensure that I communicate my feelings and needs openly with my current partner rather than breaking our monogamy agreement?
	→	
	→	

Processing the Activity

The techniques in this TIP will help you to challenge your cognitive distortions and then replace those unhelpful thoughts with a new focus on your goals and the lessons you've learned, resulting in a healthier you. In the next TIP we will further explore how to transform regrets with the help of positive reframing.

"The day I decided to change my focus from what could have been or should have been into what can be, I chose to stop being stuck in yesterday and allowed myself to embrace today."

Using Positive Reframing for a Fresh Take on Regret

Theory

David Burns, the leading authority on CBT, provides a revolutionary spin on dealing with negative self-talk in his book *Feeling Great* (2020). In TIP #36, the technique of positive reframing was introduced relating to coping with anxiety. We can also apply this technique to the topic of regret. Burns's approach suggests that negative self-talk might not be a sign of what is *wrong* with you but instead of what is *right* with you. When treating patients who struggle with regret, he encourages them to see their regrets as evidence of their goodness and appreciate what their regrets say about their core values.

Implementing Skills

You can put a positive spin on your regrets through positive reframing. Maybe the regrets that have kept you beating yourself up can help you discover how awesome you really are!

Here are some questions to help you set the stage for positive reframing:

- What does my regret show about my core values?
- What does the reason behind my sadness say about me that is positive?
- What do I like about what my regret says about my moral compass?
- How do my regrets reflect my depth of feeling?
- How have my regrets motivated me to be a better person?
- What blessings can I find in my regrets that make me a more empathetic and good person?
- How have my regrets brought me closer to feeling a shared humanity with others?

Here is an example of how positive reframing can be used for regret.

Example Situation: My daughter has struggled with addiction for seven years.

Regret	Positive Reframing
I feel guilty and at fault for her addiction.	I take my role as a parent seriously. The depth of my feelings shows that I have a lot of care and empathy.
I should have noticed the signs years ago.	I am and was a very concerned parent but she hid it so well.
I wish I knew then what I know now about addictions—I maybe could have helped her more.	I have good core values of loving and wanting the best for my child. I am educating myself now and doing all I can to support her recovery.

Regret	Positive Reframing
I should never have let her get with the wrong crowd.	I knew how important her friends were and wanted her to be happy—I had no idea until her addiction got worse how toxic they were for her.

Now It's Your Turn

Describe a situation you regret and positively reframe your negative self-talk.

Situation: _____

Regret	Positive Reframing

Processing the Activity

Positive reframing has provided a new spin on an established technique that promotes empathy, positivity, and acceptance of ourselves and others. This positive spin is, like all CBT techniques, a practice to be repeated again and again until new ways of thinking are reinforced and solidified. Positive reframing offers a practical focus to help us move past believing our cognitive distortions so that we can see and accept things as they really are.

> "I have learned to see what my regrets say about my core values. I am replacing my old, worn thinking habits with new ways of thinking."

# How to Stop Reading Old News Like It Belongs on the Front Page

Theory

One thing about regret is that once it gets hardened and stuck, it is like a boulder that weighs us down. It becomes unmovable and remains an obstacle to true happiness. It is like rereading the front page of your life's newspaper again and again, sometimes for years; the news of the day still revolves around old regrets. If you can identify with this, isn't it time to put the old regrets back at least a few pages? Sure, some regrets mixed with loss and trauma stay at the forefront of our minds throughout our lives, but if we wish to truly live in the present, we need to free ourselves from being defined by our regrets and our losses. This activity can help you get your regrets off the front page once and for all.

Implementing Skills

The template on the next page shows two newspaper front pages. On the first front page, fill in your current focuses, including regrets. Write in the main stories of what occupies your mind at present. Are there any stories or news you want to change? Then, on the alternate front page, visualize how you can change old regrets and negative thoughts to healthier thoughts that can be front page news now.

Processing the Activity

This activity can serve as a visual reminder that your regrets of the past do not have to be on the front page anymore. What did you replace your front page with? What current stories and news do you want to be center stage in your life today? How far back can you put some of the old regrets? Even the second page is better than the front page!

"My life at present will be my main focus in my life. I vow to stop rereading my old life's news as if it is front page news. Time to turn the page!"

"Old News"

DAILY NEWS

_____

_____   _____   _____
_____   _____   _____
_____   _____   _____
_____   _____   _____

Revised and Improved!

DAILY NEWS

_____

_____   _____   _____
_____   _____   _____
_____   _____   _____
_____   _____   _____

Embrace the Three Basic Components of Self-Compassion

Theory

In TIP #5 we explored how self-compassion is the main ingredient for true self-esteem and happiness in general. Judging yourself based on how you compare to others will leave you forever dissatisfied and not feeling "good enough." The truth is that you can be below average in some areas of your life and above in others—it does not make you a loser in some respects and a winner in others. Moreover, in many areas of life there is no objectively better or worse result, no winning or losing, simply differences in the choices we make or the circumstances in which we find ourselves. We are all worthy no matter how we compare with others. Self-compassion, rather than self-esteem, is the basis of personal well-being and happiness.

This TIP further explores the teachings of self-compassion expert Kristin Neff (*Self-Compassion: The Proven Power of Being Kind to Yourself*, 2015). Neff sees three main components within the foundation of self-compassion: self-kindness, common humanity, and mindfulness. This TIP focuses on these three aspects and includes a sample activity for each one.

Implementing Skills

Self-Kindness

Self-kindness involves being kind to yourself instead of critical of your missteps, regrettable behaviors, and mistakes. It includes replacing self-critical, judgmental thoughts with loving thoughts.

Consider the following example, then practice replacing your own judgmental thoughts with compassionate self-talk and loving actions.

Judgmental Thought	Compassionate Thought	Compassionate Practice
I am such an idiot for reacting with such anger to my friend that now we are estranged.	My old hurts were triggered when she questioned me and I overreacted, but I did apologize. I am proud of myself for taking responsibility and love myself for learning from this and moving on better equipped to manage my anger.	I will place my hand on my heart, massaging it, while saying kind and comforting words to myself.

Judgmental Thought	Compassionate Thought	Compassionate Practice

Common Humanity

We are not alone in our struggles. Keeping in mind our shared humanity allows us to feel connected to others as we go through hard times and setbacks. Loss, breakups, and trauma do not make us defective, but rather make us human. These experiences can increase our empathy for others and for ourselves.

Think of a regret you have that you are struggling with, and try the following practices:

1. Research it. For example, if you are struggling with a child's mental illness or addiction, look for support groups online or informational sites for loved ones affected by mental illness, such as NAMI and Al-Anon.

2. Read books on others who have gone through similar issues. On social media sites like Facebook and Pinterest, search for inspirational quotes that can help you though your particular situation.

3. Seek out support groups in your community or consider counseling. You do not need to go through your challenges alone!

4. Listen to songs (or write your own) that resonate with what you are dealing with. Music has a way of bringing us closer to a sense of common humanity when we find lyrics and music that resonate with us.

5. Open up to others you trust. Sharing our thoughts and feelings with others can be extremely healing. It is like the difference between holding a heavy pail of water alone and holding it with someone else.

Which of these practices would you like to try first? Which people, organizations, or sources of information will you seek out to share your experience?

_____
_____

Mindfulness

Mindfulness helps us focus on the here and now with nonjudgmental acceptance. Instead of engaging in judgmental self-talk in dealing with your regret, put some distance between your feelings and your thoughts while focusing on the present sensations you have. What do you see around you? What do you smell? How do your clothes feel against your skin? What are you hearing? If you are drinking or eating something, take a mindful minute to savor the sensations of the food or drink going through your throat and into your stomach.

As you focus on the present, watch any negative thoughts come and go as if each negative thought is on a cloud. For example, if you have the negative thought *I failed*, instead of buying into it, visualize watching the thought "out there." In essence, look *at* your thoughts rather than *from* your thoughts.

What thought did you use for this experience? How did it feel to be more present focused by shifting your attention to the world as it is now rather than your inside chatter? How did it feel to distance yourself from your negative thought and merely observe it floating by? What did you experience using your five senses?

_____
_____
_____
_____

Processing the Activity

This model of self-compassion developed by Neff includes self-kindness, common humanity, and mindfulness. These three areas of focus provide a foundation to understand and practice self-compassion. Self-compassion offers a path to treat ourselves like a dear friend and sets the stage for self-acceptance and self-love.

> "I deserve compassion and vow to treat myself as a dear friend instead of unfavorably comparing myself with others. After all, when I compare myself with others, I get bitter. When I learn from them, I get better."

Write a Compassionate Letter to Yourself

Theory

Building on the previous TIP, this activity will help you further increase your ability to be self-compassionate. Writing a letter focusing on treating yourself with kindness and self-compassion, even while admitting your missteps and regretful choices, can be very healing and powerful.

Implementing Skills

If you are struggling with regret, write a letter to yourself with kindness, respect, and self-love. You can write to yourself now or write to your younger self who made errors that you now regret. Reflect on your regrets and what you have learned from them. The important thing is to write from a place of love and self-compassion instead of judgment and criticism. Here are some prompts for your self-compassion letter:

- How can you be kinder to yourself? Replace any negative, judgmental, critical self-talk you have with kind words and understanding for how you erred and what you learned.
- What mindful practices can you use to stay present focused instead of mired in regrets about the past?
- What about your suffering is part of the human condition and common experiences that many feel? Does that you make you more connected and empathetic to others?
- Reflect on the pain or trauma you have experienced that triggered you to act in ways you now regret.
- Write forgiving and calming words to yourself and describe why you deserve forgiveness.
- Reassure yourself that even if you made poor choices, you did it out of hurt, not "badness."
- Are there things you know now that you did not know before?
- Think of what you would say to your hurt child inside who needs soothing and care.
- What do you need right now to heal? What are some steps you can take?
- Who could you ask for help who could be loving and nonjudgmental?
- What do you need to change to give yourself the gift of nonjudgmental acceptance?
- If a friend had the same regrets, would you react differently? How can you talk to yourself as a dear and loving friend?
- What would you like to tell your younger self with the perspective you have now?
- What encouraging words would you tell your future self?
- What other kind words can you say to yourself to keep you on the road to self-compassion?

Processing the Activity

How did you feel writing a self-compassionate letter to your younger or present self? Were you able to change criticisms into loving words? Did you identify triggers and stressors that triggered your old wounds and led you to act in ways you regret? Did you highlight lessons learned that would help you moving forward?

If you found this exercise helpful, consider keeping a self-compassion diary or journal to keep self-compassion at the forefront of your mind and heart on a daily basis.

"Leaving the past in the past is the only way I can be present in the present."

Self-Reflect on Guilt and Regret

Theory

If you are stuck in regret and guilt, it is important to be able to differentiate them from one another.

Guilt points to remorse for behaving a certain way, often knowing it was wrong even at the time, and is usually a result of acting in a way that hurt others or violated their trust. Guilt is necessary to self-correct, to be a better person, to make better choices, to feel bad for our mistakes, to take responsibility and apologize and act better based on lessons learned.

In the case of regret, behavior is often done thinking that we were right at the time, and only later realizing that we were wrong. Regret points to shame over mistakes that were made or choices and opportunities that were never taken; now, with hindsight, you realize that you would have acted or chosen differently. For example, if you wish you'd attended a different school, you are not going to feel guilty as much as feel regretful for your choice. Or regret can be a result of reacting to triggers from your own past trauma, leading you to overreact due to past emotional experiences.

In moderate doses, guilt is a good thing. Sometimes we act in ways that we know are wrong, such as betraying a loved one's trust. Guilt helps us have remorse for wrongdoing and see our behavior's hurtful effects on others, shaping our behavior to be more considerate in the future.

Whereas guilt is often more specific and situationally based, regret is more global and paralyzing because it expects that we should have known *then* what is so clear to us *now*. With this 20/20 hindsight, regret is much more consuming and shame-based, often representing a cluster of patterns of behaviors that are seen as unfortunate in retrospect. Due to its rigid, negative self-talk, regret leads to more negative and depressive symptoms than guilt, leading to self-blame for outcomes we did not expect or know how to avoid at the time.

Guilt is often a reaction to standards imposed by society, so we are more conscious of our violations. Regret, on the other hand, comes from internal standards that only in retrospect we realize we did not meet.

Implementing Skills

Here are some prompts and insights to help you sort out your feelings of guilt and regret. This will help you express your thoughts and self-reflect on how they have affected you, including what you need to do to move forward.

These are the things I feel guilty for:

_____
_____
_____

These are the things I most regret:

_____
_____
_____

How have my regrets and guilt robbed me of today's joy?

_____
_____
_____

How have my guilt and regrets impacted my life today?

_____
_____
_____

What I wish I knew *then* that I know *now*:

_____
_____
_____

Have I forgiven myself? If not, can I see a path to forgiveness? What does that look like?

_____
_____
_____

We all know that we cannot remake the past, but we can edit our story. How can I take a different view of the past and make it less shame-based?

_____
_____
_____

How have my regrets made me a better person? What positive attributes do I have because of my regrets? What do my regrets say about me that show my goodness as a person? (In reviewing guilt and regrets, some find it helpful to think "At least . . ." to help them cope. For example, if you regret who you married, you might say, "At least I have great kids.")

_____
_____
_____

List your regrets here and make each regret into a goal or action plan that you can do now or in the future. For example, if you regret raising your voice too much when your children were young, your goal might be making sure you treat your children and grandchildren with kindness now.

Regret	Action Plan or Goal

Processing the Activity

Regret and guilt can be especially difficult to overcome when you focus on past choices and behaviors rather than what you learned from them to help you moving forward. It is a challenge to take the lessons without being steeped in self-recrimination. Accept that guilt and regret are not only unavoidable emotions, but they can be our biggest motivators moving forward with lessons learned.

> "When I keep lugging my guilt and regret from the past, it leaves me little room to savor the beauty of my life now and live in the present."

Self-Forgiveness Check-In

Theory

In moderation, regrets can help you be a better person who learns from mistakes and is wiser going forward. However, some regrets can rob you of happiness today and paralyze you with rumination about what you did not know then. All too often, people beat themselves up for what they think they should have known, even though they often couldn't have known except in hindsight. Or maybe you did know all along, but other factors (such as addiction) derailed your ability to execute better choices.

It becomes tougher if others, especially those close to you, were hurt in the process. This self-forgiveness check-in will offer you a snapshot of how self-forgiving you are now and where you need to focus your inner work.

Implementing Skills

Self-Forgiveness Check-In

Using a scale from 1 to 10, with 1 being "not true" and 10 being "very true," rate how true these statements are for you.

Not true   **Very true**

1   2   3   4   5   6   7   8   9   10

____ I do not allow regrets to cloud my present day.

____ I have self-compassion for the mistakes that I have made.

____ I have compassion for those I hurt in the past and have tried to make amends.

____ I am able to put my regrets behind me to serve as learning experiences and do not ruminate about them.

____ I forgive myself for not having the foresight to know what is now so obvious in hindsight.

____ I am grateful of the lessons I learned from my regrets and am a better, deeper, and more empathic person because of them.

____ I refuse to keep on beating myself up for my arrogance or foolishness from past choices and behaviors.

____ I am working toward self-forgiveness and healing—I deserve it.

____ I am proud of myself for getting healthier and healthier as time goes on.

____ I try to keep critical self-talk at bay, since I have always done the best I could at the time.

Total score: _____

The higher the number, the more you are kind and compassionate to yourself, and the greater your tendency to be positive and optimistic. Conversely, the lower the score, the more you are likely feeling depressed, hurt, and stuck in the past.

- **85–100: Self-forgiveness expert!**—Congratulations for being able to forgive yourself for regrets from the past and building on them to make you better today.
- **75–84: Self-forgiveness semi-pro**—Self-forgiveness has helped you for the most part live a life where you have moved on and learned important lessons.
- **60–74: Self-forgiveness needs attention**—You could benefit from more self-compassion and are too hard on yourself, especially if you are doing what you can now to correct your behavior and choices.
- **40–59: Self-forgiveness impaired**—Your self-talk and regrets are weighing you down and are detracting from your joy today.
- **20–39: Self-forgiveness dangerously low**—It is likely that you are way too hard on yourself and self-compassion is just a theoretical concept that you are not integrating into your life. To help move forward from being anchored in the past, reach out for social support and another perspective, such as a friend, family member, or trusted professional.
- **0–20: Self-forgiveness danger zone**—It is hard to be happy and positive with such a negative, self-flagellating mindset. An extreme lack of forgiveness for yourself is likely reflecting a fair degree of depression and hurt. Chances are that trauma in your life, past or present, is keeping you stuck. Consider getting professional help.

Processing the Activity

How did you do on this self-test? Would you like to allow yourself to make peace with your past and forgive yourself for not handling things as well as you would be able to now? If you scored low on this self-test, how long will you beat yourself up for things that happened years and even decades ago? How long has it been? Shouldn't you be up for parole by now?

As long as you learn from your mistakes, take responsibility, and do better now with the knowledge that you have, beating yourself up has no purpose. Move forward now with better choices, better behavior, and better insight, and allow yourself to heal.

"My Self-Forgiveness Prayer:
Grant me the ability to forgive myself for past stumbles and falls,
to correct what I can, and accept what I can't,
and the wisdom and courage to try again,
this time a bit wiser."

Use Self-Forgiveness Affirmations

Theory

Affirmations are one of the most powerful tools for dealing with regret. In TIP #7 we focused on using affirmations to boost self-esteem. Now we will use affirmations for quelling the self-critical voice that nags at us when we are stuck in regretful ruminations.

Affirmations—positive self-statements often targeted on the issues that we need to overcome—are extremely powerful if repeated daily for days or weeks at a time. Sometimes people use affirmations when they need a psychological boost. And since regret can be so persistent in its focus on the past, daily repetition of affirmations can be very healing.

Long-standing negative thoughts are hard to change, so repetition is necessary to unseat the old ways of thinking and help you form new neural pathways. It does not have to be the same exact phrase each day. Affirmations around a certain topic that is relevant will likely be most effective.

Choose an affirmation or a few affirmations for the day, repeating them either a few times throughout the day or for a few minutes at one time. Mindfully meditating on the affirmations can help you focus on the message and make a dent in unseating long-standing negative thoughts. Saying the affirmation once and moving on will not be as helpful as picking an affirmation or two every day, then repeating them for a few minutes or a few times throughout the day.

Implementing Skills

The following are example affirmations for overcoming regret. Make them into notes on your smartphone or computer, or write them down on note cards to carry with you throughout the day.

- I am thankful for the lessons that my regrets have taught me.
- I will start fresh today in letting go of my past regrets but holding on to the lessons.
- I have learned better ways to handle things now and am looking forward to continuing to improve.
- I am increasing my ability to empathize and have compassion for others and myself.
- Maybe I learned some things the hard way, but the key thing is that I learned and will keep on learning.
- I will let go of rumination and embrace positivity and hope.
- My journey forward will be of self-compassion and self-love.
- I deserve kindness and forgiveness.
- I have learned from my mistakes and will be better for others with my lessons learned.
- I am increasing my empathy for others and for myself in my lessons learned.

- My past can strengthen my path moving forward instead of wearing me down.
- I deserve to heal from the past with wisdom and forgiveness.
- I am moving wisely from the past toward a freer and beautiful future.
- My challenges have helped me be a more empathetic and caring person.
- I will work hard to replace my negative thoughts with thoughts of love, compassion, and positivity.
- I can only be truly forgiving and kind to others if I am forgiving and kind to myself.
- My regrets have helped me gain insight and a chance to behave better with the new knowledge I have gained.
- I will move from unproductive regret to productive regret, where I act on the lessons learned.
- I will show myself love instead of judgment.

Now It's Your Turn

Think of your own ideas for affirmations you could use in moving on from regret. Can you add to the list?

_____
_____
_____
_____
_____
_____

Processing the Activity

Consider using affirmations in your daily life. There is no right or wrong practice. The key is repetition of saying affirmations to yourself—especially out loud, which can make more of an impact—daily for many days, weeks, or months on end. Try doing this for a few weeks and see if your affirmation practice helps you move past the past into a brighter and more forgiving future!

> "I am worthy of forgiveness and am motivated to use what
> I have learned to better myself and my loved ones."

# Self-Test to Overcome Guilt and Regret

Theory

In this chapter, we have focused on various practices to overcome guilt and regret. In TIP #53 we had a self-test on self-forgiveness. In this final TIP of this chapter we have another self-test that incorporates the lessons from all the other TIPs in this chapter and highlights their takeaways.

Implementing Skills

In the self-test that follows, rate how true each statement is for you, from 1 to 10, to assess which areas you are doing well in and which areas need some improvement. The higher the score in each item, the higher your mastery in that area. The test is not designed to give you a one-and-done score. Your self-help journey is a continual one, and the important thing is to work to keep improving on yesterday. Making several copies of this self-test will allow you to keep retaking it to monitor your progress.

At the end of this self-test you will be prompted to calculate a total score and an average score. To get the average score, divide your total score by the number of items you responded to. For any items that are not applicable to you, just write "N/A" and subtract those items from the number you divide by when calculating your average score. As you continue taking the self-tests throughout this book, compare your average scores across the different topics. This will give you a snapshot of which areas need the most attention and which areas are the strongest.

Keep this test handy whenever you want some support and reminders on what tools you can use to work on the areas covered in this chapter.

Self-Test to Overcome Guilt and Regret

Using a scale from 1 to 10, with 1 being "not true" and 10 being "very true," rate how true these statements are for you.

____ I use the double standard technique whenever I speak to myself unkindly and try to imagine talking to a dear friend.

____ I have identified my go-to cognitive distortions that undermine my ability to think clearly and work to cognitively restructure my regrets.

_____ When I notice my negative self-talk, I try to find the cognitive distortions and refute my negative self-talk.

_____ I question where I get my facts and assumptions, without immediately accepting them as the truth.

_____ I reframe my regrets from unproductive to productive regret.

_____ I try to turn my regrets into goals.

_____ I do not focus so much on *why* but rather *what's next?*

_____ I use positive reframing for my regrets, which reveals what is special and awesome about me.

_____ I commit to no longer keep rereading old stories like they are front page news.

_____ I am treating myself more and more with self-kindness.

_____ I see my challenges as part of a common humanity.

_____ I use mindfulness strategies to immerse my attention in the present and less in the past.

_____ I am increasingly focusing on using self-compassion and kindness to myself, as I would a dear friend.

_____ I am focused on learning from guilt and regret rather than allowing it to keep me stuck in the past.

_____ I am giving up the habit of rumination over what cannot be changed.

_____ I have turned my regrets into goals.

_____ I am forgiving of myself.

_____ I use affirmations to forgive myself and learn from my regrets instead of being stuck in them.

Total score: _____

Average score (*total score ÷ 18 or items answered*): _____

In the space below, process and explain your answers.

_____
_____
_____
_____
_____
_____
_____
_____

If you would like further structure to process your answers to the self-test and your reactions to the chapter, here are some prompts to guide you.

My thoughts: _____
_____

My feelings: _____
_____

My self-talk: _____
_____

What I have learned: _____
_____

Additional thoughts and strategies: _____
_____
_____
_____

Processing the Activity

Use this self-test periodically to assess your progress and to continue to master thoughts of guilt and regret that hold you back. Learning from the past, rather than living in it, is essential to emotional and mental wellness, and the tools in this chapter will be useful to helping you live more fully in the present with more wisdom and awareness.

"With practice and perseverance, I am learning to put the past in the past and give myself a chance for a brighter tomorrow."

CHAPTER 6

Managing and Growing from Stress: Learning to Be a Stress Manager and Not a Stress Carrier

When you think of the word "stress," what do you think of? If you are like most people, you likely thought of adjectives or phrases that had negative connotations. In my live presentations, when I ask participants to finish the phrase "Stress is . . ." the answers tend to go like this:

"Overwhelming."

"Exhausting."

"Too much to do, too little time."

"Bad for you."

"Uncomfortable."

"Debilitating."

Once in a while, I am encouraged to hear other responses, such as "motivating," "exciting," "meaningful," or "engaging." The truth is that stress is not inherently negative; stress is what helps us be engaged and involved in life. It is our take on stress that makes it motivating or debilitating.

Stress has even been referred to as "the spice of life" by stress research pioneer Hans Selye. After all, there are many stresses we welcome in our lives: getting married, playing or watching sports, planning a party or event, getting a new job, volunteering for an organization, going on a trip, having a baby or grandchild, moving to a new house or city, and so on. All of it is stressful, but we wouldn't trade these experiences for anything—they give us meaning to our lives.

Consider the analogy of a stringed instrument, such as a guitar or violin. If you tighten the strings on the instrument too much, the string will snap, but if it is not tight enough, the music will be out of tune. Only with just the right amount of tension in the strings can you make beautiful music.

In this chapter we will focus on how to shake hands with stress. You will learn tips to harness stress to become a stress manager rather than a stress carrier. The important thing to remember is that stress is not meant to be avoided and that it can, in fact, be the ingredient that makes our lives meaningful and satisfying. Just think of this: "Stressed" spelled backward is "desserts!"

That said, there are some stresses in life that are not like dessert—in particular, stress resulting from trauma. When we develop unhealthy habits or cannot seem to shake depression, low self-esteem, anxiety, and insecurity, some of our symptoms are likely the result of trauma. No matter how successful we are or how we good we have it in our lives, if we have experienced trauma early on, it is like being a person from a foreign country who speaks with an accent even though they moved to their adopted country at an early age. The experience of trauma stays with us and confuses us when we are triggered, leading to us feeling anxious or depressed for "no good reason." For those who grew up with mental illness in their families or who were abused, neglected, or raised in environments where they did not receive the validation needed to develop a strong foundation, the first "language" might be confusing—like "Pig Latin" where things do not really make sense. CBT helps us distance ourselves from this first language and gives us the tools to deal with our triggers, even if we keep the accent for decades.

"The best way to manage stress isn't to reduce or avoid it,
but rather to rethink and even embrace it."

–Kelly McGonigal

Make Stress Your Friend

Theory

When you think of stress, what comes first to mind? If you are like most people, your answer likely depicts the downside of stress with words and phrases such as "overwhelming," "exhausting," "problems," "debilitating," "not enough money," or "too much to do, too little time."

However, stress is really not good or bad—it just *is*. By trying to avoid stress, people cause themselves unnecessary distress. Stress expert Kelly McGonigal observes that thinking stress is bad for you is the real problem, not stress itself. In her book *The Upside of Stress* (2015), McGonigal explains that early in her career she herself taught that stress is negative and focused on how to relieve or avoid stress, but in her work in the field of mindset science she learned and subsequently taught that stress is an important part of life that only becomes negative if we label it as negative.

McGonigal also relates that research has shown that stress causes our bodies to release hormones that make us seek out others; in other words, stress has the unexpected benefit of furthering human connection. Sitting on the sidelines of life and not getting involved limits the meaningfulness and closeness in your relationships, but reaching out to help or be helped aids in establishing deeper human connection. Connecting with others over shared concerns can be one of the most meaningful and even healing experiences we could ever have. That might explain why support groups, such as AA and Al-Anon, are so healing. Having a sense of shared humanity makes our stress load a bit lighter.

An interesting factoid: The Chinese symbol for "crisis" is made up of two words: "danger" and "opportunity." It serves as a reminder that what we see as challenges and difficulties are also opportunities for growth.

Implementing Skills

First, make a list of the things that you find stressful in your life. Your list might include certain people, places, situations, activities, responsibilities, and so forth.

_____
_____
_____
_____
_____
_____
_____

Next, look at your list and consider the upsides as well as the downsides for these sources of stress. Write a plus sign, a minus sign, or both next to each item. For example, if you wrote down "children" as stressful, you likely see an upside to having children too!

Now, using McGonigal's idea that stress makes us more social, write down instances where stress helped you be more connected to others.

_____

_____

_____

_____

_____

_____

McGonigal writes in *The Upside of Stress* that chasing meaning and seeing stress as positive often entails developing *bigger-than-self goals*. Those who focus on goals for contributing to their work, society, and relationships tend to be more resilient and enjoy a more fulfilling life.

How about you? Do you have bigger-than-self goals? Commit yourself this week to one actionable bigger-than-self goal. This might be volunteer work, helping a friend or family member, or even working on yourself to be the best parent, friend, or partner that you can be.

_____

_____

_____

Processing the Activity

The main takeaway from this TIP is that stress makes us better, not worse, if we develop a positive relationship to stress. Going against common wisdom to accept that stress can improve our lives, motivate rather than debilitate, can help us embrace stress and thrive in it rather than be worn down under it.

"I will work to manage my stress, not try to avoid it.
I choose to have it enhance my life, not wear me down."

The 7 Cs of Stress Resilience

Theory

Stress is manageable or unmanageable based on our ability to be resilient. When we are resilient, we can change and adapt to new situations and bounce back from adversity even stronger than before. When we are resilient, we tend to be positive, find meaning in life's challenges, and grow deeper instead of weaker in the face of difficult situations.

Over 30 years ago, psychologist Suzanne Kobasa shared her "3 Cs" of the stress-hardy personality. In her studies of people who worked in high-stress situations, she noted that the most resilient individuals were those who exhibited a sense of commitment, control, and challenge. I have expounded on these for a total of 7 Cs that can help us make stress meaningful and more manageable. In the following paragraphs you'll find a brief explanation of each of the 7 Cs of resilience as well as space to reflect on how you can apply these traits to your own life.

Implementing Skills

The following are seven words, all beginning with C, that depict traits of the stress-resilient personality. As we learn and develop these traits, we find that stress does not need to pull us down but instead can lift us up.

The 7 Cs of the Stress-Resilient Personality

Control

We can better manage stress by focusing on what is within our control, not what is out of our control. We cannot control everything about our lives, but we have control over how we choose to react to it. Think of the mouse at your computer—you are the one who moves the mouse and the mouse is how you navigate your computer. It is a good analogy for us to keep in mind to remind ourselves that we have the ability to manage our reactions to our stress with a sense of control.

Connection

Human connection is vital for stress resiliency. Having at least one person to confide in, feeling love and being loved, and having the ability to foster close relationships are ingredients for a positive life. CBT does not downplay the importance of relationships to foster a sense of connection and emotional stability. Rather, CBT's focus on behavior offers practical skills to improve behavior and communication so as to be able to successfully navigate close interpersonal relationships.

Communication

When we communicate honestly, directly, and tactfully, we are acting assertively. With an assertive style of communication, we are much more likely to handle stress better and enlist support. In contrast, being nonassertive, fearful, or even just hesitant to share our thoughts and feelings will make us feel more anxious, depressed, and alienated. And if we communicate in an aggressive fashion, "talking at" others or being disrespectful, we will push others away, which also leads also to alienation, anxiety, and depression. Using assertive skills, as we will explore in chapter 8, is a key ingredient of the stress-hardy personality.

Commitment

Those who are committed to things outside of themselves—to other people, causes, work, or passions—find meaning and purpose in their stress. Those who feel disengaged and bored in their personal and professional lives will feel less empowered and more stressed than those with a sense of purpose and commitment. Thinking that what you are doing and what you are involved in really matters is a significant key to thriving under stress.

Challenge

Some people see setbacks and obstacles in their lives as challenges to overcome and grow from, while others feel weighed down and defeated by them. Those who thrive under stress commit themselves to growing and learning as they move through dealing with stress, using their setbacks as opportunities to grow stronger and even more self-empowered.

Compassion

In dealing with life's stresses and setbacks, we all make inevitable mistakes. The key is to have the ability to have compassion for yourself and others when setbacks occur and refrain from judgments and criticism. Having compassion for ourselves and others ensures we don't beat up on ourselves or others and offers space for healing and growth.

Creativity

Resilience requires creative thinking. Being open to develop new attitudes—looking at things with a different perspective, mental filter and lens—will ensure that you are not trapped in old, unhealthy ways of thinking that erode confidence and resilience.

Now It's Your Turn

Can you think of at least one example from your own life that you can apply to each of the 7 Cs?

Control: _____

_____

Connection: _____
_____

Communication: _____
_____

Commitment: _____
_____

Challenge: _____
_____

Compassion: _____
_____

Creativity: _____
_____

Can you think of other words that begin with C that you see as key to your resilience?
_____
_____
_____
_____

Processing the Activity

In times of difficulty and negative stress, this list of 7 Cs will serve as a framework to turn negative thinking around and help you manage your stress rather than carry it! Use this TIP as a springboard to brainstorm your own adjectives, either starting with the letter C or any other letter, to depict additional characteristics of the stress-resilient personality.

"I have a choice: berate myself for falling short and missing the mark or applaud myself for getting back up and starting over."

# Accept That Life Is Like Swiss Cheese

Theory

Analogies can crystallize life's truths in convincing ways. My favorite analogy for stress resiliency is that of swiss cheese. In 2011, together with Lora Shor, I wrote *The Swiss Cheese Theory of Life: How to Get Through Life's Holes Without Getting Stuck in Them!* In the book, we focus on how stress resiliency helps us to get through "holes" in our lives and helps us to develop more character as a result. After all, everyone's life has holes—it's how you get through them that counts!

Implementing Skills

Using the analogy of swiss cheese is a great way to honor the setbacks we have in life and use these setbacks as vehicles to make us richer and deeper in character and resilience. Consider these points:

1. Swiss cheese is one of the most popular cheeses in the world. We love it not only for its taste but also for its uniquely "holey," imperfect look!

2. Life is not smooth and predictable like cream cheese or American cheese. Living a full life means you go through many small and large "holes," but it is how you get through them and what you can learn from them that counts!

3. The larger the holes, the sweeter and more pungent the cheese. Holes are produced by bacterial fermentation—not exactly a sweet process—yet it is these bacteria-ridden holes that make the flavor stronger and deeper. In the same way, the more holes we get through in our lives, the more depth of character we develop.

4. We do not judge that a slice of swiss has too many or too few holes. We accept the cheese as it is. Likewise, when you stop judging your thinking because it "should" or "should not" be a certain way, you can get through the holes (challenges) in life much easier.

5. There are some types of swiss with no holes—they are called "blind swiss." In the book, we refer to that as "cheese in denial." Rather than deny, wish away, or avoid life's holes, we need to keep our eyes wide open for them so that we can get through them and emerge better and stronger as a result.

The following graphic shows swiss cheese with large and small holes—an analogy for the "holes" in your life. In each hole, write down a setback, mistake, challenge, loss, or failure you have experienced. Then, by the same hole, write down the life lesson that came from that hole, describing how it made you a deeper, more empathetic, and all-around better person.

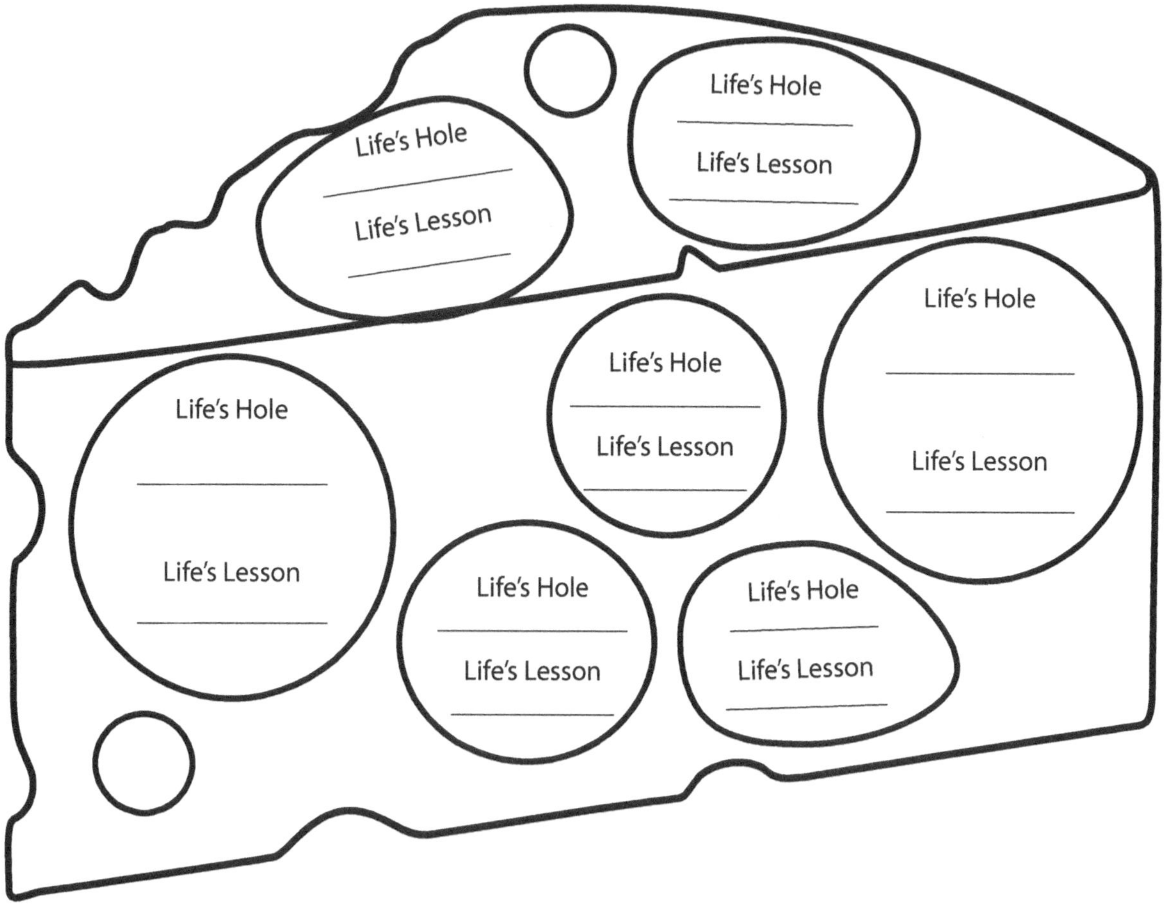
Life's Hole
Life's Lesson
Life's Hole
Life's Lesson
Life's Hole
Life's Lesson
Life's Hole
Life's Lesson
Life's Hole
Life's Lesson
Life's Hole
Life's Lesson
Life's Hole
Life's Lesson

Processing the Activity

Getting through the holes in our lives requires resilience. Stress that pushes us to overcome challenges and be better people can make us deeper instead of weaker. As horrific as some personal challenges are, many people make peace with the difficulties that have happened to them because getting through those difficulties helped them become who they are today.

> "I will accept life's holes and, using the skills I am learning, will get through those holes without getting stuck in them!"

Keep a Stress Diary

Theory

Stress is a fact of life. There is no avoiding it, and in light of what we are focusing on in this chapter, we would not really want to avoid it anyway. We need stress for a full and meaningful life. The following stress diary can be a tool to help you manage stress rather than be "stressed out." Keeping a stress diary can help you withstand large and small stresses with healthy thinking skills to manage your emotions and responses to your stressors. The three areas of CBT—thinking, emotions, and behaviors—can all be managed and controlled. No matter what types of stress come your way, you can empower yourself to grow and thrive from them, especially if you apply CBT tools.

Implementing Skills

A stress diary, with entries like the example shown here, can help you recognize thoughts and subsequent feelings and behaviors, identify your degree of certainty about those thoughts, and replace any cognitive distortions so that you can feel better and behave differently. (For full descriptions and examples of the cognitive distortions, see TIP #13.)

Example Stress Diary Entry

Beliefs (Interpretations)	Certainty of Beliefs (0%–100%)
I'm inferior.	75%
I should have tried harder.	80%
My coworker is so much better than me.	90%

Cognitive Distortions	
Comparing	All-or-nothing thinking
"Shoulds"	Jumping to conclusions
Labeling	

Feelings	Behaviors
Distraught	Withdraw
Devastated	Angry outbursts at home
Dejected	Drinking or eating too much

Challenge Negative Beliefs	Certainty of New Beliefs (0%–100%)
I am not inferior.	90%
I need more experience.	90%
I am no less worthy.	90%
This might motivate me to find another job.	100%

New Feelings	New Behaviors
Confident	Consider a job change
Motivated	Try harder at work

Now It's Your Turn

The next page contains a blank template for a stress diary entry. You can make copies to log your own situations and reactions.

Processing the Activity

This stress diary helps you identify your cognitive distortions and replace them with alternative thoughts that are healthier and kinder to yourself, as well as more accurate. This stress diary can be used whenever you have stressful thoughts that are disturbing. The reason why it is important to rate your degree of certainty about your thoughts is to realize that your degree of confidence in your way of thinking is very important, and if you are less certain of your irrational thoughts and more certain of healthier thoughts, it might help you choose healthier thought alternatives.

"I will learn skills to make sure my challenges will make me deeper, not weaker."

Stress Diary Template

| Beliefs (Interpretations) | Certainty of Beliefs (0%–100%) |

Cognitive Distortions

| Feelings | Behaviors |

| Challenge Negative Beliefs | Certainty of New Beliefs (0%–100%) |

| New Feelings | New Behaviors |

Humor Check-In

Theory

There is no doubt that a sense of humor is an important aspect of mental health. People who can inject humor into even upsetting situations are much more stress-resilient than those who take themselves way too seriously. Humor is a way of getting over difficult situations and serves as a social lubricant in dealing with stressful situations with others. This short quiz is designed to highlight the importance of having a sense of humor in bringing lightness into your life.

Implementing Skills

Do you know anyone who loves to laugh? Do you know anyone who, no matter how serious the situation might be, seems to find something to laugh about? We are not extolling the virtues of nervous laughter to pretend things are great when they are not. Rather, it is the ability to see a silver lining in every cloud that gives us lightness. Laughter makes life more fun, more enjoyable, more playful. As the adage goes, "Laughter is the shock absorber that eases the blows of life."

Humor Check-In

Rate each item on the scale from 1 to 5, with 1 being "completely false" and 5 being "completely true."

_____ I have a hard time "lightening up."

_____ I find myself more irritated than amused by life's absurdities.

_____ I tend to be serious and find little to laugh about.

_____ I tend to worry about what others think of me and feel anxious a lot.

_____ I have a hard time feeling light enough to laugh.

_____ I am not much of a smiler.

_____ I have not had a "good laugh" in quite some time.

_____ I find it annoying when people try to find the bright or funny side of things.

_____ I have so many things on my plate that it is hard to "lighten up."

_____ Having a sense of humor is not a high priority for me.

Total score: _____

Where does your score fall?

- **0–10: Superb**—Your humor quotient is unusually high! Keep up the good work!
- **11–20: Very good**—You have a very good ability to see the lightness in life!
- **21–30: Average**—Your humor quotient could use some boosting.
- **31–40: Needs work**—Look for more opportunities to lighten your load.
- **41–50: Needs a lot of work**—Life is too serious to be taken so seriously. If you find yourself consistently unable to find humor or lightness in any circumstance, consider getting professional help.

Processing the Activity

This check-in will give you a quick snapshot of how much humor is a part of your life, underscoring the importance of having a sense of humor to lighten your stress level. What was your score and what are some ways that you can improve your "humor quotient?" Can you think of ways that you can bring more lightness and humor into your life? Notice what items you scored the lowest and highest on and think of ways to boost your scores in the lowest areas. Even just trying to smile more might help you bring more lightness into your life and will help you deal with stressors in your everyday life.

"I will look to find the lightness and humor in things and will try to find things to laugh about. After all, life is too serious to be taken so seriously!"

Triggers, Triggers... and More Triggers

Theory

Anyone who has experienced trauma, as most of us do at one point or another, cannot avoid triggers from that trauma, no matter how long ago the traumatic event or situation was. People often think of trauma as resulting from a direct experience of physical violence, such as veterans who have been involved in combat, but there are other forms of trauma as well. Societal or collective trauma can result from events that have far-reaching effects, such as the 9/11 attacks or the COVID-19 pandemic. Even if we were not personally affected by the most immediate danger of such an event, it still can trigger feelings of vulnerability and horror in our present lives, even years or decades later.

A trigger can be anything that reminds you of the past experience and that causes you to have an emotional response—you may feel as if the danger from the past is actively a threat now, in the present moment. It is important to understand that while triggers remind us of the past threat, that doesn't mean they are an accurate indicator that we are unsafe in the present. For example, someone might be triggered by dogs due to a frightening past experience with a dog, but that doesn't mean they are actually in danger most of the times they encounter dogs in their current, day-to-day life.

So, although many people try to avoid their triggers, thinking this will keep them safe, it does just the opposite—it gives the triggers too much power over you. Avoidance results in a tendency to act in unhealthy ways, which only leads to more anxiety. Furthermore, if you continue to keep the trauma to yourself out of embarrassment or anxiety about sharing it, it negatively impacts the rest of your life. When you have experienced any type of trauma, there is no shortage of triggers that will bring you back to that trauma. The trick is to understand your triggers and master your reaction to them. In this TIP there are prompts to get you in touch with your triggers, while in the next TIP we will focus on how to move from posttraumatic stress to posttraumatic growth and even posttraumatic wisdom.

Implementing Skills

Trauma does not only result from suffering through war or terrorism. It can arise from a problematic childhood; experiencing the loss of family members through death, divorce, or estrangement; being painfully shy and introverted; being bullied at school—and the list goes on. The following prompts will help you get in touch with your own triggers from past hurts and trauma. These prompts may trigger a lot of thoughts and emotions, so you may wish to consider using additional paper to respond or even keeping a diary of your triggers and reflections.

Have you ever felt that you overreacted to a seemingly innocuous situation that just "set you off?" If so, you likely had a trigger from old hurts and trauma. For example, if you found yourself "losing it" with a friend or family member over a low-stakes situation or misunderstanding, leading to an out-of-proportion reaction, chances are that an old pain that was triggered by the situation. Especially if the trauma took place a long time ago, you might not even be aware of why you are so triggered now. Of course, apologizing for the blowup and trying to learn from it and work on controlling your anger in the future is advisable. But what do you do with the trigger and what the trigger unleashed in you?

- Think back to a recent situation that had triggered some extreme negative emotions and even negative behaviors.
- Think about what hurt was caused in the past that triggered your overblown reaction in the present.
- Consider writing in a journal, talking to a friend or family member, or seeking the help of a professional to process this reaction.
- Use self-compassion in processing your overreaction. It came from a place of pain and hurt, and the hurt child in you was too overwhelmed by emotion to process rationally.

Do you act in ways you don't understand sometimes, overreacting to a minor event, and then feel overwhelmed and guilty later? Explain.

_____
_____
_____
_____

Have there been times when you were taken aback by someone else's behavior as it if were different from what you had learned to expect from others? For example, a client reported that when a friend drove her and two other women to another friend's house for lunch, she was struck with a sick feeling when her friend made the wrong turn off the highway. In examining what struck her, it was not the wrong turn that bothered her; it was a flashback she had to being in the back seat of a car while her parents fought as her father took wrong turns and her mother yelled at him. As a youngster, she felt scared and powerless. Fifty years later, she realized that her sick feeling, and her surprise that no one admonished her friend who was driving, showed how that childhood trauma was still with her.

Have you experienced situations like that? If so, explain.

_____
_____
_____
_____

I have heard many clients pooh-pooh the notion of triggers for their past hurts, thinking at some point they should "get over it." However, if the first emotional language that you learned was laced with emotions such as fear, sadness, and anxiety, it is still within you. Honor those triggers, learn from them, and move on, wiser than before. Can you relate to this? Explain below.

_____

_____

_____

_____

The great healer of triggers is compassion for self and others. Understanding where the triggers came from will help you to be more forgiving of your reactions. Recognize the hurt child inside of you that was never completely healed from the old hurts. Instead of thinking you should be over it, have compassion for and forgive that child for not having fully healed. Ironically, that will help you heal more than anything else you could imagine.

When you want to yell out "What is wrong with you?" it's a sign that person is triggered and is reacting to an old hurt in a new situation. Do you treat yourself and others with compassion for being triggered or do you tend to be critical? Explain.

_____

_____

_____

_____

Realize that some triggers worsen your symptoms instead of getting you to take stock and "wake up." This can cause a relapse into old self-numbing habits such as substance abuse or other maladaptive behaviors. You might also notice that happening in someone else. Instead of being puzzled by extreme behavior and setbacks, realize that old wounds are now open and that professional help can be beneficial to prevent a cascade of aftereffects. Does this apply to you? Explain.

_____

_____

_____

_____

Triggers come in all forms: sounds, smells, words, sights, music, events that re-enact old ones, and more. You might witness an argument, hear a certain song, be startled by a loud noise, or simply feel rejected or judged—and suddenly you're overwhelmed by anxiety, fear, anger, or grief. The intensity of emotion in a triggered reaction seems completely out of proportion to the event because in some ways, the triggered person is reliving their trauma. Have you experienced this? Have you noticed others reacting disproportionately to an objectively nonconfrontational situation? Explain.

_____
_____
_____
_____

Perhaps the most important focus in emotional self-care is to heal from your past pain, which can range from small disappointments to deep trauma. What events from the past still hurt or affect you to this day? What past hurt or trauma can help explain your emotional triggers and negative thoughts that continue to show up?

_____
_____
_____
_____

Processing the Activity

How did these prompts make you feel? Did you gain any insight into yourself or others by looking at triggers and overreactions as the result of past pain and trauma? Were you able to feel compassionate toward yourself or others re-experiencing old hurts? In the next TIP we will focus on moving from posttraumatic stress to posttraumatic growth.

> "No matter what has happened to me before, every day is a new day and it is never, never, never too late to make my life the most beautiful that it has ever been. The sunrise is the gift we get for getting through the dark."

Moving from Posttraumatic Stress to Posttraumatic Growth

Theory

Trauma happens in a variety of ways. Many types of events can cause a setback that is hard to move past. Some examples of unrelenting trauma include going through a difficult breakup, becoming estranged from a loved one, getting a life-threatening diagnosis, suffering a huge financial setback, losing a job or business, not being able to realize a life dream, surviving a war or a natural disaster, experiencing physical assault or a tragic accident involving you or someone close to you, or grieving the loss of someone close to you. It might also be something from deeper in the past, such as growing up in a family where there was abuse, neglect, or chronic dysfunction and conflict.

Author and lecturer Shawn Achor writes about healing from posttraumatic stress to posttraumatic growth in his book *The Happiness Advantage* (2010). He uses the term "falling up" instead of "falling down" to describe the process of recovering from stressful events and changing for the better because of the trauma. We cannot change the past, but we can use it to become stronger. Achor believes that great suffering paves the way for the greatest changes. When you fall up, you are never really the same—you can actually become better because of the growth you experience as you recover.

Jane McGonigal, sister of stress researcher Kelly McGonigal, whose work is also referenced in this chapter, says this about posttraumatic growth: "Scientists have demonstrated that dramatic, positive changes can occur in our lives as a direct result of facing an extreme challenge, whether it's coping with a serious illness, daring to quit smoking, or dealing with depression. Researchers call this 'post-traumatic growth'" (Biegel & Cooper, 2019, p. 143).

Implementing Skills

In his book, Shawn Achor focuses on how difficult times in his life led to personal growth and a higher level of empathy for others. He credits his own period of depression as a graduate student with helping him understand how to overcome adversity and stress to change his mindset, enabling him to be more compassionate, understanding, and able to help people though his life's work on happiness.

Using Achor's idea of *falling up*, you can transform posttraumatic stress into posttraumatic growth by taking the following steps:

Step 1

Write down the three greatest moments of personal growth in your life.

_____
_____
_____

Describe how you have grown from these three moments, aided by these prompts:
- Did the greatest times of growth result from adversity?
- What lessons did you learn?
- How have these experiences helped you be a better person?
- Have you developed more empathy for others?
- Have these experiences made you wiser?

_____
_____
_____
_____
_____
_____
_____

Step 2

Write down some concrete actions you can take to empower yourself to face the challenges in front of you now. For example, if you are suffering a health scare, think of concrete ways that you can take control of your health.

_____
_____
_____

Step 3

Tell someone you can confide in about your plan of action. Research has shown that seeking social support and having a strong social network are the best predictors of growth after setbacks. Telling someone is like sharing a heavy bucket of water. Holding it alone can be unbearable;

however, holding it with someone else makes it much easier to carry. After trying this, write your reaction here.

_____
_____
_____

Step 4

Write out a list of at least three ways to build your support system and community of caring. Building a close network can take many forms, including reaching out to friends, making an effort to find new friends, joining a new club or activity, and opening up to others you trust.

_____
_____
_____

Step 5

Be compassionate to yourself and others. Never critique anyone's feelings as "too sensitive." Honoring your trauma and not belittling or judging it will lead to posttraumatic growth and posttraumatic wisdom. Forgive yourself for any past actions you regret. Forgive others for not being able to give you what they do not have to give in the first place. Use gentle self-talk that is loving and accepting. What are some soothing self-statements you might try?

_____
_____
_____

Step 6

If you spend too much time looking back on how things "should" have been, then you will never be able to fully live today. After all, what's done is done. There's a long list of things that have happened to us or we have done that we can repeatedly mull over. The only hope for moving forward is to focus more on what's left rather than on what we lost or left behind. This transitions us from posttraumatic stress to posttraumatic growth. What persistent thoughts or memories do you need to leave behind?

_____
_____
_____

Step 7

If you find yourself suffering from posttraumatic stress, have you made a plan to shift to posttraumatic growth as you seek support, open yourself to asking for help, and widen your circle of caring? Explain.

_____
_____
_____

Think of how each loss or trauma has helped you grow and become the person you are today, leading to posttraumatic growth or posttraumatic wisdom. Find the positive things that result from your life circumstances. Think of examples of posttraumatic stress and how you have moved on to posttraumatic wisdom.

_____
_____
_____

"'Finding the path up' is what separates the successful from those who give up. It requires that you look for the opportunity in any setback, rather than settling into despair."

—Shawn Achor

Processing the Activity

Giving yourself the opportunity to look for the blessings in your stresses, setbacks, and challenges will help you move from posttraumatic stress to posttraumatic wisdom. When you do that, past stresses and hurts become opportunities for growth and healing. I have been taken aback by many clients who experienced unbelievable pain in the past who said they would not trade a thing now, as that pain made them who they are today. Sometimes we grow stronger from the places that were broken. Reflect on how your old hurts have increased your empathy, wisdom, and character, helping you now in your relationships and in all aspects of your life.

"Some memories continue to haunt, some continue to heal, but for all of them I feel blessed. They have helped shape who I am today."

Ten Ways to Move Forward No Matter What

Theory

In this TIP we will focus on ways to move forward after trauma. No one goes through life unscathed by loss, disappointment, or hurt. Of course, the amount and degree vary greatly, and some people have more than their fair share of setbacks and challenges. The important thing is to honor your past and the unique set of circumstance that have affected you. All too often, yesterday's blows become today's negative pull that grips us and limits our enjoyment of now. But we have the power to make our past setbacks a setup for a richer and more meaningful life. We have control over how we respond to the trauma now. Yesterday's pain, disappointments, losses, and failures do not have to set the stage for the rest of our lives. It is never too late to change. To quote the wise words of Forrest Gump, "My mama always said you've got to put the past behind before you can move on."

Implementing Skills

Here are some ways to move forward no matter what.

1. Realize that some things you never really "get over" but you still can "get through."

There are some things that are so life-altering that we never can truly leave them behind us. Extreme and heart-breaking hurts such as the loss of a loved one, life-altering accidents, or severe medical illnesses are just a few examples. Some things we might never truly get over, but life can still be good and even beautiful on the other side of loss, trauma, and heartbreak. We can heal by finding meaning in our life challenges to improve us and deepen us.

2. Things that you can't get over are great warnings!

Think of the gas light in your car. The gas light signals that action needs to be taken—that you must get to a gas station and refill. Likewise, the things in our lives that we cannot get over are telling us something: that we still have things to learn and heal from, and it is up to us to discover what!

3. Focus on what you have the power to change.

Instead of focusing on what cannot be changed, focus on what *can* be changed. In most cases, events or other people do not cause us to feel a certain way—we are the gatekeepers of our feelings and reactions! Taking responsibility for your own thoughts and feelings will get you out of a victim mentality and empower you to make stepping stones out of your past stressors, setbacks, and disappointments instead of wearing them as millstones around your neck.

4. Beware of negative self-talk holding you back.

Often, we cannot get over something because of stories we tell ourselves with a negative spin, especially stories not based on facts. For example, someone who has lost their job might blame themselves and think they are a failure, which makes them feel unworthy and incapable of finding another job. However, another person in the same scenario might be disappointed but still have the confidence to move on, realizing that there might be better opportunities instead of thinking that they failed. The key is not to personalize life's cruel twists as somehow reflecting your worth as a person, thinking it forbodes a long-standing pattern of defeat. Beware of your negative self-talk and hold tight to your motivation to change it!

5. Honor the grieving process.

Whether it be the loss of a loved one or a dream we held dearly, grieving is a process we all need to go through at many points in our lives. Elisabeth Kübler-Ross's five-stage model of grieving—denial, anger, bargaining, depression, and acceptance—is something we all can identify with in varying amounts and intensities. From large-scale collective grief to private heartache, the process of grieving is vital to the healing process. Using the model of the five stages of grieving will normalize feelings such as anger and depression. These are often necessary steps to reach the stage of acceptance, where you grow from the hurt.

6. Don't go it alone.

People grow best through support and relationships. Those who retreat inward and shut people out so as not to be hurt again will keep on re-traumatizing themselves. Keeping trauma in and not expressing hurts that keep you stuck only begets more trauma. Those who become better rather than bitter after a setback will seek support to soothe their sense of loss. Healthy and supportive relationships can help heal wounds. Even if others cannot fix your trauma, they can support you and help you express your feelings.

7. "It's never too late to be what you might have been."

Remind yourself that it's never too late to start over. As the famous saying attributed to George Eliot reads, "It's never too late to be what you might have been." If you learn lessons from what you cannot "get over," and make healthy decisions now based on what you learned, you will truly give yourself new life to an old issue. Changing your behaviors to cope with or prevent unfortunate things from happening again will empower you. Being proactive instead of reactive, while making changes based on your life lessons, can heal past hurts and traumas.

8. Move forward with forgiveness.

Whether you need to forgive yourself, others, or even a higher power or life itself, forgiveness will release you from the chains of bitterness. The more you can forgive, the more you can accept life as it comes. Forgiveness opens your heart to gratitude, focusing on what is good in your life rather than what is sorely missed. Imagine you are looking at a bagel—do you focus on the hole or on the whole? Give yourself a gift by trading bitterness and powerlessness for acceptance and gratitude.

Do any of these ideas resonate with you? Explain.

_____
_____
_____
_____
_____

Can you think of other ways to move on in your life no matter what?

_____
_____
_____
_____
_____

Processing the Activity

If you find yourself stuck in grieving what you cannot get over, use these suggestions as a model for processing. If these tips are followed, even the most difficult setbacks can serve as a slingshot into making your tomorrows richer and more meaningful. The key is not to go it alone. Seek support from others, including professional help, if you find yourself stuck and unable to move forward or simply want additional support as you work through your hurt.

> "I know there will be things I will never get over, but I can get through—and it still can be beautiful on the other side."

Fifteen Tips for Emotional Resilience

Theory

The 15 tips in this handout crystallize the characteristics of the stress-resilient personality. The more you possess these 15 qualities, the more likely you are to bounce back from adversity and handle stress in a positive way. Use this handout as a handy reference if you feel stressed out. It is a good reminder of what truly makes us happy. Happiness should never have preconditions, such as thinking *I will be happy once I* . . . [lose 20 pounds, meet someone, have children, graduate, etc.]. Rather, it is our emotionally resilient mindset that truly makes us happy. Resilient thinking will help us get through life strong and empowered, not reaching for a goal outside of ourselves. Material possessions and outward success are nice, but they are no substitute for the emotionally resilient mindset. Wherever you go, whoever you are with, wherever you travel, you bring your mindset along.

Implementing Skills

15 Tips for Emotional Resilience

1. **Be self-compassionate.** This is the basic building block of self-esteem and gives you the ability to bounce back from adversity. Treat yourself with kindness, like you would a loved one.

2. **Forgive yourself.** Forgive yourself for not having the foresight to know what is now so obvious in hindsight. Refuse to kick yourself or beat yourself up for not knowing then what you know now.

3. **Forgive others.** You deserve to let go of the pain of the past. Forgiveness does not mean condoning or allowing others' hurtful behavior to continue. You can still set limits to the point that others who have hurt you are no longer in your present life, but you can free the space in your head from harboring blame and bitterness. You deserve better. Blame keeps you stuck in a moment in time that cannot be changed.

4. **Connect, connect, connect.** Connection with others is one of the most important factors in stress resilience. Social support and having at least one person you can self-disclose to is crucial to resilience. Ask for help when you need it.

5. **Let stress motivate you, not reduce you.** Stress is an important part of life. It makes us deeper and allows us to develop character. It offers us meaning and purpose. Don't wish it away; rather, be motivated by it.

6. **Be creative.** Play, laugh, enjoy doing things you have not done before or want to do more of without worrying about your innate ability or talent.

7. **Shift your perspective.** Look at things from different perspectives. Don't get stuck in old thinking habits that don't work for you. Sometimes it takes only small shifts in our focus to make *big* changes in our lives.

8. **Be grateful.** Grateful people are happy people. They don't compare themselves to others who have it better. They focus on what life gives them rather than being steeped in bitterness about what life has not offered them.

9. **Limit unhealthy thinking habits.** Identify unhealthy habits, called cognitive distortions, that lead to exaggerated, negative, all-or-nothing thinking.

10. **Don't shy away from challenge—it creates depth of character.** The Chinese symbol for crisis is made up of two words: "danger" plus "opportunity." Learn from adversity and grow from it.

11. **Make self-care a priority.** It is not selfish to care for yourself. In fact, loving and caring for yourself is the best gift you can give to others, since your relationship with yourself sets the foundation for your relationships with others.

12. **Have a growth mindset, not a fixed mindset**. Focus on your efforts and your enjoyment of learning, flexibility, and growth, rather than rating your worth and value based on your accomplishments or your innate abilities.

13. **Strive for goodness, not perfection!** Strive to be good, not perfect. Accept mistakes, failures, and shortcomings, and do your best without fear of failure.

14. **Focus on what you *can* control, not what you can't.** Have the wisdom to know the difference! Don't blame others for your feelings, and don't blame yourself for their feelings. We all are in control of our own feelings and choices.

15. **Be mindful.** Be present focused, instead of excessively ruminating about the past or anxieties about the future. Live in awe of life *now*.

Looking at that list, which areas do you think you are mastering? Reflect on which items resonate most with you and explain why.

_____
_____
_____
_____

Which areas are most challenging for you? Explain.

_____
_____
_____
_____

What goals can you make based on this list that can help you build resiliency? Remember, all of the items listed here can be learned and practiced, helping you develop an emotionally resilient mindset.

_____
_____
_____
_____

Processing the Activity

Use this list as a reference whenever you feel stressed and need help and support in managing your stress. The 15 items serve as reminders of the cornerstones of the positive life. If you would like to do more work on developing your resilience, you might take one item each day and journal about how you can incorporate that tip into your own life. Recognize the barriers that get in your way, such as the pulls from the past or your cognitive distortions. Reflect on solutions and goals to overcome these barriers.

> "I will work hard to improve my relationship with stress, and I will empower myself by using healthy thinking skills as I move forward, freeing myself from negative thought habits."

Have Goals That Are Bigger-Than-Self

Theory

According to psychologist Kelly McGonigal, when you are committed to something greater than yourself, you increase your stress resiliency. McGonigal refers to this as *bigger-than-self goals*. Getting involved with others in causes you believe in, for example, requires our time and energy and can even be stressful, but it is positive stress because it is motivating, helps us heal, and provides purpose and meaning to our lives. As Norman Vincent Peale said, "The more you lose yourself in something bigger than yourself, the more energy you will have." McGonigal's research shows that when we are generous with our resources of time, money, care, and compassion, we end up feeling better than those with a self-focused mindset. Happiness is less correlated with IQ or even success than with how much you pursue goals for a common good. McGonigal believes that having bigger-than-self goals ends up making you more productive and successful in your personal goals as well.

Implementing Skills

One of the surest ways to feel better about yourself is to help others. Perhaps that is why volunteerism often helps the person volunteering as much as those who are helped. In fact, the link between happiness and helping others is well documented. Many people have found that the rewards reaped from the causes and activities they devote themselves to far outweigh the inconvenience of the effort given to them. Volunteerism and nurturing others help us stay connected to others and provide us with a sense of serving a higher purpose outside of ourselves. That is why I have a favorite motto: "Want to feel better? Help someone else!"

Bigger-than-self goals do not have to be grandiose. They can involve raising children and growing a family, working on a project or business that you believe in, pouring your talents into a creative pursuit that you find meaningful and enjoy, volunteering for a cause, or finding other endeavors that you can share with others. A bigger-than-self goal can even be simply to treat everyone you meet with kindness and compassion.

Do you have bigger-than-self goals? This does not mean you cannot have personal goals just for yourself, but do some of your existing goals include a commitment to something outside of yourself? Explain.

_____
_____
_____

If you do not have any bigger-than-self goals, or if you would like to cultivate more of them, the following questions will help guide you.

What are you committed to? What would you like to commit yourself more to?
_____
_____
_____

What gives, or would give, your life more meaning?
_____
_____
_____

How can you make a positive impact on those around you?
_____
_____
_____

What inspires you?
_____
_____
_____

Instead of feeling in competition with others, how can you facilitate cooperation?
_____
_____
_____

What would you like to contribute to the world?
_____
_____
_____

What is one positive action you can take every day this week to move toward a bigger-than-self goal? Remember, it does not need to be a major undertaking—it can be a purposeful practice of treating everyone you meet with warmth and kindness.

_____
_____
_____

Now think long-range of how you can be in a supportive network to pursue bigger-than-self goals. Perhaps you would like to join a spiritual or religious group, volunteer with a political or social organization, or participate in community service that can provide a forum for engagement and connection with others. The choices we make to pursue a meaningful life within a context of involvement can help us feel connected, supported, and loved. What would this look like for you?

_____
_____
_____

Processing the Activity

One benefit of having bigger-than-self goals is that it will make you feel more connected to others. Social support can be transformative in itself. We grow best through our relationships with others. Whenever you feel alone and distant from others, think of how you can commit yourself to bigger-than-self goals that will provide you with a sense of involvement, connection, and meaning.

"Ironically, having a goal to help others ends up helping me tremendously by offering me a sense of purpose and connection with others, some of whom may even become my family of choice."

Self-Test for Managing and Growing from Stress

Theory

This self-test for relieving stress is a summary of the main points of this chapter. Using this TIP as a review of the chapter's main points and an opportunity for reflection will help you gauge how well you thrive under stress and grow and learn from life's setbacks instead of being held back by them. In this chapter we focused on the motivational effects of stress and even trauma in making us the people we are today. Understanding your triggers and learning from old hurts can help you move from posttraumatic stress to posttraumatic growth and even help you attain posttraumatic wisdom.

As in every other chapter, the key to your success will be practice, practice, and more practice.

Implementing Skills

In the self-test that follows, rate how true each statement is for you, from 1 to 10, to assess which areas you are doing well in and which areas need some improvement. The higher the score in each item, the higher your mastery in that area. The test is not designed to give you a one-and-done score. Your self-help journey is a continual one, and the important thing is to work to keep improving on yesterday. Making several copies of this self-test will allow you to keep retaking it to monitor your progress.

At the end of this self-test you will be prompted to calculate a total score and an average score. To get the average score, divide your total score by the number of items you responded to. For any items that are not applicable to you, just write "N/A" and subtract those items from the number you divide by when calculating your average score. As you continue taking the self-tests throughout this book, compare your average scores across the different topics. This will give you a snapshot of which areas need the most attention and which areas are the strongest.

Keep this test handy whenever you want some support and reminders on what tools you can use to work on the areas covered in this chapter.

Self-Test for Managing and Growing from Stress

Using a scale from 1 to 10, with 1 being "not true" and 10 being "very true," rate how true these statements are for you.

Not true ⟵ 1 2 3 4 5 6 7 8 9 10 ⟶ **Very true**

____ I do not avoid stress and in fact am often motivated by it.

____ I embrace stress as something that helps me grow as a person.

____ I see myself as having a stress-resilient personality, using the 7 Cs of resilience: control, connection, communication, commitment, challenge, compassion, and creativity.

____ I accept that life is not fair and has holes in it, just like swiss cheese, and I have become stronger because of the holes in my life.

____ I find it helpful to keep a stress diary where I can reflect and process my stresses and stressors.

____ I use a sense of humor and find that humor has helped me with life stresses.

____ I understand my triggers and am compassionate with myself, as well with others who overreact due to their own triggers.

____ For any trauma or hurt from the past, I have reached some degree of posttraumatic growth and wisdom.

____ No matter what my setback is, I try to move forward even stronger and deeper with lessons learned.

____ I honor the importance of bigger-than-self goals and strive to be motivated by them in my life.

____ I have reviewed the list of the 15 tips for emotional resilience and consider myself to be high in emotional resilience.

Total score: _____

Average score (*total score ÷ 11 or items answered*): _____

In the space below, process and explain your answers.

_____
_____
_____
_____

If you would like further structure to process your answers to the self-test and your reactions to the chapter, here are some prompts to guide you.

My thoughts: _____
_____

My feelings: _____
_____

My self-talk: _____
_____

What I have learned: _____
_____

Additional thoughts and strategies: _____
_____
_____
_____

Processing the Activity

Use this self-test periodically to assess your progress and to continue to improve your ability to handle stress. Your general overall score will vary over time, and it would be helpful to keep a record of your scores to see if you are improving in your skills to manage stress. The important takeaway from this chapter is that stress is not to be avoided, but rather embraced for a full and meaningful life!

"I am thankful for my strength and motivation to embrace the stress in my life, which makes me a more empathetic and deeper person. I am proud of my resilience."

CHAPTER 7

Managing Anger: Control Your Anger So You Won't Lose Control

Anger is an important and useful emotion. It can serve as a motivator to stand up for yourself and not allow others to mistreat you. It can be a driver to make the world a better place. Like anxiety, anger can be compared to the indicator light in a car that lets us know when the fuel is low—it is giving us information that something is not right. Thus, we need to address and honor our anger.

However, many people do not regard anger as a desired emotion. All too often, people ignore their feelings of anger because they see it as a "bad" or unwanted emotion that they should not feel. Furthermore, anger is often confused with aggression—yet they do not need to go hand in hand. Anger is a feeling, while aggression is a behavior, and differentiating these is an important part of anger management. It's okay to feel angry, but it is not okay to lash out at others in anger, even if they provoked you or "started it."

Aggressive behavior is not limited to physical violence or what we typically think of as bullying. The definition of an argument is trying to prove you are right and change the other person's mind. If your goal is to change someone else, even their opinions, your goal is an aggressive one. Behaviors like giving someone the silent treatment, rolling your eyes, or making a loud sigh are also aggressive forms of communication (in this case, nonverbal communication).

We will delve more into aggressive behavior in chapter 8, which focuses on communication skills and improving interpersonal relationships, but since uncontrolled anger and aggressive behavior are closely linked, this topic will also be addressed in this chapter. Uncontrolled anger most often originates from distorted, out-of-control thinking. CBT offers tools to talk ourselves down from extreme ways of thinking as we replace irrational thoughts with more rational ones. For example, a statement like "You make me so mad" puts the blame for your feelings on the other person, which is not true or fair in most cases. You own your feelings, not anyone else. Rather than making statements like that, be more specific and use "I" statements, such as "I feel frustrated when you do not wash the dishes as we'd agreed."

This chapter will help you cope with your angry feelings without getting aggressive. It will help you accept anger as a rightful and useful feeling that can motivate you to heal old wounds, set limits, do good in the world, and work toward bettering your life and the lives of others. The important thing is not to hold on to it any longer than we need to give us the impetus to use our anger to motivate us for positive actions.

"Holding on to anger is like grasping a hot coal with the intent of throwing it at someone else; you are the one who gets burned."

—attributed to the Buddha

The Benefits of Separating Thoughts and Feelings

Theory

Learning to separate thoughts from feelings is important in many areas of our lives, including managing our anger. When we're in the height of emotion, thoughts and feelings are often mixed together in one confusing mess. This lack of clarity often results in anger spiraling out of control, leading to regrettable outbursts and rude behaviors. Thinking more clearly by separating your thoughts and feelings will help calm you and the situation, leading to healthier reactions.

Implementing Skills

For the following angry reactions, put an F next to the statements that represent feelings and a T next to the statements that represent thoughts.

_____ She makes me so mad!

_____ I feel like I was thrown to the wolves!

_____ You're upsetting me!

_____ I feel that I was treated unfairly!

_____ I don't deserve to be treated this way!

_____ I feel like you are criticizing me!

_____ I feel like you don't respect me!

_____ I feel like you are always trying to "one up" me!

_____ I can't forgive you for what you said to me!

_____ You have no right to upset me like that!

Tally your score. How many statements did you mark as feelings and how many did you mark as thoughts?

In fact, they were *all* thoughts. The use of "I feel" in many of these sentences can throw you off. However these are thoughts that are emotionally charged.

It is important to differentiate thoughts from feelings. Challenging irrational thoughts can change the subsequent feelings. You then will be better able to manage your anger rather than have it spiral out of control and cause you to lash out.

Let's use a couple of the preceding examples to differentiate thoughts from feelings.

- "She makes me so mad" is an irrational thought because no one can directly make you mad. This view makes you a victim of someone else, which furthers the feelings of being angry and trapped. A more rational way of saying it would be "I was mad when she said that."

- "I feel like I was thrown to the wolves" is also a thought, despite the use of the word "feel." The implied feelings in this expression are anger and indignation at not receiving the support you had expected from someone else. A more clear, factual, and rational statement would be "I feel upset and hurt because I had hoped you would support my points in that discussion."

Can you rephrase the other statements from the list in similar ways to separate the feelings from the thoughts and make the thoughts more factual?

You're upsetting me! _____

I feel that I was treated unfairly! _____

I don't deserve to be treated this way! _____

I feel like you are criticizing me! _____

I feel like you don't respect me! _____

I feel like you are always trying to "one up" me! _____

I can't forgive you for what you said to me! _____

You have no right to upset me like that! _____

Processing the Activity

Confusing thoughts with feelings is such a common phenomenon that it often goes undetected, which can cause our anger to spiral out of control. Using CBT skills to differentiate thoughts from feelings is one way to ensure that anger will be a useful feeling to motivate you to stand up for what you believe in rather than engage in aggressive behaviors you later regret. Anger can help you identify what does not work for you, but that does not give you the license to act aggressively.

"I can control my anger and find peace in managing it with clear thinking."

Learning Communication Skills to Express Anger Assertively

Theory

In the last TIP we focused on separating thoughts and feelings so that our angry feelings do not spur us to behave aggressively. This TIP will focus on developing skills for managing anger in a healthier way. To do this, we must first establish the differences between the three main types of communication: assertive, non-assertive, and aggressive.

In *assertive* communication, emotions are managed calmly and without being hurtful to others; the person expresses their feelings, needs, and desires in a clear but respectful way. In *aggressive* communication, strong emotions, such as anger, go unchecked and lead to bullying, bossy, or otherwise hurtful and disrespectful behavior toward others. Conversely, those who stuff their feelings because they want to avoid confrontation at all costs end up using *non-assertive* communication by keeping their true feelings, wishes, and needs to themselves. Anger turned inward leads to depression, anxiety, resentment, and feelings of being isolated and misunderstood that accumulate over time and often end in aggressive outbursts.

Implementing Skills

The following chart shows how the three types of communication deal with angry feelings. Which communication style do you most identify with when you are angry?

How the Three Communication Styles Deal with Anger

Feelings		
Non-Assertive	**Assertive**	**Aggressive**
Unconfident	Confident	Self-righteous, indignant
Afraid of "making waves"	Comfortable setting boundaries and limits	Focused on getting what they want at others' expense
Afraid of being judged	Nonjudgmental	Judgmental
Seeks others' acceptance	Seeks self-acceptance	Focused on being "right"
Feels inferior	Feels worthy	Feels superior
Feels controlled	Has self-control	Seeks to control others, while their own feelings are out of control

	Behaviors	
Non-Assertive	**Assertive**	**Aggressive**
Suppresses their anger	Accepts their anger	Lashes out in anger
Simmers quietly	Expresses their feelings honestly and tactfully	Expresses their feelings honestly but tactlessly
Denies their feelings	Accepts responsibility for their feelings	Blames others for their feelings
Avoids conflict	Is honest and open to resolve issues	Instigates arguments or takes revenge
Avoids risks	Open to risk and vulnerability in service of their goals	Behaves or speaks with little regard for consequences
Keeps their thoughts and feelings hidden	Uses "I" statements	Uses "you" statements
Permits their rights to be violated	Stands up for their own rights while respecting others' rights	Violates others' rights

Processing the Activity

As we can see in this TIP, anger does not need to lead to aggressive behavior. You can use an assertive communication style to ensure healthy expression of even the strongest emotions. Be careful of angry words, as they are just like feathers released to the wind—once you let them out, you can't take them back. As a saying attributed to Benjamin Franklin goes, "Whatever is begun in anger ends in shame." At the same time, be careful not to stuff down your emotions, as they will likely grow over time and burst out as aggressive communication despite your efforts! Staying assertive across the board will improve your relationships, your confidence, and your life. Remember that no one can make you angry or have power over you unless you give it to them.

"I have a right to express myself so long as I do so assertively and respectfully to others."

No One Makes You Feel Angry—You Own Your Feelings!

Theory

When people are angry, they often blame others for "making" them feel that way, even to the point where they blame others for their own aggressive reactions (having a "you made me do it" mentality). Taking responsibility for your feelings away from others and into your own hands will turn you from a victim into a victor. This TIP will help you regain control over your own emotions, which will empower you and help you manage anger instead of offloading it to others.

Implementing Skills

In most human interactions that do not involve abusive behavior, we are directly responsible for our own feelings and reactions. This exercise gives you an opportunity to practice changing "you" statements into "I" statements when expressing anger, which, as we learned in the previous TIP, is one of the hallmarks of a healthy, assertive communication style. Here are a few examples to get you started.

Turning "You" Statements into "I" Statements

"You" Statement	"I" Statement
"You make me so mad!"	"I feel angry when you raise your voice at me."
"You should know better!"	"I did not realize you did not know that."
"You offend me."	"I felt offended when you said that."
"Stop being so nosy."	"I won't discuss personal matters."
"You'd better not do that again!"	"I am asking you to please not do that again."

Now It's Your Turn

Are there some "you" statements that you have made (or thought) in the heat of anger? How can they be changed into "I" statements?

"You" Statement	"I" Statement

Just as it is important to focus on your communication style in dealing with others, especially in the heat of anger, make sure your self-talk is also assertive. If your self-talk is aggressive and blaming toward others, the words you say out loud likely will be as well. Here are some examples of negative self-talk and how to replace them with more rational self-talk, which will in turn make it easier for you to communicate with others assertively.

Turning Negative Self-Talk into Healthy and Rational Self-Talk

Negative Self-Talk	Healthy and Rational Self-Talk
"What a jerk!"	"I am disappointed in the way he is acting."
"I hate her!"	"I do not like her or admire her right now."
"He makes me furious!"	"I am very upset with him."

Now It's Your Turn

Practice changing your angry, blaming self-talk into healthier, rational self-talk.

Negative Self-Talk	Healthy and Rational Self-Talk

Processing the Activity

This TIP demonstrates how irrational self-talk and giving up control of your feelings to others leads to unhealthy and aggressive communication skills. To keep your angry thoughts in check, keep in mind that "anger" is one letter short of "danger!" One moment of not keeping your anger in check can lead to a lifetime of regret.

"When I am in control of my anger by controlling my self-talk and my reactions, I feel empowered and calm."

Avoid Put-Downs Disguised as Questions

Theory

When anger is unchecked, anger-fueled rhetorical questions are not uncommon. The interesting thing about rhetorical questions is that they are really put-downs and criticisms disguised as questions. They are rude, offensive remarks meant to hurt or demean another person. In the heat of anger, watch out for these judgmental put-downs. Underneath the rhetorical questions are faulty thoughts that show out-of-control thinking and behavior.

Implementing Skills

Here are some examples of angry rhetorical questions:

- What's wrong with you?
- What were you thinking?
- Didn't I already go over that?
- Why are you being such a brat?
- Are you for real?
- How many times do I need to tell you that?
- Why can't you listen the first time?

Can you think of rhetorical questions that you have said (or thought) in the heat of anger?

_____

_____

Can you identify the irrational thoughts behind the rhetorical questions, using either the examples given or your own? For example, thoughts such as *They should know better* or *They should not be acting that way* show an indignant, self-righteous, and judgmental way of thinking.

_____

_____

Processing the Activity

Rhetorical questions are in fact aggressive statements disguised as questions. Identifying when you have such thoughts will help you fine-tune your communication from assertive to aggressive.

"I will work on being less judgmental and critical so
that I can be healthier for myself and others."

Anger Is Not Aggression!

Theory

One of the most surprising things that clients have asked me over the years is whether or not they have a right to feel the way they do. I have always been taken aback by that, as having any feeling is our undeniable right. We need to accept our feelings without judgment, just as it is important to accept the feelings of others without judgment. As we have seen in the previous TIPs in this chapter, it's another thing to act on feelings such as anger with assertiveness versus aggression. Remember that anger is a feeling while aggression is a behavior. Thus, feelings of anger are always acceptable, but acts of aggression are not appropriate in most human interactions. Assertive behavior is the key to good interpersonal relationships.

Even if you feel like you are wrongly accused of something, and try to prove you are right with righteous indignation, you are actually being aggressive. It is fine to stand up for yourself, expressing your alternate view of things, but if the goal is to defend yourself by proving how wrong someone is, you will lapse into aggression. Consider the adage that it is better to be kind than be right.

Implementing Skills

Anger management, like most of the skills in this book, is a trainable skill. In this chapter, we have been exploring the hallmarks of assertive versus aggressive communication. The following check-in will help you see whether you tend to confuse the two or whether you have learned how to identify them.

Read each of the following statements and circle whether it represents aggressive or assertive communication.

1.	"I am angry with you right now."	Aggressive	Assertive
2.	"You make me so mad."	Aggressive	Assertive
3.	"You shouldn't get so angry with her."	Aggressive	Assertive
4.	"I was angry when you said that."	Aggressive	Assertive
5.	Yelling back when someone yells at you first.	Aggressive	Assertive
6.	Glaring at someone without saying a thing.	Aggressive	Assertive
7.	Giving someone the "silent treatment" after they insulted you.	Aggressive	Assertive

8.	"You have no right to say that to me!"	Aggressive	Assertive
9.	"You hurt my feelings—you should know better!"	Aggressive	Assertive
10.	"I think you are incredibly rude."	Aggressive	Assertive

After filling in your answers, check them against the key at the bottom of this page.

How did you do? Notice that the only items in the list that are assertive are "I" statements. All the others are "you" statements because they are blaming others, telling others what to do, or being judgmental. Still, just because you start with an "I" does not mean it is an "I" statement. Notice the last statement starts with an "I" but is actually aggressive because it labels the other person.

If you missed a few (or more) of these questions, it will be helpful to review the other TIPs in this chapter for additional practice and even continue on to chapter 8, which further explores assertive communication skills, then retake this test to see if your score improves.

Processing the Activity

Differentiating anger from aggression is one of the most important things you can do, whether you have problems controlling your anger or find yourself denying your anger and stuffing it in. If you need further help managing anger, try writing out some of your own thoughts and then, just as you did in this check-in, identifying whether each one uses aggressive or assertive communication to express your anger. Although anger often leads to aggression, by knowing the difference and recognizing when you feel angry, you can get in the habit of handling your anger assertively rather than aggressively.

"I will keep in mind when I am angry that expressing anger aggressively makes my anger one letter short of danger."

1. Assertive, 2. Aggressive, 3. Aggressive, 4. Assertive, 5. Aggressive, 6. Aggressive, 7. Aggressive, 8. Aggressive, 9. Aggressive, 10. Aggressive

Anger-Producing Cognitive Distortions

Theory

Throughout this book we have focused on how distorted and twisted thinking provides a negative mental filter, which is at the base of many emotional and mental health problems. In this chapter we have differentiated between aggressive communication and assertive communication, which we will continue to focus on in chapter 8. In this TIP we will show how twisted, irrational thinking leads to anger management issues. As with other harmful emotions we've discussed, cognitive distortions are at the core of angry behavior, whether it is in the form of angry outbursts or silently glaring at someone. By identifying your cognitive distortions, you can calm your thinking down and will have more control over your anger.

Implementing Skills

The following table shows the cognitive distortions often that underlie angry behavior, with examples of healthier "I" statements that challenge the distortions. (For a list of the cognitive distortions, see TIP #13.)

Anger-Producing Cognitive Distortions and Solutions

Anger-Producing Thought	Type of Cognitive Distortion	Anger-Reducing Thought
He's a jerk.	Labeling	I do not like it when he talks over me.
She shouldn't have said that.	"Should" statement	I wish she had not said that to me.
He burns me up.	Blaming	I felt angry when he said that.
He never listens!	All-or-nothing thinking	I am not getting my point across.
You are so rude to me.	Discounting the positive	I find some of your comments critical of me.
She will always treat me like a child.	Fortune telling	I would appreciate her treating me more respectfully going forward.
You think you are better than me.	Jumping to conclusions	I feel insulted by your teasing.

Now It's Your Turn

Write down some examples of angry thoughts from your own situation, then identify the cognitive distortions behind them and come up with more helpful, anger-reducing alternative thoughts using "I" statements.

Anger-Producing Thought	Type of Cognitive Distortion	Anger-Reducing Thought

Processing the Activity

Using a table like the one in this TIP can help you manage anger so it does not turn into aggression. Although anger is a perfectly normal emotion, always remember to use "I" statements in expressing anger. You will be able to do that if you are not thinking in twisted and distorted ways. If you find yourself acting or speaking in aggressive ways, try to detect the type of distortion underneath the unhealthy behavior, and replace this distortion with healthier ways of thinking.

"I will identify my anger and honor it, but I will watch out for
distorted thinking that leads me to act aggressively."

Strategies for Keeping Anger in Check

Theory

As we have previously focused on, the triad in the CBT model is *thoughts, feelings, and behaviors*. In the last TIP we focused mostly on the cognitive distortions (thoughts) that lead to unmanaged anger. In this TIP we will focus on both the feelings and behaviors that stem from your angry thoughts. Although focusing on distortions and replacing our self-talk is often vital to control angry impulses, understanding our feelings and behavioral reactions is also necessary to make sure anger does not spill out aggressively.

This TIP provides the opportunity for self-reflection and insight to help you manage your anger behaviorally while honoring those feelings of anger. It can also help you gain insight into what is behind the anger of others in your life.

It might be helpful to consider that anger is a normal part of the grieving process. Maybe you need to grieve the loss of a relationship or of the image that you had of someone in your life. Forgiving others for not giving you what they didn't have to give can help you move through grief and toward acceptance. It is about mourning the loss of a reality that is different from the one you hoped for.

Implementing Skills

This worksheet is designed to help you identify and clarify your thoughts and feelings, as well as develop strategies to keep your anger in check. It will help you differentiate your thoughts from your feelings. Developing your awareness and control over your anger will help you keep your anger in check, so you will be less likely to lapse into aggressive behavior.

Identify Thoughts

Identify what triggers your anger.

_____

_____

Identify your feelings.

_____

_____

Identify your thoughts—are they factual or irrational?

_____
_____

Identify any underlying cognitive distortions.

_____
_____

Replace any irrational thoughts with healthier thoughts.

_____
_____

Identify whether your anger may be part of a grieving process.

_____
_____

Identify Feelings

Anger often is the tip of the iceberg; underneath anger there may be many other emotions. Think of a situation that causes you anger and identify the feelings underneath the anger.

ANGER

STRESS   DEPRESSION   SADNESS   GRIEF
LONELINESS   HURT   LACK OF FORGIVENESS
SHAME   HOPELESSNESS
HELPLESSNESS
JEALOUSY   PARANOIA
ANXIETY
RESENTMENT

What feelings do you identify most with?

_____
_____

What situations trigger the most anger in you? Can you identify the feelings that are fueling your anger in these situations? When you focus on your feelings, you are better equipped to manage anger effectively.

_____
_____

Have you been disappointed by someone you care about? Can you forgive that person for not being who you hoped they would be or acting the way you hoped they would act?

_____
_____

Can you consider your anger a grief reaction, coming to the realization that the person cannot give you what you thought they were capable of giving? If so, explain.

_____
_____

Behavioral Strategies for Anger

The following strategies can help you manage your anger. Check off the ideas that resonate most with you, and make a plan to practice them the next time you notice your anger rising.

____ Count to ten or twenty before responding.

____ Remember to differentiate the feeling of anger (which is okay) from aggressive behavior (which is not okay).

____ Remember to respond with "I" statements instead of "you" statements.

____ Identify and dispute any cognitive distortions.

____ Keep calm with healthy self-talk.

____ Talk to a friend or family member about your feelings.

____ Write your thoughts and feelings out in a journal.

____ Take a walk or exercise to cool down.

____ Set limits with the other person.

____ Take slow breaths.

____ Draw your feelings.

____ Make coping cards to remind yourself how to handle anger.

____ Make sure your goal is an assertive one, not to control or seek revenge.

____ Forgo the need to be right—be kind instead!

____ Forgive, forgive, forgive—people cannot give you what they don't have to give.

How will your life be different if you are able to put these ideas into practice?

_____
_____
_____
_____

Processing the Activity

Focusing on the triad of CBT—thoughts, feelings and behaviors—will help you understand your own anger and that of others. Anger is a legitimate emotion, but unbridled anger spilling into aggression is not okay. If you can differentiate anger from aggressive behavior, you will be better equipped to handle strong emotions effectively. You will be able to express your feelings and assert your needs with empathy and understanding for the other person as well.

> "I will give others a piece of my heart, not my mind."

Keeping an Anger Log

Theory

An anger log can help you process your thoughts and feelings to keep your anger in check. This log will give you the opportunity to put the three areas of focus—thoughts, feelings and behaviors—together.

Implementing Skills

Use the log on the next page to keep track of situations that trigger anger and your responses in each of the areas listed. This includes the use of SUDs (subjective units of distress), which you may remember from the chapter on anxiety. As a reminder, you can rate the SUDs level resulting from your angry feelings from 0 (no distress) to 100 (the most intense distress possible). If your SUDs level is very high, remember that you can dial down the anxiety or anger by identifying and challenging irrational thoughts.

Processing the Activity

Using this anger log can help you put things into perspective so that you can manage your anger so it does not manage you! Understanding the cognitive distortions underlying your anger can be quite helpful. Anger can help you set limits and stand up for your rights, but be careful of putting up walls that are not actually needed in that situation.

"I will keep my anger in check by identifying my thoughts, feelings, and behaviors, as well as the intensity of my feelings of distress, which will help me gain objectivity and insight."

Anger Log

Situation/ Trigger	Thoughts	Cognitive Distortions	Feelings	SUDs (1–100)	Behaviors	Challenge	New Behaviors	SUDs (1–100)
Friend called me too sensitive	She should not have said that!	"Should" statement, labeling	Mad, righteous	80	Give her the cold shoulder	I wish she hadn't said it, but I forgive her	Tell her I did not like her labeling me	35

Writing a Letter to Move Past Anger and Toward Forgiveness

Theory

Forgiveness has become increasingly recognized as an important factor in mental health and wellness. The ability to forgive lessens the grip that anger has over you and leads to self-empowerment, healthy thinking, and assertive communication. Forgiveness is a choice to let go of what has hurt and angered you. Forgiveness allows us to move past our anger at how we have been wronged. With forgiveness, we are able to replace righteous indignation with insight, compassion, and acceptance. Forgiveness does not mean condoning the actions and behaviors of others (or ourselves), and it does not mean you must continue to allow another person to mistreat you or even remain in a relationship with them—you can forgive from afar. However it's done, forgiveness can help you make peace with limitations and disappointments, freeing you from the bitterness and resentment that keeps you stuck.

Implementing Skills

Forgiveness is not really about the other person. It is about your need to not be stuck in bitterness. One way to work on forgiving what you might consider unforgivable is to write a letter of forgiveness. This can release you from the negativity that holds you back. Writing a letter is to help you—you do not need to send it out. Even if the letter is addressed to someone who is no longer in your life, writing it can help you get your thoughts and emotions "out there" and crystallize them so you can best put past hurts behind you.

Here are some ideas to structure your letter of forgiveness:

- Describe why you are angry and hurt, honoring those feelings by expressing them. Share other feelings you might have, such as regret, guilt, and sadness.
- Explain what you would like to forgive and why it is hard to do that.
- Include the limits you need to set going forward.
- Write how the anger and hurt has affected you and might have triggered past hurts.
- Write what you learned to help you moving forward.
- Write how your life would be better if you could achieve forgiveness, and why you deserve it.
- Keep in mind that forgiveness does not mean letting others off the hook or condoning hurtful behavior—it just means you have disengaged from the cloud of bitterness that that hovers over you and robs you of today.

- Sometimes the person we need to forgive the most is ourselves. If you can't stop reliving your worst moments and keep on beating yourself up for actions and words that you cannot take back, writing a forgiveness letter to yourself can be very therapeutic. Forgive your younger self for not knowing what you now do or being healthy enough to act differently back then.
- No matter how you felt hurt, make sure the letter shows kindness and empathy for yourself.
- Keep in mind that admitting feeling is a sign of strength.
- If this letter is about forgiving yourself, make a plan of how to make amends to those you have hurt, including yourself.
- Consider sharing your letter with a trusted loved one, friend, or therapist for support and further insight. When you share something important with someone you trust, opening up and expressing your thoughts and feelings, you allow for more healing.

Processing the Activity

Whether you are seeking to forgive others, yourself, or both, honoring the anger and pain while working on forgiveness will be helpful in putting the past behind you. Letting go of being steeped in blame and moving toward acceptance can help to ease the anger and trauma following the experience.

"I forgive myself and others because I deserve to live in peace and not be defined by moments in the past. Every day is an opportunity for a fresh start."

Quiz: How Forgiving Are You?

Theory

Forgiveness is a choice that has tremendous healing power over negativity and anger. Having a quick check-in at your fingertips can help you ensure that bitterness and negativity will not keep you stuck. This quiz highlights some important aspects of forgiveness to keep in mind.

Implementing Skills

Rate each of the following questions from 1 to 5, with 1 being *strongly disagree* and 5 being *strongly agree*. If you are not sure how to answer, you can place yourself in the middle of two numbers to give yourself a fractional score, such as 4.5.

Quiz: How Forgiving Are You?

____ I do not feel ready to forgive.

____ Some people in my life who have wronged me do not deserve my forgiveness.

____ I am consumed with anger and other negative emotions and cannot seem to let it go.

____ Unless someone admits they were wrong, I will not be able to forgive them.

____ If I forgive others, that means I am letting them off the hook.

____ Forgiving someone who has hurt me makes me feel that I am letting them win.

____ I am unable to forgive myself for my failures, poor choices, and regrettable behaviors.

____ My trauma over the actions of others or myself continues to haunt me and robs me of being truly happy today.

____ I continue to hold grudges when I feel I have been wronged.

____ Being unforgiving is interfering with my relationships with others.

Total score: _____

The lower the number, the more you forgiving you are. Conversely, the higher the score, the more you are likely feeling angry and bitter. Here are some ranges that break it down further:

- **45–50: Self-help alert!**—Your inability to forgive might very well be the result of unresolved trauma. Consider getting professional help.
- **37–44: Forgiveness impaired**—A difficulty with forgiving is preventing you from living a positive and happy life. Consider seeking professional help.

- **28–36: Forgiveness challenged**—There are some areas of forgiveness that pose a challenge for you and need attention.
- **19–27: Forgiveness student**—You are still holding on to the toxic effects of the hurt and pain caused by others or yourself. Keep working on it!
- **11–18: Forgiveness master**—You have mastered many areas of forgiveness, but you need to keep working to become a forgiveness expert!
- **0–10: Forgiveness expert**—Congratulations! You have used forgiveness to help you heal and grow. This attitude will help you live in the present without the past weighing you down.

Processing the Activity

This quiz gives you a snapshot of your ability to forgive. Although the overall score is useful, also look at the specific questions you rated the highest and the lowest. This will help you identify your strengths and areas to work on.

Remember, forgiveness does not mean condoning someone's behavior or going back for more. It just means that you release yourself from the power that others have over you, refusing to be stuck in blame. In the case of self-forgiveness, offer yourself empathy and compassion for not having the clarity, skills, or mental health back then to change what you now regret.

Whether it is forgiving yourself or forgiving others, your ability to let go of the anger and hurts of the past is truly a gift you give to yourself, no matter how wrong you were or how much you were wronged.

"The more I can forgive, the more I leave the chains of past hurt behind. I will no longer give my past more power than my present."

Self-Test to Manage Your Anger

Theory

In this chapter we have touched on various ways to understand and handle anger. This final TIP serves as a summary for key takeaways in the form of a self-test, along with additional space to reflect and process your feelings and ideas. Using this self-test can help you keep your anger in check and serve as an objective tool to use when negative emotions are high and in danger of spilling over to others. Learning to control your anger will also limit the chance that you will resort to self-destructive behaviors such as substance abuse or any other unhealthy behaviors.

Implementing Skills

In the self-test that follows, rate how true each statement is for you, from 1 to 10, to assess which areas you are doing well in and which areas need some improvement. The higher the score in each item, the higher your mastery in that area. The test is not designed to give you a one-and-done score. Your self-help journey is a continual one, and the important thing is to work to keep improving on yesterday. Making several copies of this self-test will allow you to keep retaking it to monitor your progress.

At the end of this self-test you will be prompted to calculate a total score and an average score. To get the average score, divide your total score by the number of items you responded to. For any items that are not applicable to you, just write "N/A" and subtract those items from the number you divide by when calculating your average score. As you continue taking the self-tests throughout this book, compare your average scores across the different topics. This will give you a snapshot of which areas need the most attention and which areas are the strongest.

Keep this test handy whenever you want some support and reminders on what tools you can use to work on the areas covered in this chapter.

Self-Test to Manage Anger

Using a scale from 1 to 10, with 1 being "not true" and 10 being "very true," rate how true these statements are for you.

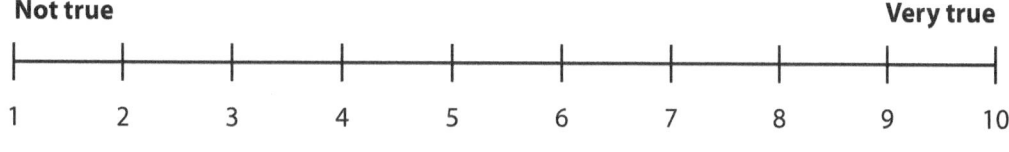

____ I am able to separate thoughts from feelings.

____ My self-talk is rational and not exaggerated.

____ I honor my feelings of anger without resorting to behaviors of aggression.

____ I am not focused on blaming, but rather take responsibility for my feelings.

____ I am looking to learn and grow from my anger, not be held back by it.

____ I use "I" statements to express my anger and avoid "you" statements.

____ I think before I respond when I am angry.

____ I am avoiding rhetorical questions in my communication with others and even with myself.

____ I have identified my cognitive distortions that lead to difficulties managing anger.

____ I do not "should" on myself or others.

____ If I find it helpful, I can process my thoughts and feelings of anger in a log, journal, or letter to myself.

____ I am able to forgive others.

____ I am able to forgive myself.

____ I can admit when I am wrong and say I am sorry.

____ I can identify the feelings underneath my anger.

Total score: _____

Average score (*total score ÷ 15 or items answered*): _____

In the space below, process and explain your answers.

_____
_____
_____
_____
_____
_____
_____

If you would like further structure to process your answers to the self-test and your reactions to the chapter, here are some prompts to guide you.

My thoughts: _____

_____

My feelings: _____

_____

My self-talk: _____
_____

What I have learned: _____
_____

Additional thoughts and strategies: _____
_____
_____
_____

Processing the Activity

Managing anger effectively using assertive skills without lapsing into aggressive communication is one of the great challenges to managing anger. As we have seen in this chapter, anger can be the tip of the iceberg for a gamut of issues, and noticing triggers, identifying irrational thoughts and cognitive distortions, and practicing forgiveness are all part of healing from deep-seated pain that can lead to anger and even aggressive behaviors. Keep in mind that anger itself is not "bad"—it is a necessary emotion and can be a great motivator for change.

*"I can learn skills to manage my anger
to make sure it does not manage me!"*

CHAPTER 8

Improving Interpersonal Relationships: Increasing Empathy and Improving Assertive Communication Skills

CBT recognizes how the quality of our thoughts affects our lives. It also acknowledges the need for social support and human connection. Having a strong sense of belonging to a network of family and friends correlates to a happier life. The quality of our relationships is a predictor of our general level of happiness and life adjustment. Clear thinking alone will not make us satisfied with life if we are isolated and feeling lonely. That is why communication is one of the most important behavioral aspects of CBT. Good communication skills come more easily to some, but any of us can learn them by making an effort.

In the previous chapter, I touched on the importance of managing anger assertively rather than aggressively. In this chapter we will explore more deeply the hallmarks of healthy communication, learn to differentiate assertive from non-assertive and aggressive communication, and practice assertive skills. Conflict arises when people communicate in unhealthy ways; often, they do not even recognize it. With the tools in this chapter, you will be able to more easily spot and alter problematic communication habits. Often these patterns are learned early on in our lives, like a first language, a product of not only our personal situations but also our socialization. For example, women are more conditioned in our society to communicate in non-assertive ways, while men are conditioned to be more aggressive. Recognizing your own patterns will allow you to focus on where you can improve your skills to communicate more assertively.

Communication skills help us develop close relationships and gain social support, which benefits not only our mental and emotional well-being but also our physical health. Many studies have supported the notion that good relationships help us deal with stress, stay healthy, and even live longer!

"Communication is a skill that you can learn. It's like riding a bicycle or typing. If you're willing to work at it, you can rapidly improve the quality of every part of your life."

—Brian Tracy

Recognizing Styles of Communication

Theory

As we discussed in chapter 7, there are three general styles of communication: *assertive*, *non-assertive* and *aggressive*. Understanding these styles, and learning how to use assertive skills, is vital to healthy communication. Communication is something we all do—it is so basic and necessary—but most of us never learn the guidelines for healthy communication.

To differentiate the three styles, I like to riff on the title of Thomas A. Harris's (1967) bestselling book *I'm OK—You're OK*. His original phrase, "I'm okay—you're okay," characterizes the assertive communication style. In aggressive communication, the motto would be "I'm okay—you're not," and in non-assertive communication, it becomes "you're okay—I'm not."

Being able to distinguish between assertive, non-assertive, and aggressive communication in ourselves and others helps us to communicate effectively in healthy ways, allowing us to reap the huge benefits of creating strong bonds with other people.

Implementing Skills

The following table describes the goals, feelings, and behaviors that characterize the three types of communication, as well as their typical outcomes.

The Three Communication Styles

Goals

Non-Assertive	Assertive	Aggressive
To be liked	To be honest, kind, and tactful	To feel "right" and superior to others
To not offend others	To be respectful to themselves and others	To assert dominance or get revenge
To be accepted by others	To connect authentically with others	To have power and control over others

Feelings

Non-Assertive	Assertive	Aggressive
Unconfident	Confident	Overconfident
Anxious, hurt	Disappointed but accepting of themselves and others	Angry, indignant
Afraid of "making waves"	Comfortable setting boundaries and limits	Focused on getting what they want at others' expense
Afraid of being judged	Nonjudgmental	Judgmental
Seeks others' acceptance	Seeks self-acceptance	Focused on being "right"
Feels inferior	Feels worthy	Feels superior
Feels controlled	Has self-control	Seeks to control others, while their own behaviors are out of control
Often feels "wrong"	Interested in mutual understanding and respect, not "rightness"	Needs to be "right"

Behaviors

Non-Assertive	Assertive	Aggressive
Allows their feelings to build and then might end up exploding	Attends to their feelings and expresses them with care	Is overwhelmed by their feelings and reacts without regard for other people
Hides or minimizes their feelings	Expresses their feelings honestly and tactfully	Expresses their feelings honestly but tactlessly
Denies their feelings	Accepts responsibility for their feelings	Blames others for their feelings
Avoids conflict	Is honest and open to resolve issues	Instigates arguments or takes revenge
Avoids risks	Open to risk and vulnerability in service of their goals	Behaves or speaks with little regard for consequences
Uses people-pleasing behaviors	Uses "I" statements	Uses "you" statements
Speaks indirectly, such as dropping hints	Speaks directly and clearly	Speaks bluntly and even harshly
Soft-spoken or silent (latter is passive-aggressive)	Speaks respectfully	Raises their voice or gives the "silent treatment"
Does not speak up	Talks *with* the other person	Talks *at* the other person
Avoids eye contact	Maintains good eye contact	Stares or glares angrily

Results

Non-Assertive	Assertive	Aggressive
Permits their rights to be violated	Stands up for their own rights while respecting others' rights	Violates others' rights
Is often taken advantage of	Respects their own and others' boundaries	Takes advantage of others
May avoid confrontation, but also avoids productive conversations	Pursues healthy, productive conversations	Sparks or fuels unproductive confrontations
Strained relationships	Healthy relationships	Strained relationships

How would you describe your communication style? Does it differ depending on whom you are dealing with, such as your friends, children, spouse, or coworkers? If so, how?

_____
_____
_____

What communication styles are used by those close to you? How do their communication habits affect you? How do you react?

_____
_____
_____

Are there things you would like to change in your communication skills? If so, what would you change? With whom?

_____
_____
_____

Processing the Activity

Since the quality of our relationships is so important, it is extremely important to understand the differences between the three communication styles and their associated behaviors. Healthy communication is the key to success in all areas of your life.

In my live presentations and webinars, it has always amazed me how differently people interpret the communication role-plays we do. After I explain the three types of communication carefully and do a role-play where I act aggressively, many interpret my aggressive communication as assertive or even non-assertive. Once I emphasize how important "I" statements are instead of "you" statements, they can see more clearly when, as part of the role-play, I am trying to change someone else (aggressive) and when I am confidently expressing myself while being respectful to the other person (assertive).

To explain more about this, in the next TIP we will focus on replacing "you" messages with "I" messages.

"I will pay more attention to my communication skills to show respect to others rather than show an attempt to control and judge them."

Using "I" Messages and Avoiding "You" Messages

Theory

This TIP models how to change "you" messages into "I" messages for healthier communication. "You" messages are judgmental, dismissive, and controlling, while "I" statements stick to the facts, are sensitive and respectful, and show compassion to others. In the examples that follow, you will see that "you" statements do not necessarily have to include the word "you" or "I" statements the word "I"—it may instead be implied. What's more important is identifying whether the statement as a whole is arrogant, critical, and rude or respectful, validating, and nonjudgmental.

Implementing Skills

Turning "You" Messages into "I" Messages

"You" Message	"I" Message
What's wrong with you?	I see you are going through a tough time.
You burn me up!	I am upset with what you just said.
Don't interrupt me!	I would like to finish my statement.
You're trying to railroad me!	I would like to stick to the facts and not make it personal.
You are much too sensitive!	I see how much this topic means to you.
Don't worry about it.	I can see how worried you are about it.
It's not so bad!	Wow—that sounds tough!
Stop saying that!	I feel uncomfortable when you say that.
How could you say that?	I do not agree with that.
You took it the wrong way.	I did not mean it that way.

Now It's Your Turn

Change the following "you" statements into "I" statements. Then add your own "you" messages that you or others have said in your own life, and change them into better "I" statement alternatives.

"You" Message	"I" Message
You're always late!	
You're not being considerate!	
Just listen to me!	

Processing the Activity

As you can see, the assertive "I" statements promote closeness whereas the aggressive "you" statements lack empathy and compassion and will likely push people away. A lot of people mistakenly think that if they are in a position of power, such as the boss or the parent, then they are justified to act more aggressively. However, an authoritative boss or parent is much more effective than an authoritarian one. Even the words themselves show the difference: The suffix *-ative* means "tending toward," which suggests more flexibility, while the suffix *-arian* means "having the occupation of," which suggests more rigidity. Authoritative bosses and parents tend to engender healthier relationships than those who use authoritarian approaches based on power and control.

"I commit myself to using 'I' statements instead of 'you' statements to show respect for myself and others."

Assertive Rights and Responsibilities

Theory

Underneath the ability to be assertive is to identify your own personal rights. Those who deny their rights out of a lack of confidence end up trusting the opinions of others over trusting themselves. Giving up a sense of personal power often leads to feeling misunderstood and discounted. Those who are aggressive step on the rights of others due to feelings of superiority. When you are assertive, you stand up for your own personal rights but also balance those rights with responsibilities to others. This is important to set the stage for assertive communication. If you do not identify your rights and your responsibilities to others, you will end up either feeling violated or violating others. In this TIP we will focus on the rights and responsibilities to keep in mind as we try to improve our assertive skills.

Implementing Skills

Basic Assertive Human Rights	Basic Assertive Human Responsibilities
To be treated with respect	To be respectful of others
To express your anger assertively	To accept feelings of anger in others
To say no and set limits	To accept others' limits
To not live up to others' expectations	To not be judgmental of others
To ask for help	To help others in need
To make mistakes	To accept the flaws of others
To be responsible for your own feelings	To accept others' feelings
To change your mind	To accept changes in others
To have privacy	To respect others' privacy
To not be responsible for others' choices	To respect others' choices
To be self-accepting	To accept others
To feel sad, upset, or down	To accept others feeling sad, upset, or down
To forgive yourself	To forgive others

Are there any rights in this list that you have difficulty accepting? Explain what makes it hard to accept these rights. (For example, have you received messages from your family, society, or others that said you do not deserve these things?)

_____
_____
_____
_____
_____
_____

Which of the items in this list resonate the most with you? What other rights and responsibilities might you add to this list?

_____
_____
_____
_____
_____
_____

Processing the Activity

Identifying our rights and responsibilities is at the foundation of healthy assertive communication. These rights and responsibilities serve as guidelines for improving our assertive behavior. Keep them in mind, especially in dealing with difficult people or when you find it challenging to assert yourself. By identifying your rights, you will improve your ability to stand up for yourself and express yourself honestly and tactfully.

> "I have a right to express my thoughts and feelings and accept myself, even if I do not fit the standards that other people impose on me."

Be NICE

Theory

Perhaps the biggest gift you can give to others is to be NICE. A kind word, a considerate gesture, showing warmth and empathy—these are all too often lacking in human communication. The NICE acronym sums up the most essential ingredients in being a good communicator and a loving human being.

Implementing Skills

In good times and bad, remember this acronym to guide you in keeping your relationships positive and healthy through good communication skills.

Characteristics of a NICE Person

- **Nonjudgmental:** All too often we make judgments about the way others should be and have preconditions for accepting them. From raising children to interacting with your next-door neighbor, the more you try to impose your judgments on others, the more issues and conflicts will arise. If you are angry at someone, chances are you have judgments about the way they "should" be that have resulted in conflict. Recognize any judgments that lead to anger and feeling self-righteous. Strive to replace judgment with radical acceptance and unconditional love.

- **"I" Statements:** One of the hallmarks of good communication is using "I" statements instead of "you" statements. When you use "I" statements you are expressing your own feelings and thoughts without passing judgment on the thoughts and feelings of others. One of the most valuable gifts you can give to anyone is the gift of assertive communication. You can learn new habits of assertiveness by intentionally focusing on being honest and nonjudgmental in your communication toward others, without expectations attached.

- **Compassion:** Being kind, showing that you care, not being sarcastic or belittling—all this leads to strong and caring relationships. Compassionate communication involves showing sensitivity and respect, which includes nonverbal communication such as your tone of voice, body posture, and eye contact. The compassion people show is more memorable than the exact words they speak.

- **Empathy:** Empathy is the ultimate social connector. It is the art of not only showing concern for another but also attempting to recognize and connect with their feelings without pushing your own agenda or offering solutions (unless asked). Sympathy is different from empathy in that sympathy shows concern that might border on pity. Empathy is focused on an emotional connection. When you are empathetic, you are attempting to walk in someone else's shoes.

Are there examples from your own life where you recognize that you have used these skills?
_____
_____
_____

Is there an area that you would like to improve upon? For example, do you tend to show empathy and compassion to certain people more than others? How can you improve upon your skills to be NICE?
_____
_____
_____

How would your life be different if you further developed these skills?
_____
_____
_____

How would your life be different if others showed those skills to you?
_____
_____
_____

Processing the Activity

The NICE acronym is a good reminder that in dealing with others it is important to be nonjudgmental, assertively using "I' statements, compassionate, and empathetic. All these traits show respect and caring for the other person and will contribute to healthy connections with others. They allow you to convey positive and warm feelings toward others, embodying the meaning of this quote from Maya Angelou: "People will forget what you said. People will forget what you did. But people will never forget how you made them feel."

"Honoring others with respectful, healthy, caring, compassionate, and empathetic communication will improve my relationships."

Communication Pitfalls to Avoid

Theory

To further delve into the basics of healthy interpersonal relationships, this TIP builds on the understanding of the three types of communication. There are common pitfalls to avoid in communication that can strain relationships. Learning skills and avoiding pitfalls in relating to others is important in ensuring the ability to enlist supportive and healthy relationships, which are vital for healthy growth.

Implementing Skills

The following are common pitfalls in communication to watch out for.

Rhetorical Questions

Watch out for put-downs disguised as questions! Rhetorical questions are not questions at all, but are in fact "you" statements with a question mark. They are quite aggressive in the way they are used to berate, belittle, and judge.

Here are some examples:

- "What's wrong with you?"
- "Didn't I already tell you that?"
- "How many times do I have to tell you that?"
- "What were you thinking?"
- "Didn't you learn that lesson the last time?"
- "What are you, crazy?"

To avoid rhetorical questions, suspend the judgment and be more compassionate and kind in your response. For example, "What's wrong with you?" could be replaced with "Sounds like you are having a tough time."

Can you think of times you used rhetorical questions or someone said them to you? How could those put-downs be rephrased to reflect acceptance and compassion?

_____
_____
_____
_____
_____

Negative Nonverbals

It is estimated that 80 percent of our communication is actually nonverbal. Sometimes we communicate in ways that need no words but convey a lot of feeling, especially when anger is involved! Here are some examples of negative and positive nonverbal communication.

Negative	Positive
• Scowling or glaring	• Smiling conveying warmth
• Grunts or sighs	• Encouraging sounds like "uh huh"
• Aggressive gestures like pointing your finger or rolling your eyes	• Friendly gestures like nodding or smiling
• Angry tone of voice	• Calm tone of voice
• Looking away; poor eye contact	• Good eye contact

Another example of nonverbal communication is how you emphasize your words. For example, take this phrase: "I never said she took your ring." Can you see how the meaning changes with each of these words accentuated?

- "*I* never said she took your ring."
- "I *never* said she took your ring."
- "I never *said* she took your ring."
- "I never said *she* took your ring."
- "I never said she *took* your ring."
- "I never said she took *your* ring."
- "I never said she took your *ring*."

Statements Full of Cognitive Distortions

Watch out for faulty self-talk that leads to conflict within yourself as well as in your relationships with others. Here are just a handful of examples of cognitive distortions commonly found in negative communication.

- **Blaming:** "It's your fault he is so screwed up."
- **All-or-nothing thinking:** "You never listen to me!"
- **Fortune telling:** "You will never get it together!"
- **Mind reading:** "You are trying to gaslight me!"
- **Emotional reasoning:** "I feel unappreciated, so you must not value me."

Which of these examples (or those in TIP #13, which features a more complete list of the cognitive distortions) resonate most with you? How do these distortions interfere with your ability to communicate assertively?

_____
_____
_____
_____
_____

Processing the Activity

Avoiding these common pitfalls in communication will likely help you improve your relationships and, in turn, the quality of your life. Hopefully this TIP and others in this section will help you become clearer on the guidelines for healthy communication. Understanding the common pitfalls will help to ensure that your communication is more assertive than aggressive or non-assertive.

> "I will take care to examine my verbal as well as nonverbal communication to make sure I convey warmth and respect to others."

The Underlying Reasons for Aggressive and Non-Assertive Behavior

Theory

Since assertive communication is so important to relationships and general life adjustment, it is vital to understand why people act aggressively, non-assertively, or assertively. People do not act aggressively because they are fundamentally bad people, but because they are unhealthy and lack the insight and skills to be assertive. In the case of non-assertiveness, some people have learned early on that if they speak up, others will get mad at them, make fun of them, or discount their importance. Beneath this non-assertiveness is a fundamental lack of self-esteem and self-confidence. Women in particular often act non-assertively because they have been taught that this is polite behavior and that expressing themselves would be selfish. Conversely, men are conditioned to be aggressive in their communication, as for men this is often seen as being "strong."

Implementing Skills

The following are some insights into what causes aggressive and non-assertive behavior.

Aggressive Behavior: Underlying Reasons

- **Prior non-assertion:** Keeping things in often results in anger building up until it reaches a boiling point, leading to angry outbursts. Sometimes the outbursts are not even directed toward the source of the anger but might instead be displaced onto others close to you.

- **Violation of rights:** If you feel that you have not stood up for yourself or have "allowed" yourself to be mistreated too many times, the tension and anger builds until it comes out, often in inappropriate ways.

- **Triggers from the past:** Trauma and pain from earlier on in your life may cause you to react in explosive ways when you are triggered. Often it is not a conscious decision, but rather an overreaction to the past.

- **Revenge:** Aggressive behavior is often geared toward lashing back and seeking revenge for having been hurt. That is what happens in an argument—our behavior seems justified to us if the other person "started it."

- **Need to be "right":** Aggressive behavior is motivated by the goal of being "right" (instead of being kind), which often comes from insecurity and an underlying sense of inferiority.

- **Wanting to get one's way:** Aggressive behavior can be an attempt to control others in order to get what you want, regardless of the human cost.

- **Indignance over having been wronged:** As the saying goes, two wrongs don't make a right—but when someone is boiling over with anger, they don't see that!

- **Wanting to be "in control":** Ironically, the need to be in control leads to acting out of control. That is because the goal is not self-control but rather to control another person.
- **Skills deficit:** Most people do not know that aggression is unhealthy. Maybe you learned that behavior early on or were rewarded by friends and family when you used aggression to get your way. This leaves you without the skills to control your anger.
- **Cognitive distortions:** A belief that people "should" be a certain way can cause you to lash out or try to change them if they are not.

Non-Assertive Behavior: Underlying Reasons

- **Anxiety and fear:** Many people who behave non-assertively feel anxious about saying the "wrong" thing and fear rejection or criticism.
- **Lack of self-esteem:** Not having a strong sense of "self" leads to worrying too much about what others think of you, rather than what you think of yourself.
- **Lack of confidence:** You may feel it is safer to avoid speaking up than to risk saying something "stupid" or "wrong" that could lead to feeling foolish, being disliked, or even being ridiculed.
- **Confusing assertiveness with aggression:** You may be afraid of being considered bullyish or selfish if you were to express yourself.
- **Wanting to appease others and avoid conflict:** In being non-assertive, you stay under the radar in the hope that people will not get mad at you.
- **Mistaking non-assertiveness for politeness:** Many people are taught—erroneously—that it is not polite to express your thoughts and feelings.
- **Cognitive distortions:** Catastrophizing, labeling, and mental filtering are just some of the cognitive distortions underlying non-assertive behavior. Irrational thought blocks lead to irrational interpretations and fears.

Processing the Activity

In looking at these descriptions of the reasons behind aggressive and non-assertive behavior, where do you see yourself? Can you identify the reasons for non-assertiveness or aggression in yourself and others? Insight is the first step to change. Using this handout as a reference to understand non-assertive and aggressive behavior can help you uncover why you and the people close to you act the way they do and can help you learn new skills to communicate assertively.

"I will work to stop the cycle of keeping things in to avoid disapproval or confrontation, as this only causes resentment to build, leading to my blowups at those close to me."

How to Listen—and Not Just Hear!

TIP #84

Theory

Communication is not mostly about talking—it is a balance between talking and listening. People often are so focused on what they are saying that they do not focus on how they are listening and showing validation for the other person.

All too often, the words *listening* and *hearing* are interchanged, but they are far from the same. Hearing is taking in audible sounds passively. Effective listening requires more action, including summarizing and clarifying what the other person has said and paying attention to their nonverbal communication to better understand how they are feeling. Active listening shows empathy and interest in the other person, while simply hearing does not show that type of engagement.

If you are a good listener, you will be a better communicator than someone who talks a lot but shows little empathy or interest in others. Just think of how many altercations and misunderstandings people could avoid by using good listening skills! Let's further explore the difference between hearing and listening.

Implementing Skills

Effective Listening Skills Versus Merely Hearing

Active Listening	Hearing
Reflects what the other person is sharing	Does not reflect on what the other person is communicating
Encourages the other person to speak	Remains quiet with no input or reacts without showing sensitivity
Conveys general interest in others	Does not always show interest
Clarifies what the other person is saying	More intent on getting own point across
Restates and summarizes what is being said	Might challenge or discount what the other person is saying
Focuses on the feeling and message behind the words	Focuses on perceiving and reacting to what is being said with little reflection
Validates and accepts the other person	Judges, challenges, or negates the other person
Shows empathy	Empathy is not shown

Active Listening	Hearing
Tries to express and understand the other person's point	Does not try to understand; is focused on getting their own point across
Accepts the other person's perspective even if they do not agree with it	Might argue their case
Is kind and caring	Can be disinterested or argumentative
Uses open-ended questions	Uses closed questions that do not invite sharing
Thoughtful responses	Reactive responses that might be insensitive and discounting
Seeks to understand	Is more concerned with being understood
Shows concern	Is more likely to show judgment

Examples of Listening Versus Hearing

Active Listening	Hearing
"I can see you are worried."	"Don't worry about it!"
"I am sorry you are so upset."	"Why are you so upset?"
"Sounds like you did not expect that."	"Things happen—get used to it!"
"I don't remember saying that."	"You misheard me!"
"I feel bad when you raise your voice at me."	"Don't talk to me like that!"
"I can see that really hurt you."	"You're too sensitive!"

Processing the Activity

Do you tend to listen . . . or just hear? If you would like to improve your relationships, keep in mind that listening is as important as talking. Showing empathy and using sensitivity makes the other person feel heard and you will be a safer person to be with in good and bad times. In an argument, people are hearing and thus reacting—they are not really listening or empathizing. To really listen is a gift you give yourself and others.

"In dealing with others, I will strive to understand
as well as to be understood."

Handy Guide to Effective Communication

Theory

Having an assertive goal for your communication is crucial. Often people erroneously think their goal in communication is assertive since they mean well—they want only the best for someone and want to be helpful. But if you are trying, for example, to change someone's mind or get them to agree with your point of view, the goals are outside yourself and are in actuality aggressive goals. Therefore, when you communicate, you will likely be more aggressive than assertive.

As we've noted, aggressive behavior does not have to mean raising your voice or getting into an argument. It can be merely judgmental, insensitive behavior that tells other people what they "should" be doing. It might be well-intended—for example, giving someone unsolicited medical advice because you are concerned about their health—but this kind of communication can actually be rude and unwelcome. Intentions don't matter if they end up "shoulding" on some else.

It's worth noting that we are not talking here about making decisions for your young children—we are referring to general communication skills where safety issues are not involved. However, if you are an authoritarian parent versus an authoritative parent, your communication with your child will easily lapse into aggression. For example, with young children, setting limits is far more effective than trying to convince them to see it "your way."

In times of conflict, or if you feel hurt by someone's words and want to talk it out, this checklist will be handy for planning your communication strategy and communicating your thoughts without bordering on aggression. Think of it like an inspection on your car. The car will not pass inspection unless certain items are checked off. In the same way, this checklist offers a user-friendly guide to how to communicate assertively, with an assertive goal.

Implementing Skills

Here is a checklist to keep in mind when dealing with challenging interpersonal situations. Each item in the list is followed by an example to illustrate it. Use this guide to remain assertive, even if someone is not assertive with you.

Handy Guide to Effective Communication

1. **Clarify your goal in specific terms.** This first step is crucial for the rest of the checklist. If your goal is aggressive, your communication will be aggressive. Even if you have good intentions and just want to have someone see things your way to help them out, that is an aggressive goal, as its outcome is not in your control.

   My friend told me that I was being "self-centered and lazy" and that I "always spoil everything." My goal when we meet for lunch this week is to tell her assertively that I felt hurt by her words.

2. **Decide on your major points.** Think of at least one or two points to make sure you won't get sidetracked. Others might try to take you off the subject—keep your goals in mind and remain focused.

   My major points will be:
   - *Let her know I feel hurt and don't feel comfortable being called names or labeled.*
   - *Let her know our relationship is important to me, but not at the expense of being treated disrespectfully.*
   - *Ask her to let me know if she has specific issues with some of my words or actions, without criticizing me as a person.*

3. **Identify your personal rights and corresponding responsibilities.** It is crucial to stand up for your rights and express yourself, but you are also responsible for treating others with respect. (See TIP #80 for a full list of your assertive rights and responsibilities.)

   Rights:
   - *To feel offended and disappointed*
   - *To express what is bothering me*
   - *To stand up for myself and tell her I do not deserve to be treated with disrespect*
   - *To set limits and remove myself from the situation if she continues disrespecting me*

   Responsibilities:
   - *To treat her assertively and not name-call, even if she did that to me*
   - *To not "should" on her or try to teach her lessons*
   - *To stand up for myself in a way that does not demean her*

4. **Clarify your thoughts.** Evaluate whether your thoughts are irrational or rational. Irrational thoughts lead to aggressive or non-assertive behavior, with cognitive distortions like "shoulding" on yourself, labeling yourself and others, and being judgmental (for a list and definitions of the common cognitive distortions, see TIP #13). For any irrational thoughts, come up with a more accurate and helpful alternative thought.

Irrational Thought	New Rational Thought
Maybe I shouldn't say anything—she might get mad at me.	*I have no control over her reaction. I can only stand up for myself and express myself.*
She shouldn't be so rude!	*I wish she had not spoken to me like that—it was hurtful and I will tell her that.*
Maybe I am just too sensitive.	*I will not be unkind or label myself as "too sensitive." I refuse to put myself down and give so much power to someone else.*

Irrational Thought	New Rational Thought
I'm not as good as her—maybe that is why she does not respect me.	I refuse to compare myself with anyone else except where I was yesterday. I am a worthy human being and do not deserve to compare myself unfavorably with others. I am equally important. I am worthy of respect from myself and others.
She made me so mad!	I was mad when she said that.

5. **Clarify your feelings.** It is important to identify your feelings and respect your feelings without judgment. Your feelings are in direct reaction to your thoughts. You cannot change your feelings directly, only through changing your thoughts as in the previous step. Rational thoughts tend to result in calm, confident feelings and irrational thoughts lead to low self-esteem, depression, and anxiety.

    I feel disappointed by my friend's behavior. I also feel worthy and confident that I can respectfully set a limit with her, regardless of how she responds.

6. **Think about how you will express your feelings.** Consider how you can express your feelings in a way that honors both your own rights and your responsibilities toward others. Remember the difference between anger and aggression—while you have the right to feel any emotions, including anger, and to communicate your feelings assertively, you do not have the right to behave aggressively.

    I will tell my friend, "I was really angry and hurt when you said that."

7. **Commit yourself to listening and not just hearing.** When you actively listen, you paraphrase, summarize, and show empathy. You are not just focusing on the audible sounds, but rather seek to understand where the person is coming from.

    My friend may be taking anger out on me that isn't really about me; I know she's been arguing a lot with her daughter lately. I will actively listen to what she says and show empathy, such as saying, "It sounds like you did not know what to do with all that hurt and anger, and you must have felt in a lot of pain to take it out on a good friend."

8. **Anticipate positive and negative scenarios.** Anticipate how the other person might react by asking yourself, "What's the *worst* thing that could possibly happen?" and "What's the *best* thing that could possibly happen?"

    The worst case is that she will try to justify her aggression and continue to be rude, and I might lose a friendship. The best case is that she will tell me she is sorry and is glad I said something, as it had been bothering her and she did not know how to bring it up.

9. **Weigh the benefits versus risks of being assertive.** Sometimes it is an assertive decision not to assert yourself. At times, you might decide to remain silent, not out of fear of disapproval or other non-assertive reasons but because you have decided asserting yourself is not important to you in that particular situation (for example, if you do not interact with that person often and their behavior only bothers you a little bit).

The benefits outweigh the risks in this situation, since I value this friendship and I want to try to repair it rather than allowing my resentment to build.

10. **Rehearse.** Practice the planned conversation in front of a mirror or visualize it in your mind. Or, even better, role-play with a trusted professional, friend, or family member. Role-playing is a great way to practice expressing and asserting yourself. Think of what the other person might say that would challenge your assertiveness, such as "It's not such a big deal," "You are way too sensitive," or "I never even said that." Practice responding to such statements in an assertive (not aggressive) way—for example, "It's important to me," "I do not appreciate you judging me," and "I do remember you said that."

    Make sure you:

    - Keep your goal in mind.
    - Make sure the goal is assertive.
    - Use "I" statements.
    - Do not use "you" statements.
    - Show empathy.
    - Don't overexplain or overapologize.
    - Don't get sidetracked.
    - Focus on the behavior, not the person.
    - Be descriptive, not judgmental.
    - Don't personalize or catastrophize.
    - Remain assertive, not aggressive (even if they communicate aggressively).

I will bring these notes to my therapy session tomorrow and ask my therapist to role-play the conversation with me. This will prepare me to have the actual conversation with my friend when I see her next week.

Processing the Activity

This handy guide can help you learn skills to become more assertive. By applying these ideas to your own situation, you will have important tools to express yourself assertively and confidently. If there is a situation from the past that is affecting you, whether or not the person is still in your life, you can role-play the scenario of what you would have liked to say to help you learn the skills and clarify your own thoughts and feelings from here on.

Note for mental health professionals: You can use this guide in your role-plays with your clients to help them develop assertive skills and approach problematic situations with confidence. It is especially helpful in group therapy, as a checklist for group members to use in preparing and evaluating role-plays with one another.

"I will focus on my own self-control when dealing with others rather than try to control them. After all, trying to change other people is like trying to change the weather. Better to just carry an umbrella!"

Comparing Effective Communication and Ineffective Communication

Theory

Since communication skills are the key to successful relationships, and in turn are the essentials to a sense of well-being and lifelong happiness, let's use this TIP to further reinforce the skills needed for healthy, assertive communication in the way of specific examples. Effective communication is always assertive, whereas ineffective communication is either aggressive or non-assertive. It is important to note that assertive "I" statements and aggressive "you" statements do not necessarily have the word "I" or "you" in them; it may instead be implied. Any response that is discounting and rude—which may even involve no words at all, such as quietly giving someone the silent treatment—is aggressive and ineffective.

Implementing Skills

Hallmarks of Effective and Ineffective Communication

Ineffective Communication	Effective Communication
"You" Statements "Stop yelling!"	**"I" Statements** "I feel angry when you yell at me."
"Should" Statements "You shouldn't feel upset."	**Accepting Statements** "It's hard for me to see you upset."
Devaluing Statements "Don't worry about it!"	**Empathetic Statements** "I can understand why you're concerned about that, but I don't think that will cause a problem."
Judgmental Statements "You are so defensive with me!"	**Nonjudgmental Statements** "Looks like you are feeling upset with me."
Rude Statements "You have that long face again!"	**Kind Statements** "I'm sorry you are feeling bad."
Rhetorical Questions "Are you out of your mind?"	**True Questions** "Are you having a hard time with this?"
Aggressive Nonverbals Glaring or staring, raising voice, silent treatment	**Assertive Nonverbals** Good eye contact, moderate voice, smile

Ineffective Communication	Effective Communication
All-or-Nothing Statements "You're always complaining about your coworkers!"	**Specific Statements** "I've noticed you have complained about your coworkers a lot in the last few weeks."
Blaming "You're sidetracking me!"	**Taking Responsibility** "I am getting off track."
Labeling "You are such a chauvinist!"	**Not Labeling** "I do not appreciate you generalizing about women."
Tactless "You don't know what you're talking about!"	**Tactful** "I do not agree."
Demanding a Change "Stop cursing right now!"	**Requesting a Change** "I am asking you to stop cursing."
Discounting Your Importance "I can't make the meeting, so just go ahead without me. It does not matter to me." (when it really does)	**Honest and Direct** "Can we agree on another time for the meeting?"
Complimenting Evaluatively "You got an A—you are so smart!" (What happens if she gets a C—is she stupid?)	**Complimenting Specifically** "Great job getting that A. You worked hard!"
Authoritarian Parenting "You're not listening!"	**Authoritative Parenting** "I would like for you to listen carefully to me."

Communication Stoppers and Enhancers

Communication Stoppers	Communication Enhancers
No way!	I don't see it that way.
That will never work!	I don't think that it will work.
You're not listening to me!	I don't think you have grasped my point.
It's impossible.	I don't feel like it's practical.
You're always short with me!	It seems like you are short with me often.
That's wrong!	I don't agree with you.
You shouldn't do that.	I would appreciate it if you didn't do that.

Communication Stoppers	Communication Enhancers
Keeping quiet out of fear of disapproval	Expressing your thoughts
Overapologizing	Apologizing

Now It's Your Turn

Give examples from your own life, making your communication more healthy.

Ineffective Communication	Effective Communication

Processing the Activity

This TIP containing examples of the dos and don'ts of communication can be a helpful guide if you are working on your skills to tone down aggressive behavior or to express yourself more confidently if you tend to be non-assertive. Often people are assertive in some areas of their lives but have ineffective communication in others. For example, a parent might be perfectly assertive at work but bossy with their children at home. Striving to be assertive across the board will improve not only your relationships with others but also your relationship with yourself.

"I will watch the way I express myself to others, because once you say something it is like releasing feathers to the wind—you can never take it back."

Forgiveness Check-In

Theory

Since the topic of forgiveness is so important for mental health and wellness as well as for interpersonal relationships, this TIP offers another forgiveness quiz to build upon TIP #76.

Forgiveness is truly one the of the biggest gifts you can give yourself and others. If you feel slighted or wronged, it is not unusual to be self-righteous and indignant, yet indignance just leads to more anger and bitterness, which often leads to vindictive behavior. In so many cases, clinging to the importance of being right is overrated, and being able to forgive the slights and mistakes of others will offer much more peace moving forward. This check-in will give you a snapshot of your ability to forgive, which is a good indicator of general life satisfaction and a sense of well-being.

Implementing Skills

Forgiveness Check-In

How forgiving are you? Using a scale from 0 to 10, with 0 being "not at all true" and 10 being "very true," rate how true these statements are for you:

____ When I am wronged, I have a hard time forgiving the other person because they don't deserve it.

____ I can only forgive someone if they are sorry and admit it.

____ If I forgive others, I feel like it is giving them a pass and condones unacceptable behavior.

____ Forgiveness is something that you feel or do not feel—it is not something to work at.

____ I need to protect myself from being hurt again; feeling wronged protects me from going back for more.

____ I have a hard time giving up a grudge when I feel I have been wronged.

____ I am a bit stuck in the past because I am holding on to bitterness.

____ If I forgive someone, it means I will expose myself to hurt again by letting them back into my life.

____ When someone hurts me, I instinctively want to hurt them back.

____ My lack of forgiveness has led to feelings of anger inside.

Total score: _____

The lower the number, the better you see the benefits of forgiveness for your own mental health.

- **0–15:** Congratulations! Your ability to forgive has helped you choose to be better instead of bitter.
- **16–29:** You have given yourself the gift of being able to forgive and are able to stay positive because of this ability.
- **30–49:** Forgiveness is a work in progress. You can intentionally try to release chains of the past by boosting your ability to forgive.
- **50–69:** Bitterness takes over too much of your life. The benefits of learning to forgive will help you in staying positive in the present.
- **70–84:** You are very stuck in bitterness and that impacts the quality of your life. Learn more about the benefits of forgiveness and work toward uncovering the trauma that keeps you stuck. Consider seeking professional help.
- **85–100:** This level of hurt and bitterness is crippling and often tied to depression and anxiety. Holding on to hurt from the past will prevent you from living in the present and moving forward to a better future. Psychological help is needed.

Processing the Activity

How forgiving are you? By looking at the questions in this check-in, you can see some of the hallmarks and drawbacks of being unforgiving. This might help crystallize areas to work on to set you free from bitterness and past hurts. An important point to keep in mind is that you can forgive someone from afar. Forgiveness benefits you because that happens inside your head. Forgiveness does not mean you go back for more. It is not necessary to allow someone back into your life who is not healthy for you. You can forgive from afar and set limits on your future interactions, including no contact.

> "I deserve to forgive so I do not feel pulled down by the past. I can choose how I will proceed with people who have been hurtful, and I will not allow them to occupy too much space in my head."

Self-Test for Improving Interpersonal Relationships

Theory

In this chapter we have focused on how to improve your relationships with others by learning how to improve your assertive communication and avoid non-assertive and aggressive communication. If you are struggling with conflict with others in any areas of your life, keep on revisiting the TIPs in this chapter so you can continue, for example, to use "I" statements instead of "you" statements, as well as to show empathy and convey acceptance while still respecting your own rights and limits.

Implementing Skills

In the self-test that follows, rate how true each statement is for you, from 1 to 10, to assess which areas you are doing well in and which areas need some improvement. The higher the score in each item, the higher your mastery in that area. The test is not designed to give you a one-and-done score. Your self-help journey is a continual one, and the important thing is to work to keep improving on yesterday. Making several copies of this self-test will allow you to keep retaking it to monitor your progress.

At the end of this self-test you will be prompted to calculate a total score and an average score. To get the average score, divide your total score by the number of items you responded to. For any items that are not applicable to you, just write "N/A" and subtract those items from the number you divide by when calculating your average score. As you continue taking the self-tests throughout this book, compare your average scores across the different topics. This will give you a snapshot of which areas need the most attention and which areas are the strongest.

Keep this test handy whenever you want some support and reminders on what tools you can use to work on the areas covered in this chapter.

Self-Test for Improving Interpersonal Relationships

Using a scale from 1 to 10, with 1 being "not true" and 10 being "very true," rate how true these statements are for you.

____ I tend to be assertive, speaking my mind confidently without being offensive or discounting to others.

_____ I tend to speak to others in "I" statements instead of "you" statements, even in times of stress or when I strongly disagree.

_____ The goal of my communication is to express myself, not to change others.

_____ I avoid rhetorical questions.

_____ I stand up for myself and make sure I do not allow others to violate my rights.

_____ I am respectful of my assertive responsibilities to others.

_____ I try to communicate in a way that is nonjudgmental and accepting.

_____ I show compassion and empathy to others.

_____ I am conscious of my nonverbal communication and work to improve my assertive nonverbals.

_____ I have identified and addressed my cognitive distortions that interfere with my ability to be assertive.

_____ I have insight into the aggressive communication of myself and others, understanding the results and reasons.

_____ I have insight into the non-assertive communication of myself and others, understanding the results and reasons.

_____ I am careful to use active listening skills with others.

_____ If I have challenging relationships with others, I try to address it assertively by keeping my assertive goal in mind.

_____ I view my communication skills as generally effective and can identify the people in my life that pose more assertive challenges for me.

_____ I am forgiving to others and do not hold grudges.

Total score: _____

Average score (*total score ÷ 16 or items answered*): _____

In the space below, process and explain your answers.

_____
_____
_____
_____
_____

If you would like further structure to process your answers to the self-test and your reactions to the chapter, here are some prompts to guide you.

My thoughts: _____
_____

My feelings: _____
_____

My self-talk: _____
_____

What I have learned: _____
_____

Additional thoughts and strategies: _____
_____
_____
_____

Processing the Activity

Use this checklist periodically to assess your progress and to continue to improve your assertive skills. Your score will vary over time, and keeping a record of your scores will allow you to see whether you are improving your ability to communicate assertively. It might be helpful to answer all the questions in this self-test while focusing on one subset of people in your life, such as your parents, children, coworkers, or friends. Your answers might be different for various people in your life. For example, some people have more difficulty being assertive with close family members, and others have more difficulty with people at work or in their social network.

There are times in life that, despite our best efforts to be assertive, others continue to be aggressive and violate our rights. In those cases, we need to set good limits. It might even be that at times you need to give up on someone so as not to give up on yourself. After all, if they can't accept you for who you are, you may need to let them go. We need ourselves much more.

"I will continue to improve my assertive skills with everyone in my life, and be as honest and authentic as I can."

CHAPTER 9

Staying Mindful: Learning to Be Present with Nonjudgmental Awareness

CBT is known as the second wave of behavioral psychology (the first wave being Skinner's behaviorism). The second wave focuses on challenging and changing the quality of your thoughts to change the quality of your feelings and your life. In the third wave, the cognitive approach is softened by the principles and practice of mindfulness, an increasingly important component in the newer practices of CBT.

Therapeutic orientations including mindfulness practice that have grown out of CBT include dialectical behavior therapy (DBT), which focuses on life skills and emotional regulation for treatment-resistant personality disorders such as borderline personality disorder, and acceptance and commitment therapy (ACT), which uses CBT practices combined with acceptance and mindfulness strategies. Mindfulness-based cognitive therapy (MBCT) also melds the use of cognitive strategies with mindfulness practice.

Many people think of mindfulness as synonymous with meditation. In fact, mindfulness is much more than that. Sitting quietly and breathing deeply with your eyes closed is just one example of mindfulness. Mindfulness, as modern psychological treatments define it, doesn't isolate you from the world, but rather makes you more aware of yourself and the world in the present moment. Simply put, mindfulness is the practice of nonjudgmental awareness. It is being present focused and receptive to what is around you.

When you are mindful, you are not a victim of your past or caught up in the what-ifs of your future. Mindfulness helps you distance yourself from your negative thoughts, feelings, and anxieties, instead noting them without reacting. Whether you are sitting in lotus position on the beach, driving in a car during rush hour, working, playing a video game, watching a movie, bathing, walking, washing dishes, or doing laundry, mindful awareness will help you experience life in the moment without being torn by rumination from the past or worries about the future.

"Mindfulness helps you see with greater clarity how you may approach your moment-by-moment experience skillfully, taking more pleasure in the good things that often go unnoticed or unappreciated, and dealing more effectively with the difficulties you encounter, both real and imagined."

—MBCT.com

Take a Mindful Moment

Theory

Taking time during the day to have a mindful moment will help to limit stress and anxiety. It can stop the "monkey mind" from churning repetitive and negative thoughts that rob you of present joy. Mindfulness can set you free from anxieties about your future and help you appreciate life as it is now. When you are mindful, you are more grateful for what you have, rather than lamenting what you don't.

Getting in the habit of taking a mindful moment at various times throughout the day will help set you on the path of present-centered gratitude. Mindful moments help you appreciate the little things in life, while letting go of expectations for things that are out of your control. Learning the art of acceptance will help you be nonjudgmental in your thinking habits, which decreases anxiety and depressive thinking.

Implementing Skills

The following are ideas for bringing mindfulness into your everyday life. Throughout the day, at least a few times, practice mindful awareness with some of the following suggestions.

1. Make a positive intention for the day to focus on during your mindful moments. Do you want to be loving to yourself today? Do you want to work on self-acceptance, flaws and all? Do you want to focus on asserting yourself today and expressing your thoughts and opinions without worry about what others will think? Write down a positive intention for today. Focus on the intention without judging how you are doing or how you did yesterday. Just mentally note the intention and develop the habit of using positive intentions in your daily life.

   _____
   _____

2. Breathe slowly for a few moments with your hand on your abdomen, imagining a balloon in your stomach inflating and deflating to ensure you will have deep belly breaths. As you breathe, look around you and notice, without judgment, things you may not have noticed before: marks on the wall, the feel of your clothing against your skin, how much water is left in your glass, the reflection on the glass coffee table, the trees swaying outside though the window, and so on. Give yourself a few moments to absorb your surroundings without judging if it is too messy, shabby, or unattractive. What do you notice?

   _____
   _____

3. Do you ever miss a snack or a meal? Besides actually not eating, this could also mean being so preoccupied with thoughts, distractions, busyness, or passive activities like watching TV that by the time the food is almost gone, you realize you were not even conscious of having eaten. Slow down your eating and try to savor each sensation. Mindful eating like this helps with training your mind and is healthier for your body too!

_____

_____

4. When you walk, instead of being preoccupied in thought, pay conscious attention to the scenery around you. Note the sensations you experience from the temperature, breeze, smells, sights, and so on. If you are walking outside, you might notice the flowers around you and appreciate the beauty and uniqueness of each one, or look at the clouds in the sky and notice their shape.

_____

_____

5. Take a mindful moment to identify what sensations you're experiencing right now via your five senses, without judging what you are experiencing. For each sensation, choose one thing that you are aware of that you might not have been aware of a moment ago, and use it as a prompt to unleash your feelings of gratitude and appreciation for experiencing life.

_____

_____

Processing the Activity

These practices are just a few examples of how you can take a moment for mindfulness in your day. How else can you consciously connect with your present experience in a way that centers you and makes you calm? Many people enjoy practicing yoga, meditation, and other spiritual mind-body practices. Others practice mindfulness by immersing themselves in music or art. Consider having a mindful moment journal—every day, write down some experience that has helped you more fully experience the present. The most important thing is to find what works for you to reduce stress, calm your mind, and offer you an appreciation and renewed enthusiasm for life.

"I will take note of the beauty around me and enjoy mindful moments where I practice the art of unconditional acceptance and gratitude. I will stop taking my life for granted—after all, I don't get another one."

Develop a Beginner's Mind

Theory

Consider a child's innocence and freshness of perspective as they discover how the world works. Things we take for granted are not seen by young children in the same way—they are fascinated by what we often ignore. In the exercise that follows, we focus on developing a beginner's mind, where everything seems fresh and enticing about the world. This helps you stay present and focused on gratitude and appreciation, rather than being steeped in "woulda coulda shouldas" from the past or anxieties about the future.

Implementing Skills

1. Imagine or observe a young child in your own life. Watch or visualize them learning about the world. What do they find interesting? Everything! They touch, explore, watch, and are mesmerized by things we take for granted. Spend a few moments experiencing your surroundings as if you have never seen them before. What do you notice? What do you smell? What do you feel? What do you hear? Notice the colors, shapes, textures, smells, and sounds around you.

2. Now imagine you are looking at your surroundings through the eyes of a pet, such as a dog or cat. Or watch your pet or someone else's pet and observe their total immersion in the present. What do you notice? Are they absorbed in thinking of the past or future, or are they living in the now? Watch how they go through life being immersed in the present.

3. Do a mindful activity such as blowing bubbles, even if you are an adult and there are no kids around! Watch the bubbles float and disappear. Take delight in the process of noticing how the bubbles move and reflect subtle colors as they float away. Or light a candle and watch it flicker. Finding mindful activities like these can help you appreciate the wonders of the world again.

4. Slow down! Consciously try not to rush and instead give yourself time and space to immerse yourself in the beauty of the moment. In everything you do today, give yourself enough time so you are not stressed or rushing and can instead savor the experience of living. Make an effort to notice something that you have not noticed before.

5. Note the judgmental thoughts that go through your mind about what you are experiencing. For example, if you are in your kitchen and it is cluttered with dirty dishes, you might tend to focus on what needs to be washed or put in the dishwasher. Now look at the same things without value judgments or labels. Simply describe what you see, such as three dishes and two forks, some orange peels and eggshells in the sink, a red rim around the plate, and so on.

6. Use a beginner's mind to look at yourself in the mirror. If you have low self-esteem, your descriptions of yourself will likely be made of some negative interpretations. Many people focus on their perceived flaws, such as a large nose or wrinkles. Replace those negatively biased descriptions with statements from the fresh perspective of a beginner's mind, with no judgments. Focus what you see without a critical eye—for example, two brown eyes, creases under your eyes, earrings in your ears, and so forth.

7. Describe yourself in a loving way, focusing on what you admire about yourself. All too often, our self-view is jaded by our negative self-talk. Allow yourself to instead describe yourself in kind and loving terms with a fresh perspective. What is special about you? What do you admire about yourself?

Processing the Activity

Having a beginner's mind will allow you to be curious about the world and approach life with openness and excitement, while suspending your old judgments. It will help you develop a fresh perspective on yourself and your intrinsic beauty and worth. Especially if you tend to be judgmental in your self-talk, reminding yourself to use the perspective of a beginner's mind will help you see yourself in a loving, nonjudgmental way without negative preconceptions that you might have learned along the way.

"No matter how old I am, I can choose every day to look at the world with fresh eyes and a sense of childlike wonder."

Be an Observer of Your Thoughts

Theory

Cognitive defusion is a technique developed by Stephen Hayes, who originated acceptance and commitment therapy (ACT) to combine CBT techniques with mindfulness techniques. ACT does not focus on changing persistent unhealthy ways of thinking, but rather on changing your relationship with those thoughts and distancing yourself from them. Rather than disputing negative thoughts, cognitive defusion helps you become an observer of those thoughts, which helps "de-fuse" or loosen their hold on your brain. By distancing yourself from those thoughts, you change their believability and their emotional fallout is minimized. Cognitive defusion is not meant to diminish the importance of cognitive reframing and disputing irrational thoughts, but rather offers an additional tool if negative thoughts prove to be too ingrained and persistent.

Implementing Skills

The following are ways to use cognitive defusion to distance yourself from upsetting thoughts by observing them rather than being attached to them.

Negative Thought	Using Cognitive Defusion
I failed.	There I go again thinking I am a failure. I realize that is all-or-nothing thinking.
I'll never find someone to love.	Barbara is thinking again that she will never find anyone to love [*speaking to yourself in the third person to further distance those thoughts*].
I will never get myself together.	I am looking *at* the thought that I will never get myself together.
I failed as a parent.	I am noting and observing my thought that I am a bad parent, but I do not need to buy into it.

Now It's Your Turn

What are some persistent and irrational negative thoughts that you would like to get out of your mind so you can get into your life?

Negative Thought	Using Cognitive Defusion

Processing the Activity

Cognitive defusion is a tool to detach from your existing negative habits of thinking. It is a very effective technique to use when you constantly are battling with yourself over automatic negative thoughts. Instead of actively challenging or disputing the thought, you accept the thought but distance yourself from believing it by "defusing" it from your brain. Instead, simply observe those thoughts, looking *at* them rather than *from* them. In the next TIP we will explore some visualizations that can help distance us from unhealthy thinking.

"I will use distance in my relationship to my negative thoughts and merely observe them rather than identify with them and believe them."

Use Cognitive Defusion Visualizations

Theory

Visualizations can be a great tool to distance yourself from upsetting thoughts. The visualizations described here will be helpful in imagining that your thoughts are far apart from you and will give you more opportunity to watch your irrational thoughts rather than identify with them. Using these visualizations regularly, along with traditional CBT techniques, will change your relationship to your negative thoughts and open space in your head for healthier thoughts.

Implementing Skills

- **Ticker tape:** Imagine your negative thoughts are on an old-fashioned ticker tape or a chyron (i.e., electronically generated captions, such as the bar at the bottom of a TV news show that lists the major headlines). Let the thoughts on the chyron come and go as you simply watch.
- **Thought train:** Imagine a train is passing by as you watch from a bridge. Each boxcar is painted with one of your negative thoughts. As each car rattles by, you see your negative thoughts chug by, passing out of view. Watching the train go by rather than getting on it will help you look *at* your thoughts rather than looking *from* your thoughts.
- **Thoughts on the big screen:** Visualize your negative thoughts on a movie screen. Imagine sitting in the back of the theater, with a lot of distance between you and those thoughts on the screen. Look at the thoughts like you would credits or subtitles, with no emotional reaction.
- **Leaves on the stream:** Visualize your unwanted thoughts lying on various leaves floating down a stream. As you sit by the water, place one thought on one leaf at a time and watch each one float away and disappear down the stream.
- **Clouds in the sky:** Put your thoughts up high in the sky and imagine you are reading them on the clouds. As the clouds float by, watch your unwanted thoughts float by as well.

Processing the Activity

These visualization techniques are extremely powerful to help you detach from your nagging negative thoughts as you still note their existence. Cognitive defusion helps to minimize the intensity of those nagging thoughts. Practice these visualizations often to work on distancing yourself from particularly persistent thoughts. The less you identify with them, the more you will be able to replace them with healthier thoughts.

"I will give myself a break from my critical thinking about myself and others and will allow more objectivity into my view of myself and the world."

The Gift of Radical Acceptance

Theory

Another third-wave offshoot of CBT using mindfulness strategies is Marsha Linehan's dialectical behavior therapy (DBT). Linehan developed DBT in response to her work with treatment-resistant patients, such as those with borderline personality disorder, who often need more than traditional CBT strategies to regulate emotions and tolerate distress.

One of the main features of DBT is the practice of *radical acceptance*, which is a tool for tolerating extreme distress and hard-to-manage feelings and behaviors. Practicing radical acceptance is like observing things with a Teflon mind to which upsetting thoughts don't stick—they just come and go. Of course, you do not need to have a personality disorder to appreciate the value of radical acceptance. We all have strong emotions at times, and learning how to regulate ourselves with the skills of radical acceptance can be quite helpful.

Implementing Skills

The following are some elements in the practice of radical acceptance:

- Observe the upsetting situation without extreme emotional reactions to it.
- Accept and make peace with the fact that life can be unfair.
- Remind yourself not to fight what you cannot change.
- Acknowledge that when things are out of your control, they can only be accepted. By not struggling to change what cannot be changed, we gain some type of peace. For example, by radically accepting trauma or upsetting situations from the past, we don't give these experiences and memories as much power to upset us in the present.
- Use a nonjudgmental view of what is out of your control, using forgiveness for yourself and others as well as self-compassion to soothe and comfort.
- Learn to take lessons from a situation without dwelling on the pain with it by using mantras or affirmations for coping. Here are some examples:
    - I can accept what I cannot change.
    - I did not deserve what happened to me, but I have become resilient and stronger through my experiences.
    - What's done is done.
    - I love myself just as I am.
    - I am a survivor, not a victim.
- Make a behavioral plan of how to cope and move on.

- Use relaxation exercises, breathing exercises, or mind-body practices like physical exercise, meditation, or yoga to help cope with issues out of your control.
- Recognize that resistance, the opposite of radical acceptance, will only prolong pain and suffering.

Processing the Activity

Think of radical acceptance like accepting a rainbow. We do not think there should be more pink or blue in a rainbow; we accept the rainbow as beautiful no matter what. The practice of radical acceptance helps us let go of what we can't control and enables us to make peace with it. It is embodied in the Serenity Prayer by Reinhold Niebuhr: "God, grant me the serenity to accept the things I cannot change, the courage to change the things I can, and the wisdom to know the difference."

"I will let go of what 'should be' and accept things as they are."

Using Visualizations for Radical Acceptance

Theory

Thinking in new ways is a key to acceptance as we change old habits. In the previous TIPs, we used some cognitive defusion techniques such as visualizations and metaphors to encourage flexible thinking. Since visualizations, metaphors, and analogies are so powerful in unlocking insight, here are some additional examples that relate to the topic of radical acceptance.

Implementing Skills

- **Mountain:** A mountain remains unwavering despite extreme weather changes like storms and lightning. Planes fly over and people climb on it, but it remains majestic and standing no matter what. It does not react to people, the weather, or any other activity on or near it.

- **Beach ball:** If you push a beach ball into a body of water, it just keeps popping up to the water's surface. Imagine that the ball represents reality and the act of pushing it down represents an attempt to reject reality. We find that the lower we push the ball, the higher it pops up. This metaphor represents how when we resist reality, it comes back to haunt us stronger and more vehemently than ever. However, when we cease to resist and allow the ball to stay afloat, it will not pop up in our face!

- **Eraser:** An eraser reminds us to accept our mistakes and flaws, once and for all. We are human and make mistakes—that's why we need erasers!

- **Quicksand:** A person sinking in quicksand will only sink deeper when they struggle and fight to get out. The more we fight our reality and refuse to accept what we cannot change, the more we become mired in that reality. Only by lying spread-eagle in the quicksand can you stop sinking in it. Likewise, surrendering to the inevitability of pain and struggle will help us to figuratively stay afloat.

- **Balloon:** When we blow up a balloon and let it go, we cannot control or direct where it goes. Instead, we recognize that we must accept its journey away from us and out of sight. Likewise, we need to accept our persistent thoughts that we cannot change and allow them to exist while we try to be more objective about them.

- **Yellow Jeep:** Think of a yellow Jeep. Now try to stop thinking about it. Of course, the image is hard to shut off; in fact, you are likely still visualizing a yellow Jeep right now. When you resist thoughts, you will only think of them more.

- **Meditative practice:** Breathe deeply and try to quell your racing thoughts by being present focused while breathing slowly and deeply. It might be helpful to imagine a color going into your body with each breath, going even to the tips of your toes and fingers, and then with each breath out, the color withdraws and goes into the air. Savor the warm feeling of being present in this visualization.

Processing the Activity

These ideas are a small sample of how visualizations, metaphors, and analogies can unlock feelings and ideas to encourage us to practice the art of acceptance. Can you think of others? Creative and mindful practices like these help us to accept what can't be changed in a way that evokes peaceful images and a sense of calm.

"I will not 'paint myself into the corner' with unhealthy and negative thinking. Visualizations and analogies will help me learn the art of accepting the things that are out of my control."

Mindfulness-Based Relaxation and Calming Practices

Theory

In this TIP we will focus on Dr. Jon Kabat Zinn's mindfulness-based cognitive therapy (MBCT), another third-wave treatment approach that made the practice of mindfulness mainstream in the US. Meditative practices have long been a part of many Eastern traditions, and Dr. Kabat Zinn's research into the medical benefits of these practices helped in their being recognized in the US as legitimate treatment for medical and psychological problems, as well as for general wellness.

Mindfulness-based relaxation exercises give us structure for keeping a present-centered focus while calming the mind and body. These exercises involve opening yourself to the world around you and help combat the tunnel vision and depressive thinking that limits your awareness of present sensations, sights, sounds, and so forth. For those who tend to ruminate or feel depressed or anxious, mindfulness practice offers hands-on activities that ward off the "monkey mind." When you are mindful, you are not ruminating about the past or obsessing about the future. Instead, you are anchored in the here and now.

Implementing Skills

The following are some of MBCT's meditative practices for promoting nonjudgmental awareness, relaxation, and healing from and coping with psychological and medical challenges.

Body Scan

Lie down and close your eyes while consciously slowing your breath. Progressively focus your attention on various parts of your body, from your toes through your left leg to the right side and progressively up your body to your head. Notice the sensations in each part of your body, scanning for any tension you might feel. Consciously try to relax any area where you feel tension. You can think of your body as an instrument and consider the body scan as a way to gently tune it.

Progressive Relaxation

This is a variation of the body scan described previously. Lie down, close your eyes, and slow your breathing while you consciously tense up various parts of your body one at a time. Start with tensing your toes, holding the tension for a few moments, then releasing it. Notice the feelings of relaxation in your toes as the tension leaves your body.

Gently shift your awareness to the sensations of each part of your body as you move up from your feet to your head, tensing and then relaxing. Notice the feelings of relaxation in contrast to the tension immediately preceding them. Once you move from your toes to your head, you might want to do the same thing in the opposite direction, moving from your head back down to your toes. This practice makes some people realize how tense they often are without even knowing it!

Exhale Bitterness, Breathe in Gratitude

Slow your breathing and imagine yourself exhaling your bitter thoughts and inhaling thoughts of gratitude. Breathe out bitterness, breathe in gratitude. Imagine yourself breathing out a negative thought, then breathing in a thought of gratitude related to your bitter thought. For example, "I am bitter that my marriage fell apart" can be replaced with a thought of gratitude such as "I am grateful to be able to love again, this time a bit wiser."

Mindful Eating

This classic mindfulness exercise uses a raisin to encourage awareness of the senses and staying in the present. Raisins are small but have an interesting texture and a burst of flavor as you eat them. One raisin can take a few minutes to eat it due to the fact it does not dissolve as easily as many foods. (Other foods, especially dried fruits, would work just as well for this exercise.)

Sit comfortably, consciously slow your breath, close your eyes, and put a raisin in your mouth. Experience the raisin as something new, cultivating a beginner's mind. How does it taste? How does the texture feel? What sensations are you experiencing with this one raisin? Can you describe it?

While focusing on the raisin, you are taking your attention away from thoughts about yesterday and tomorrow, allowing yourself to be open to only the present. You can do this exercise with any food or drink; you can even practice it at mealtimes.

Mindfulness with Music

Many of us find music to be healing and restorative—it can evoke powerful emotions and soothe us in a way that words alone often can't. How about practicing mindfulness with music? Listen to a favorite song while slowing your breathing, relaxing your body, closing your eyes, and experiencing the music while limiting your outside thoughts and worries. What are some of your favorite songs? Why are they special to you? How has music helped in good times and bad? What feelings and sensations does the music evoke in you? Reflect on how they feel. Make a commitment to listen to a song every day from your favorite playlist.

Mindfulness with Your Five Senses

Sit comfortably, slow your breath, and focus on one of your five senses at a time. For example, when you focus on sight, look at your surroundings with a beginner's mind, as if you are seeing things for the first time. Look around with nonjudgmental awareness. What do you see? What do you notice that you have not noticed before? How would you describe what you are seeing? What is beautiful about what you are seeing?

Continue with each of your other senses: hearing, touch, smell, and taste (if you are eating or drinking).

What do you notice that you were not aware of a few moments ago?

Mindfulness Using One Word

Often in meditative practice, people focus on a mantra as they are breathing in and out. Using a word like *om*, *kind*, or *love* can give you a focus for your attention to limit the internal chatter in your head. Breathing deeply while focusing on that one word will help you gently shift away from other distracting thoughts.

Mindful Visualizations

Some people find it helpful to visualize a beautiful, peaceful scene while focusing on their breathing and letting their distracting thoughts move away from the forefront of their minds. Use soothing imagery like being by the ocean—imagine hearing the waves crash, smelling the air, and feeling the warmth of the sun's rays emanating through your body as you take each breath.

Processing the Activity

These exercises are a sample of how you can incorporate mindfulness into your everyday life. There are many variations to practice mindful awareness, and there is no-one-size-fits-all. If you would like to explore mindfulness practice, use the examples in this TIP for at least a few minutes every day, trying different variations to see what works best for you. Some find it helpful to use a timer for even a few minutes, a few times each day, to take a mental break for peace and calm.

"I will use mindful practice to help me focus on the here and now and focus on each breath with gratitude and love."

Gratitude Prompts and Putting Gratitude into Action

Theory

Mindfulness and gratitude go together. When we are grateful, we are often mindful of what we appreciate in our present life. As you become mindfully aware of your present, limiting the negative chatter in your head, you end up being more open to accepting things as they are and can appreciate yourself and your surroundings much more. Being tuned into the present this way will help you be more aware and in awe of life around you. It's hard to live a happy life if you feel bitter, but with gratitude, you are always looking for the good.

Implementing Skills

The following prompts and practices will help you incorporate more gratitude into your life.

Do you tend to be grateful for what you have or bitter about what you don't?

_____
_____

What are some things you are grateful for about yourself?

_____
_____

What are some things you are grateful for about others in your life? How do you show them your gratitude? If you tend to keep those thoughts to yourself, how could you express them more?

_____
_____

Do you tend to find the good in others rather than focus on being critical?

_____
_____

Do you set limits with the people in your life who tend to be negative?

_____
_____

Do you look for the positives in most situations (the "bless" in life's mess)?
_____
_____

How do you express joy?
_____
_____

Using your five senses, name at least one thing you are grateful for experiencing right now:

- What I hear: _____
- What I see: _____
- What I feel: _____
- What I smell: _____
- What I taste: _____

What material possessions are you most grateful for?
_____
_____

What are you grateful for in nature?
_____
_____

How have you improved your life recently?
_____
_____

What are you grateful for about your body and your physical health?
_____
_____

What are you grateful for about your mind and character?
_____
_____

How have the down times in your life made you stronger?

_____

_____

Put Gratitude into Action

- Consider having a gratitude journal, in which you write three new things each day that you are grateful for. That will help you keep gratitude at the forefront of your mind.
- Brainstorm several things that you are grateful for and write or print them on cards or slips of paper. Put them in a gratitude box and pick one to focus on each day.
- Spread positivity to others by saying one thing each day to someone that shows gratitude, such as thanking them for something they said or did. The more you incorporate gratitude in your life, the more likely you are to feel happy, optimistic, and loving.
- Wayne Dyer suggests that every morning when you get out of bed, you should start with "thank" as you put one foot down on the floor and "you" as you place the other foot down.
- To keep gratitude on the top of your mind, choose words for your computer passwords that relate to things you are grateful for. (Be sure to still include elements to make those passwords secure, such as using numbers and special characters within the words!)
- Expressing yourself creatively can be a great way to allow more mindful feelings of gratitude into your life. Draw something you are grateful for, or cut pictures or words from magazines that reveal what makes you grateful.
- The following is a great activity for adults and children alike. Cut out a small circle and petals out of construction paper to make a flower. In the middle of the flower, write "gratitude." On the petals, write things you are grateful for. You can make many flowers with different answers on the petals. Then glue your flower onto a craft stick and put it in a planter with your real flowers.

Processing the Activity

How did it feel to process your thoughts about how gratitude fits into your life? How can you incorporate gratitude into your life moving forward? What ideas from the list would you like to try? With a focus on gratitude, not only are you filling yourself with positive words of appreciation and directing your energy toward what you are thankful for, but you are also making mindfulness part of your daily life. How can you adopt an attitude of gratitude in your life moving forward?

"Once I can let go of the bitterness of what life could not give me, I can embrace with gratitude everything that life is able to give."

Mindful Conversation

Theory

Incorporating the focus of present-centered nonjudgmental awareness to improve our relationships is a great way to apply mindfulness. Especially in relationships that have some conflict and friction, mindful listening can help tremendously in calming down the communication and ending conflict. After all, arguments arise when two or more people try to prove that they are right or change the other's mind or even their behavior. Not only does this make their goal an aggressive goal, but it also fills their communication with judgment and negativity.

Mindful conversation replaces judgment and negativity with acceptance, kindness, and empathy, which are often lacking in times of conflict. Focusing on mindful conversation is helpful anytime, even when people are in agreement. It will increase your awareness and acceptance of what the other person is saying.

Implementing Skills

The following are some guidelines for having a mindful conversation. Keep these guidelines in mind when you communicate. They will be especially helpful if you anticipate a conversation that could be difficult, as they will help ensure that you stay the course and do not devolve into an argument (talking *at* each other instead of *to* each other). You can practice these strategies in advance by role-playing with a family member, friend, or therapist.

Mindful Communication Tips

- Set a positive intention for the conversation, such as "I will suspend judgment and communicate with loving kindness."
- Express your thoughts and feelings with "I" statements.
- Avoid "you" statements.
- Paraphrase, summarize, and show empathy and concern.
- Use good eye contact (without glancing at your cell phone!).
- Avoid labeling the other person. Instead, be open and accepting of what the other person is saying. Refrain from judging them—or yourself, for that matter.
- Notice the other person's verbal and the nonverbal communication. Do their verbals and nonverbals match?
- Be aware of your own nonverbals. Do they match what you are saying?

- Be aware of your thoughts while you are talking. Are they sticking to the facts or their interpretations? Are they nonjudgmental?
- If you notice your mind wandering, bring your thoughts back to the present conversation.
- Be aware of your emotions while talking. If you are upset or angry, choose your words carefully, because once you say them, there is no turning back!
- What are the sensations you feel in your body? Is there tension? Do you feel relaxed? Are there any symptoms of anxiety, such as rapid heart rate, pressured breathing, or sweaty palms?
- Do you observe any intrusive thoughts? Gently let them go while you focus on the conversation. If you find yourself listening to your negative or judgmental thoughts, you will be too focused on your internal dialogue to really attend to the other person.
- Make sure you focus on being kind rather than on being right. How does it feel to have no agenda to change someone's mind or get them to see it your way?
- Are you refraining from criticism?
- Are you interrupting or monopolizing?

Is there anything that struck you about your focus on mindful listening?

Processing the Activity

The guidelines just presented, along with the active listening tips in TIP #84, will help you be mindful and present in your communication with others. Especially when there is disagreement and conflict, these guidelines will ensure that the communication does not devolve into yelling or other aggressive communication. Using mindful communication, you might find you have more tact in communicating with others; you will be more observant, more present-centered, and more skilled in defusing potentially contentious communication.

"I will be more aware of conveying love and respect to others. After all, nothing I can tell them is more important than the love and respect I can give them."

Mindful Self-Compassion

Theory

In previous TIPs (such as #25, #50, and #51) we focused on the importance of self-compassion in overcoming negative self-talk. As you might recall, Kristin Neff's work on self-compassion identifies mindfulness as one of the three major components to self-compassion, the other two being self-kindness and common humanity.

Self-compassion is a mindful antidote to negative and judgmental self-talk. It replaces beating yourself up and self-sabotage with self-kindness, self-acceptance, and loving self-awareness. Persistent, critical self-talk is negatively biased to the point that cognitive distortions are seen as facts rather than fiction. When we are compassionate, we soothe ourselves with self-statements and reminders that pain is a part of the human condition and we are not alone in our pain.

Self-compassion replaces shame and doubt with confidence and self-love. Whenever you find yourself putting yourself down or thinking depressive, negative thoughts, intentionally use self-compassion to shift away from this negative self-talk. Even in times of frustration and anger, compassion soothes the sharp edges of our critical thoughts and softens the sting of our negative thoughts and feelings.

Implementing Skills

Soothing yourself with self-compassion—instead of listening to negative self-evaluations you would never say to anyone but yourself—will help you shift your focus to self-acceptance and self-love. The following prompts will guide you to improve your self-compassion practice.

Sit comfortably and spend a moment or two being aware of your breath. Slow your breath. Consciously note how you breathe in and out for a few minutes.

Now that you are focusing with present-centered awareness, note any negative self-talk or thoughts that are going through your head. Consciously take them out of your head and observe them as you write them down.

_____

_____

Ask yourself if these self-statements are true. Where is your evidence? Are they just stories you are telling yourself from an old narrative that is tainted with stains of the past? Can you identify cognitive distortions?

_____

_____

Ask yourself if you deserve this negative spin on yourself. Would you continue to be friendly with anyone else who talked to you like that? Chances are, the answer is no. Rather, see yourself as a beautiful person and a special friend. How would you rephrase these negative thoughts into more loving, accepting, positive thoughts?

_____
_____

Now see yourself as a beautiful person, without any of the shame and doubt you might carry around. What is beautiful about you? What is worthy of compassion and love? What are things you admire about yourself? What words of kindness do you have for yourself?

_____
_____

How does it feel focusing on yourself in a kind and loving way right now? How does it feel to see yourself with love and compassion?

_____
_____

How can you incorporate this nonjudgmental, self-loving stance in your everyday life?

_____
_____

Processing the Activity

How was this self-compassionate mindful practice for you? Did it feel awkward and foreign, or did it feel soothing and natural? If you find yourself constantly plagued by negative self-talk that spirals out of control, consider filling this out TIP daily for at least a few days to focus on changing your habits. Do this practice every day until you create new pathways in your mind that will be more positive. You might want put on soft music to set the stage or start with a sound, like a Tibetan bell that signals the start of a meditative practice and reverberates for a while. Find what works for you to set the stage for a present-centered activity where you compassionately observe your thoughts without buying into them, and replace them with more self-compassionate, kind self-statements. You deserve it!

"I will shift my awareness to my thoughts, feelings, and sensations of the present moment to achieve true self-compassion and peace."

Self-Test on Staying Mindful

Theory

This self-test will focus on your ability to stay mindful and use the mindfulness skills of nonjudgmental awareness. In this chapter we learned various ways to become more accepting and present focused. This self-test will crystallize the major points in this chapter. Revisit areas that need more attention as you use CBT skills to improve the quality of your life.

Implementing Skills

In the self-test that follows, rate how true each statement is for you, from 1 to 10, to assess which areas you are doing well in and which areas need some improvement. The higher the score in each item, the higher your mastery in that area. The test is not designed to give you a one-and-done score. Your self-help journey is a continual one, and the important thing is to work to keep improving on yesterday. Making several copies of this self-test will allow you to keep retaking it to monitor your progress.

At the end of this self-test you will be prompted to calculate a total score and an average score. To get the average score, divide your total score by the number of items you responded to. For any items that are not applicable to you, just write "N/A" and subtract those items from the number you divide by when calculating your average score. As you continue taking the self-tests throughout this book, compare your average scores across the different topics. This will give you a snapshot of which areas need the most attention and which areas are the strongest.

Keep this test handy whenever you want some support and reminders on what tools you can use to work on the areas covered in this chapter.

Self-Test on Staying Mindful

Using a scale from 1 to 10, with 1 being "not true" and 10 being "very true," rate how true these statements are for you.

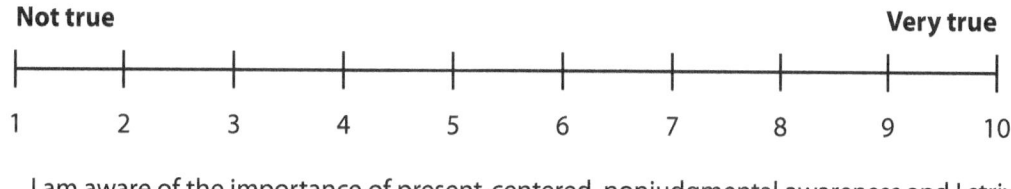

_____ I am aware of the importance of present-centered, nonjudgmental awareness and I strive to use this focus in my life.

_____ I use positive intentions to set the stage for a positive mindset for the day.

_____ I use some relaxation techniques that work for me, such as to slow my breathing and become more aware of my surroundings in times of stress.

_____ I try to be aware of the sensations of all my five senses in the course of the day to bring me to a present-centered focus.

_____ I find it helpful to practice a "beginner's mind," where I look at things with a fresh perspective.

_____ I am practicing the skill of radical acceptance, where I do not judge things but rather accept what I cannot change.

_____ When I have upsetting thoughts, I try to look *at* them rather than *from* them.

_____ I use visualizations and metaphors to help myself observe my thoughts and distance myself from negative thinking.

_____ I tend to be a grateful person and look for reasons to feel grateful.

_____ When I converse, I try to use the skills of mindful conversation, where I actively listen and give the other person my full attention.

_____ I understand the importance of mindful self-compassion and use this skill to combat negative self-talk.

Total score: _____

Average score (*total score ÷ 11 or items answered*): _____

In the space below, process and explain your answers.

_____
_____
_____
_____
_____
_____

If you would like further structure to process your answers to the self-test and your reactions to the chapter, here are some prompts to guide you.

My thoughts: _____
_____

My feelings: _____
_____

My self-talk: _____
_____

What I have learned: _____
_____

Additional thoughts and strategies: _____
_____
_____
_____

Processing the Activity

The higher your score in this self-test, the more you use mindfulness skills in your everyday life. As you periodically redo this self-test and total your scores, you will have something to compare your newer scores to. The purpose of this self-test is not to have a fixed score, as each time you take it the scores will reflect where you are on that day.

Compare your average score with your average scores for the other chapter self-tests to see which of the 10 areas focused on in this book need the most attention. This will fluctuate over time as you master some areas and struggle with others. The important thing is to keep on practicing, revisiting the exercises, and evaluating your progress with these self-tests. Repetition is the key to developing your ability to be mindful.

"Mindful practices will help me become less judgmental and more loving and compassionate to myself and others."

CHAPTER 10

Wellness Tips for a Happier You: Going from Surviving to Thriving

Even those of us who do not have any identifiable mental health issue or disorder can benefit from tips to not only survive, but thrive. We all have stress, and whether we are debilitated or motivated by our stress will determine whether it makes us better or breaks us down. In the same way, no life is unscathed by some loss and trauma; we need to dig deep for resilience and thrive with a sense of personal challenge, going toward something greater for a sense of life purpose.

A full and complete life is never free of ups and downs. Living a meaningful life requires that we learn the tools and develop the courage to rise above adversity and embrace our vulnerability as we evolve. After all, a positive life is much more about possibilities and growth than it is about limitations. This mindset can help you keep moving forward no matter what. Think of your attitude like your mind's paintbrush—it can color any situation.

In this chapter we will use some of the concepts included in the field of positive psychology, of which CBT is a cornerstone. Concepts such as optimism, gratitude, and resilience are part of a wellness journey that all humankind can relate to. They are ingredients in a well-actualized life, whether or not you are dealing with particular problems or mental health issues. Mental health is not just about coping; it is about self-actualizing, growing, developing as a person, showing empathy, and being capable of truly loving yourself and others.

All too often people think that being positive and optimistic means expecting things will always turn out okay. However, true optimism recognizes that sometimes things do turn out terribly wrong, but nevertheless believes you can make the best out of whatever comes your way. No matter our circumstances, we can all strive to be the best that we can be. This chapter will offer you tools to live a happier life and be your best self!

"Our greatest glory is not in never falling, but in rising every time we fall."

–Oliver Goldsmith

Develop Happiness Traits

Theory

Although we often strive for things outside of ourselves, such as being admitted into a prestigious school, having a successful career, getting a promotion, finding a mate and having children, or increasing our material possessions and wealth, none of these things ensure true happiness. That is because happiness is an inside job. Most of us know people who seem to "have it all" yet are not happy, while others who have very little seem to feel blessed with their lot in life. In this TIP we will focus on what really makes people happy. Even though things from the outside certainly help, the habits of happy people show us that true happiness comes from within.

Implementing Skills

The 15 Traits of Happiness

1. **Happy people like themselves!** It's not what you have; it's who you are! Happy people do not wait to like themselves until they achieve a goal or prove their worth—they like and even love themselves along the way. They have high self-esteem because they admire themselves not just based on what they do, but for the beautiful souls that they are.

2. **Happy people don't compare themselves to others.** The only person happy people compare themselves to is themselves, based on how they have grown since yesterday. They don't need to be better than others; they just seek to improve and build on yesterday.

3. **Happy people have a strong sense of social support.** Happy people love to love and be loved. They know the importance of having people to whom they can self-disclose and do not put up walls between themselves and others. They treat others kindly and get kindness in return.

4. **Happy people are forgiving of themselves and others.** Those who do not hold grudges against themselves or others tend to be happier people. They realize that we are all works in progress, and they do not spend too much time looking back at their own worst moments or the worst moments of others. They do not subject themselves to toxic people from their past and, more importantly, they do not "rent space in their heads" to such people. Instead, happy people forgive others for not being as healthy as they wished, and move forward, with or without them.

5. **Happy people spend little time looking over their shoulders.** Happy people live life picking themselves up and moving forward. The past is useful only to learn from, not to live in. They might have regrets, but they make their regrets productive and learn from their missteps and mistakes, using those regrets to become deeper instead of weaker.

6. **Happy people fully realize that there are some things they will never get over.** Happy people realize that some things are never really healed, but that you can be happy despite the thorns in life. They don't deny the thorns; they just don't dwell on them. Instead, they have a sense of gratitude for what remains.

7. **Happy people are trusting of themselves and don't spend much time being self-protective.** Happy people are trusting of others, mostly because they trust and like themselves.

8. **Happy people are optimistic.** Optimism means looking at things in a positive light. Happy people are not pretending things are okay when they are not, but rather making the best of things as they are.

9. **Happy people are proactive, not reactive.** Happy people don't wait for things to happen—they *make* them happen! They focus on what they can change, not what they can't.

10. **Happy people are filled with self-compassion and compassion toward others.** Happy people focus on acceptance rather than living steeped in judgment of themselves and others. They refuse to be collectors of injustice.

11. **Happy people look to make the world a better place.** They have a moral compass and are committed to goals outside themselves to make the world a better place, whether it be close to home with family and friends or with causes they believe in. They do not look for material things to make them happy.

12. **Happy people have a growth mindset instead of a fixed mindset.** Research has shown that people are most happy when they are flexible in their thinking and focus on their growth, improvement, and effort rather than on their innate abilities and external successes.

13. **Happy people use challenges and setbacks as opportunities for growth.** They do not see setbacks as obstacles that get in their way. They focus on solutions rather than problems. They do not expect life to always be fair, accept what they can't control, and work hard to overcome what obstacles they can.

14. **Happy people are loving people.** They are filled with love and appreciation for themselves and others. They do not spend time being bitter, comparing, being filled with anger, or expecting themselves or others to be different.

15. **Happy people are grateful people.** They are grateful for what they have in life rather than bitter about what they don't. They are mindful that life is a gift and look for the "whole" rather than the "hole."

Processing the Activity

Review the list—how many of those traits do you have at present? What areas are the hardest for you to accomplish? What traits would you like to work on?

So often we get sidetracked thinking that things outside of ourselves will make us happy. Success is great and there is nothing wrong with material wealth, but without the right mindset, outward things will not make you happy. If you want to use this list as a guide, print and post it in a prominent place, such as on your bedroom mirror or by your computer. This reminder of what really makes us happy can help us ensure we don't look for happiness in all the wrong places.

"I will stop looking to outside sources for my happiness. Although they can help considerably, I realize that my thinking habits and ability to be compassionate and loving are so much more important than things I 'get.'"

Emotional Wellness Inventory

Theory

Both CBT and positive psychology are known for their self-help quizzes, mood checks, and self-tests. When used often, self-tests can offer a snapshot of what areas of emotional wellness you are doing well in and what areas you need to work on. Comparing your results at various times can help you crystallize your growth and offer a snapshot into your progress in major areas of personal well-being. The thing you want to refrain from is comparing your score with those of other people. Your emotional wellness journey is yours alone—it is not a competition. Comparing yourself to where you were yesterday offers richer and more relevant information than comparing yourself to others.

The inventory that follows crystallizes eight important aspects of emotional wellness. These questions serve as guidelines for improving personal well-being and happiness. Using it on a regular basis will help you gain insight and self-awareness of what areas are more developed for you and what areas need more work. If you are a mental health professional working with clients, this quiz can be used at each session as an emotional wellness check. Keeping a folder of past quizzes can offer valuable information on what areas have and have not improved.

Implementing Skills

Emotional Wellness Inventory

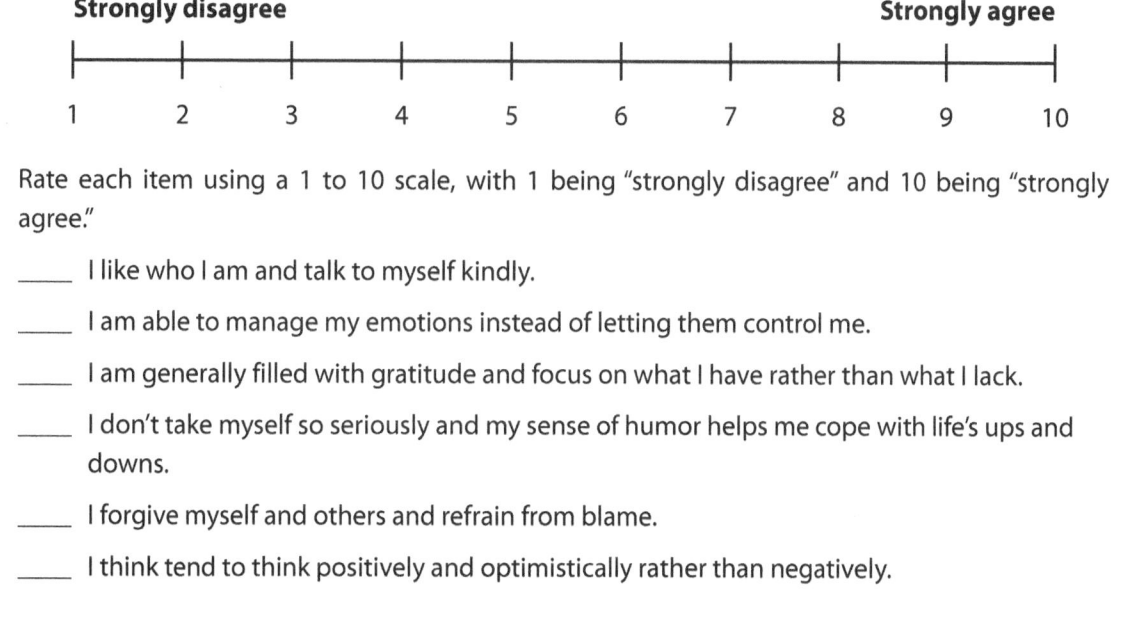

Rate each item using a 1 to 10 scale, with 1 being "strongly disagree" and 10 being "strongly agree."

____ I like who I am and talk to myself kindly.

____ I am able to manage my emotions instead of letting them control me.

____ I am generally filled with gratitude and focus on what I have rather than what I lack.

____ I don't take myself so seriously and my sense of humor helps me cope with life's ups and downs.

____ I forgive myself and others and refrain from blame.

____ I think tend to think positively and optimistically rather than negatively.

____ My regrets and hurt from yesterday do not interfere with my happiness today.

____ I feel supported and connected with those who care about me.

Total score: _____

A higher score reflects greater satisfaction with your life, while a lower score indicates lower emotional wellness and a need for further support:

- **73–80:** Your emotional wellness is awesome!
- **66–72:** You have a high level of emotional wellness.
- **57–65:** Your emotional wellness is good.
- **46–56:** Your emotional wellness could use more attention.
- **34–45:** Your emotional wellness is low, pointing to low moods and depression.
- **23–33:** Your level of life satisfaction and well-being is low and suggests depression. Seeking help from a professional is advised.
- **Below 23:** You are suffering from depressed mood and professional help is indicated.

Processing the Activity

The eight areas addressed in this quiz are well regarded as cornerstones of personal satisfaction and happiness. Whether this quiz is used once or repeatedly, it offers a great springboard for exploring how to be more satisfied with your life. If you are in the helping profession, it will help you work with clients on boosting their emotional wellness IQ.

> "My emotional wellness will be a priority in my life moving forward—my happiness depends on it."

Using a Metaphorical Toolkit for Personal Growth and Resilience

Theory

A metaphorical toolkit can boost emotional and mental wellness. It offers powerful reminders of how to cope with stress, develop resilience, and calm yourself during challenging times.

Metaphors reach us in a way that unlocks insight and makes complex topics easy to understand. Metaphors encourage flexible thinking, and thinking in new ways is a key to resilience and getting out of our own way. For example, reminding ourselves that there is a reason that cars have small rearview mirrors but large windshields show us the importance of living life with a focus on moving forward instead of focusing too much on past missteps and regrets.

In a metaphorical toolkit, we can use actual objects to remind us of metaphorical insights. For example, a toy car in your toolkit can remind you of the aforementioned lesson, that in order to drive forward in life you need to look ahead and stop looking at life through your rearview mirror. The more creative we can be with metaphors, the more potential we have to get "unstuck" and move forward on the path to growth and healing.

Implementing Skills

Here is a small sample of other metaphorical toolkit items that I use to demonstrate therapeutic points:

- **Elastic/rubber band:** This item reminds you not to let yourself get stretched too thin—say no and set limits without feeling guilty. It also reminds you that elastic is like stress: We need some stress in our lives to feel vibrant. When life feels like a limp rubber band, we will feel disengaged. But don't stretch yourself too much or you are going to snap!
- **Crayon:** This item is a reminder to put color into your world. If you see things in black and white, you will think in extreme and unhealthy ways.
- **Eraser:** Erasers remind you that you don't have to be perfect! It's okay to make mistakes—that's why we have erasers.
- **Deck of cards:** This is a reminder that we all receive high and low cards in life; what is most important is how we play the hand we are dealt.
- **Polished gem:** Craft store gems can represent the precious sparkle inside each of us, reminding us that we all have value and there is a gem inside us all.
- **Chewing gum:** This is a reminder that when we chew on an issue over and over (that is, ruminate about it), it ends up losing its flavor.

- **Magnifying glass:** This item reminds you look closely at your thoughts—to be a "thought detective" by identifying your cognitive distortions. If you turn the magnifying glass over to minimize, think of this as a metaphor for not allowing yourself to minimize your feelings and needs.
- **Dollar bill:** No matter how many times you wrinkle it, crush it, or step on it, the worth of a dollar bill stays the same. Likewise, our self-worth always remains the same even if we feel crushed by our life circumstances.
- **Hershey's Kisses:** Spread the love! Let this item remind you that kindness is more important than being right.
- **Happy face sticker:** This will remind you to stay positive and optimistic. It does not deny that you might have difficult emotions, but you can learn and grow from any adversity if you have a positive mindset.
- **Band-Aid:** Sometimes we need to remind ourselves there is a time to heal, and a bandage represents the ability to soothe yourself if you are in need of healing.

Can you add to this list? What items would you assemble in your toolkit for mental wellness?

_____
_____

Assembling objects in a metaphorical toolkit can be a great group activity in a therapeutic or even a business setting, crystallizing important concepts to keep in mind for the topic at hand and reinforcing those concepts long after the meeting or group experience.

_____
_____

Processing the Activity

Metaphorical toolkits for mental health and wellness can focus on various self-help themes. There is no shortage of ways to use them for personal development and growth. You can make your own toolkit for self-help, use them with your children to help them learn self-management skills, or use them with individual and group clients if you are in the mental health field. Metaphorical toolkits provide healing and growth in a fun, creative way.

> "I will stop 'painting myself into a corner' with my negative thinking and use a metaphorical toolkit to keep me focused on living my life with positivity and gratitude."

Mindset Matters: Shift from a Fixed Mindset to a Growth Mindset

Theory

Although many people equate a happy and fulfilling life with things like success, wealth, professional achievements, superstar kids, or natural intelligence, studies by mindset psychologist Carol Dweck (*Mindset: The New Psychology of Success*, 2007) show that the main determinant of happiness and life satisfaction is having a *growth mindset* over a *fixed mindset*. A growth mindset is characterized by determination, effort, and learning—being motivated by life's setbacks rather than being defeated by them. While innate intelligence will not necessarily lead to greater success, having a growth mindset sets the stage for knowledge and skills to be learned.

Psychologist Angela Duckworth (*Grit: The Power of Passion and Perseverance*, 2016) added to this concept with her notion of *grit*. Grit is having the ability to persevere with something that you feel passionate about, despite having times where you fall down and need to pick yourself back up. It reminds me of the Japanese proverb "Nana korobi ya oki" which means "Fall down seven times, stand up eight." That sense of passion and perseverance supersedes innate talent and ability alone. Duckworth regards grit as a key factor in having a personal sense of life satisfaction.

Implementing Skills

In the following table, notice how you can change a fixed mindset thought to one of a growth mindset.

Fixed Mindset	Growth Mindset
I'm terrible at relationships.	I'm working hard to improve my relationships with others.
I've made so many mistakes.	I have learned so many things by my mistakes to help me moving forward.
I can't believe I failed.	I am proud of myself for trying and will keep trying.
I'm not artistic or creative.	I love being creative and will take different classes to find the right hobby.
I have to be good at this.	I want to enjoy this and will learn.
I have no talent.	I don't need talent to learn and have fun.

Fixed Mindset	➡	Growth Mindset
I'm not educated enough.	➡	I am still bright and eager to learn without an advanced degree.
They have accomplished so much more than I have.	➡	I am on my own path.
It's too hard.	➡	I will keep practicing.

Now It's Your Turn

Write down some of your own self-limiting beliefs and change them into positive beliefs that reflect a growth mindset.

Fixed Mindset	➡	Growth Mindset
	➡	
	➡	
	➡	
	➡	
	➡	
	➡	
	➡	

Processing the Activity

The notion of a growth mindset can be a comfort to those who harbor regrets that hold them back in life. Whether these regrets are about not going further with a job or education, experiencing addiction, poor choices in relationships, or another area of life, having a growth mindset can be freeing. All past mistakes can be seen as learning experiences to propel growth and be motivating with lessons learned. It evens the playing field for all people who have it in their power to embrace themselves and their lives through a sense of purpose and commitment. This focus on growth is also good for self-care, allowing you to concentrate on your own development and improvement.

How about you? Do you define yourself too much by your successes or failures? How can concentrating on your growth improve your self-care?

"I will focus on growing, learning, and challenging my self-limiting beliefs that keep me from enjoying my efforts."

How Grateful Are You? Take This Attitude of Gratitude Quiz

Theory

Having an attitude of gratitude goes hand in hand with a life of positivity. Gratitude is when you focus on what you have rather than what you don't. Ideally, a focus on gratitude should be with us every day, and many times a day. Grateful people are happier people—they tend to be optimistic, forgiving, and resilient, and they do not take the little things in life for granted. As a result, such people are more likely to bounce back from adversity.

A sense of well-being and gratitude are very much intertwined. If you are positive, forgiving, and accepting, you will feel better about yourself and your life. You can train yourself to be more grateful by challenging negative thoughts and focusing not on what has gone wrong in your life but on what has gone right. Life is not always fair; it is up to us to choose to get better instead of bitter. Your attitude can be the one thing that gets in the way between you and a positive life. Choosing a positive attitude every day is a choice, so strive every day to choose gratitude!

The short quiz that follows will help you keep in mind some hallmarks of a grateful mind and prompt more positivity in your attitude. It can also help you identify areas that work well for you on your gratitude journey and those that need work.

Implementing Skills

Our ability to be grateful is at the core of our ability to think positively and optimistically. Many of us focus on what we are grateful for once a year on Thanksgiving. How about making every day a day of thanks with an attitude of gratitude?

Attitude of Gratitude Quiz

Using a scale from 1 to 10, with 1 being "not true" and 10 being "very true," rate how true these statements are for you.

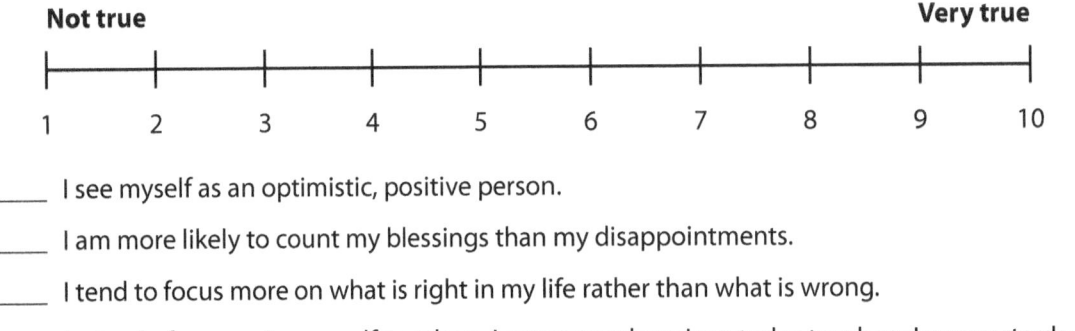

____ I see myself as an optimistic, positive person.

____ I am more likely to count my blessings than my disappointments.

____ I tend to focus more on what is right in my life rather than what is wrong.

____ Instead of comparing myself to others, I compare where I am today to where I was yesterday.

____ I generally forgive people in my life and do not hold grudges.

____ I can forgive myself for my regrets of choices and behavior in the past.

____ I generally think that I am fortunate or lucky in life.

____ I am thankful for aspects of my health that are working well.

____ My past challenges, traumas, and difficult times have helped me to be more grateful now.

____ I focus more on how fortunate I am in my life than how I have been unfortunate.

Total score: _____

The higher your total score, the more you are filled with gratitude. Conversely, the lower the score, the more hurt, bitterness, envy, negativity, and disappointment control your life.

- **85–100: Gratitude rock star!**—Congratulations for allowing gratitude to be an integral part of your outlook on life.
- **70–84: Gratitude master**—Gratitude has helped you live a life of optimism.
- **50–69: Attitude of gratitude needs work**—You could benefit from letting an attitude of gratitude into your life.
- **35–49: Gratitude challenged**—Your level of disappointment, hurt, and negativity has made it hard to feel grateful for what is good in your life.
- **20–34: Gratitude impaired**—It is likely that your gratitude score is affected by hurt, negativity, and pessimism. Getting help by opening up to a friend, family member, or trusted professional is advised.
- **0–10: Ungrateful**—It is hard to be positive with a negative mind. A low level of gratitude is often linked to depression. Chances are that past or present trauma in your life is making you stuck. Consider getting professional help.

Processing the Activity

Gratitude is a practice, not a destination. When you start each day with a grateful heart, light illuminates from within. Gratitude provides a roadmap to a more mindful and positive life. If there are blocks to your ability to be grateful due to your negative thoughts, past or current trauma, loss, or feelings of depression, be kind to yourself, use self-compassion, and try to shift your focus each day to be a little more grateful and positive than yesterday. Use this quiz as a guide to nudge you toward a more positive and resilient mindset.

"Gratitude has allowed me to count my blessings, not my disappointments, and has opened my eyes to the beauty of life around me."

Set a Positive Intention Each Day

Theory

Positive intentions are healthy thoughts that can help us maintain a positive mindset. Along with setting a nice tone for our day, they remind and guide us to stay motivated and optimistic. If you find yourself in a negative mindset, focusing on a positive intention might seem awkward, but it will help you shift your focus to looking at the world with a more positive and optimistic lens.

It is helpful to take a few moments each day to give yourself some time to slow down, breathe deeply, and think of a positive intention for the day. Choosing one or more positive intentions each day can support us in working on issues that we need to attend to within ourselves. You might use the same intention for many days in a row until you feel there is some mastery in that thought or choose a new one each day to support your focus on various areas of your mental health and wellness.

Implementing Skills

The following are examples of positive intentions:

- I am a wonderful, beautiful person and deserve to have a good day.
- I will be kind to myself and treat myself like I would a best friend.
- I will work on being less critical and more forgiving of myself and others.
- I will express my thoughts and feelings. I will be true to myself and not live in fear of what others might think.
- I will treat others and myself with compassion and unconditional acceptance.
- Today I will focus on being grateful for what I have in my life without bitterness for what is missing.
- I will find one person each day to thank for something or express my gratitude in some way.
- I will try to greet everyone with a smile today.
- I will improve my eye contact with others today and will not be distracted by glancing at my phone while interacting with others.
- I will stay present in talking to others instead of listening to commentary inside my mind.
- I will refrain from judgments about others or myself.
- I will prioritize my health by eating mindfully and healthily, drinking water instead of sugared drinks, and getting at least 30 minutes of physical activity most days of the week.

- I will focus on actively listening to others today instead of merely hearing.
- I will speak up with others and not hide from interaction with my non-assertiveness. I will be focused on communicating, not mind reading what others think.

Processing the Activity

Think of what positive intentions you need in your life and prioritize them and your mental health by using them each day. If you find positive intentions helpful, consider keeping a journal of them and adding a new one each day. Writing or printing various intentions on note cards or strips of paper and putting them into a box can provide you with an abundance of positive thoughts to guide you toward a consistently positive mindset.

Want to give your intentions a boost? Say them out loud in a mirror or to a trusted friend or family member. Sharing with others will increase your sense of social support as well as help you be accountable to the intentions you've set. Consider adding movement to your positive intention, keeping it in mind as you walk, practice yoga, dance, or enjoy other activities.

"My positive intentions will help me stay grounded and focused through the day."

# TIP #106 Using Quotes for Growth and Empowerment

Theory

The power of quotes cannot be overestimated. They offer us foundational truths that resonate with us and express in a pithy way what we feel in our hearts. They inspire us to be resilient and forward-looking. Just a short quote can normalize an upsetting experience, making us feel not so alone as we realize that others have also struggled with similar issues. This is why many people find comfort in quotes when they are going through personal adversity. Quotes can also be a source of inspiration that helps us actualize our potential.

Some of the most popular quotes in history are precursors for the foundation of CBT. Some are decades or even centuries old, yet they are just as relevant today as they were then. Quotes like the following help us appreciate the universality of the human condition.

- "God, grant me the serenity to accept the things I cannot change, the courage to change the things I can, and the wisdom to know the difference." –Reinhold Niebuhr (1892–1971)
- "There is nothing either good or bad, but thinking makes it so." –William Shakespeare (1564–1616)

Implementing Skills

Compiling a list of quotes that are personally relevant to you can be comforting as well as motivating. The following are 10 ways to use quotes in your daily life to help keep you comforted, grounded, motivated, and inspired.

Ten Ways to Use Quotes in Your Daily Life and Work

1. Keep your favorite quotes on note cards, your computer monitor or screensaver, or on sticky notes around the house.
2. Write one of your favorite quotes on a piece of paper, then draw something inspired by that quote and hang it up for inspiration. This is a good activity to do with children as well as adults.
3. Keep a box or jar with your favorite quotes and pick one each day to carry around with you and refer to throughout the day.
4. If you keep a personal journal, use a quote each day as a prompt to set a motivating and inspirational tone for your writing.
5. Quotes are great conversation starters. Sharing a favorite quote can increase communication and deepen a relationship.

6. If you are a therapist working with clients, offering clients a sheet of various self-help quotes and having them pick ones that relate to them can be a great starting point for conversation. This works well for both individuals and groups.
7. Quotes have a way of helping us get in touch with our emotions; even a short phrase can help crystallize meaningful and poignant thoughts. Choose a quote and reflect on how it describes (or perhaps changes) your feelings in this moment.
8. Make your own inspirational quote! Being inspired by the quotes of others can give you motivation to create your own inspirational saying based on your inner wisdom.
9. Make a picture or poster for your wall from a favorite quote, or consider having a wall of quotes to really inspire! In your home or place of work, consider having a Plexiglass quote card holder on your door, wall, or desk and change out the quote every couple of days.
10. Quotes can be great icebreakers and are a nonthreatening way to crystallize and share thoughts and feelings. In particular, quotes can be used in team-building exercises for groups, whether it be a therapy group or corporate team building. They can help leaders communicate values to others in the group or, if the group has a theme for the day, group members can work together to choose some quotes that epitomize that topic. The following is a small sample of some quote topics that can be used in this context:

Our Common Humanity

- "We make a living by what we get, but we make a life by what we give." –attributed to Winston Churchill
- "Be the change that you wish to see in the world." –attributed to Mahatma Gandhi

Healthy Thinking

- "Change your thoughts and you can change the world." –Norman Vincent Peale

Resilience

- "What doesn't kill me, makes me stronger." – Friedrich Nietzsche
- "Do not judge me by my successes; judge me by how many times I fell down and got back up again." –Nelson Mandela

Flexible Thinking, Creativity

- "We cannot solve the problems using the same kind of thinking we used when we created them." –Albert Einstein

Motivational

- "Learn from yesterday, live for today, hope for tomorrow." –attributed to Albert Einstein
- "The important thing is not to stop questioning." –Albert Einstein

Anger Management

- "Anybody can become angry—that is easy, but to be angry with the right person and to the right degree and at the right time and for the right purpose, and in the right way—that is not within everybody's power and is not easy." –Aristotle
- "Holding on to anger is like grasping a hot coal with the intent of throwing it at someone else; you are the one who gets burned." –attributed to the Buddha

Love

- "'Tis better to have loved and lost than never to have loved at all." –Alfred, Lord Tennyson

Forgiveness

- "Forgiveness is the fragrance that the violet sheds on the heel that has crushed it." –attributed to Mark Twain

Regret

- "Regret doesn't remind us that we did badly. It reminds us that we know we can do better." –Kathryn Schultz
- "We regret the things we don't do more than the things we do." –attributed to Mark Twain

Processing the Activity

Whether you use quotes in your personal life or as a mental health professional working with individuals or groups, quotes offer a richness of experience in an easy, meaningful way. Quotes have a healing power by universalizing common human experiences so we can gain comfort, inspiration, and a sense of connection to others.

"Quotes provide comfort and inspiration and resonate with me in a way that most words cannot. I will use them in my daily life to improve my attitude and my life."

Prioritize Self-Care Strategies with a Self-Care Inventory

Theory

One of the biggest obstacles to working on self-care is the message that it's a selfish act. All too often, people think that they are selfish if they set limits or say no. But self-care is not selfish—it is an act of love for others as well as yourself. After all, the better you can be to yourself, the better you can be for others. The happier you are, the happier you will be for others.

Although selflessness is often framed as a virtue, in reality selflessness works against any efforts of self-care. When we feel depleted by giving without getting what we need, we end up feeling depressed, alienated, and burned out. Not addressing mental or medical self-care can cost us our health and even our lives. Caring for and replenishing yourself is the greatest gift you can give not only to yourself but also to those around you. In this TIP we will focus on the most important areas of self-care that ensure we are healthy in mind, body, relationships, and spirit.

Implementing Skills

For each area of self-care, describe what you currently do and what goals you have.

Self-Care Inventory

Mental Health Self-Care

Learning to take care of your mental health is crucial to self-care. Implementing CBT strategies to challenge cognitive distortions and replacing unhealthy self-sabotaging thoughts with more rational, healthier ones will help you think more positively and change your attitude to change your life. One such strategy is replacing each negative thought with two positive ones.

Other steps toward mental health self-care include using mindfulness, relaxation, or movement techniques to keep your mind and body calm and asking for help when you need it to overcome mental health and emotional problems (whether through self-help books or by reaching out to a trusted professional, friend, or loved one).

What do you currently do for mental health self-care?

_____

_____

How would you like to improve your mental health self-care?

_____
_____

Physical Self-Care

Regular exercise or doing active activities you enjoy, stretching, eating nutritious food, and otherwise taking care of your body will help you enjoy a healthier and longer life. Be sure to get your recommended health screenings and check-ups, and do not ignore concerning medical or dental issues because you are too busy to address them.

What do you currently do for physical self-care?

_____
_____

How would you like to improve your physical self-care?

_____
_____

Vocational Self-Care

Whether we are engaging in a profession, raising a family, attending school, or volunteering our time, work can give us a sense of meaning and connection in our lives. Describe how you find meaning in your roles and how you balance your responsibilities with your personal needs and goals. Are there things you can do to make your responsibilities work more for you? What are some challenges in balancing it all? Since we spend so much of our lives in our roles as student, employee, employer, caregiver, volunteer, and so on, it is important to find a sense of control and purpose in your roles.

What do you currently do for vocational self-care?

_____
_____

How would you like to improve your vocational self-care?

_____
_____

Spiritual Self-Care

There are many ways to practice spiritual self-care. Organized religion, yoga, meditation, connecting with nature, contemplation, and reading devotions are just some examples. Committing yourself to a short practice or ritual every day to connect to your sense of higher power and life's meaning is very healing.

Seeing yourself as belonging to something larger than yourself, such as a religion, spiritual practice, group, or cause, is part of what psychologist Kelly McGonigal calls *bigger-than-self goals*. Connect with a deep inner sense of purpose that is bigger than yourself. How have you begun to lay a foundation for a better sense of purpose? How have you been nourishing yourself spiritually? Does your spiritual self-care bring you together with others who share the same values and interests?

What do you currently do for spiritual self-care?

_____
_____

How would you like to improve your spiritual self-care?

_____
_____

Social Self-Care

Self-care does not mean living in isolation—rather, it includes connecting with others and letting them into your life. Having a strong sense of social support is an important ingredient in life satisfaction and resilience. Conversely, isolation and loneliness are linked to depression and unhappiness. What is the quality of your support system? What changes (if any) would you like to make? What needs to be improved in your relationships with those close to you? Do you have people you can confide in?

What do you currently do for social self-care?

_____
_____

How would you like to improve your social self-care?

_____
_____

Creative/Interests Self-Care

Allow yourself to tap into your creative side without worrying about not having enough talent. Find a creative outlet you enjoy, such as listening to music, playing an instrument, singing, dancing, making art, crafting, writing, or reading. Hobbies and creative outlets allow self-expression and can help us become mindful in ways that very few other things do. These outlets often have the bonus of bringing you together with others who share the same passion. Taking classes and joining interest groups like a book club or an art appreciation group are just a few ways to enjoy hobbies and stretch your mind and creativity.

What do you currently do for creative/interests self-care?

_____
_____

How would you like to improve your creative/interests self-care?

_____
_____

Financial Self-Care

Do you have your finances under control? Do you have too much debt? Paying attention to your finances and keeping your expenses within your means is an act of self-care that lowers stress. If you find that you are constantly stressed over finances, do you have any solutions to get things under control? Live within your means, set financial goals you can reach, seek the help of a financial professional if you need—these are just some examples of maintaining your financial health.

What do you currently do for financial self-care?

_____
_____

How would you like to improve your financial self-care?

_____
_____

Self-Care Habits

Whether it is decluttering your living environment to make it peaceful and calming or practicing meditation, do you commit yourself to daily self-care habits? Such habits could include simple pleasures like walking outside, taking a bath, reaching out to at least one person you care about every day, or giving yourself even 5 to 10 minutes a day for self-reflection, gratitude affirmations, or meditative practice. Whatever habits you choose, carving out some time for regular practice will help you on your self-care journey.

What do you currently do for self-care habits?

_____

_____

How would you like to improve your self-care habits?

_____

_____

Processing the Activity

Looking at the areas of self-care you've just explored, what is your overall impression of your self-care? What areas do you pay a lot of attention to? What areas would you like to focus more of your energies on? Did you get some new ideas in taking this inventory? Recognize that to be the best for others, you need to be the best for yourself. Self-care is not a selfish act—it is an act of self-love that will help you value yourself and love your life.

"I will take more time to focus on my self-care so I can be the best version of me for myself and others."

Practical Goal-Setting Strategies

Theory

An important concept in CBT is *behavioral activation*. It is possible to boost your mood and encourage healthier thoughts by practicing behaviors that are healthy for you. For example, if you have realized that walking every day for a half hour is good for your mental health, you do not need to "feel like it" each day in order to get it done. You can do it because you have accepted that walking daily for 30 minutes is a good goal for your mental and physical health. By deciding in advance what activities are good for you, chances are when you accomplish them, you will feel good about what you did. Actively and consistently pursuing the goals that you have determined are good for you can spur pleasant moods that generate more positive thoughts.

In this TIP we will focus on how to make behavioral activation strategies effective. If your goals are too vague or lofty, such as "exercise a couple of hours every day," they will be harder to stick to and therefore are more likely to set you up for failure and stress. Making goals manageable means being realistic about what will work for you.

Implementing Skills

Set SMART Goals

To make your behavioral goals attainable and manageable, set goals that are SMART:

- **Specific:** I will commit myself to walking 45 minutes a day for at least four days in the week. I will change routes often so I will not get bored.
- **Measurable:** I plan to walk 5,000 steps a day, four days per week.
- **Attainable:** I have time to commit to this plan. I will set my alarm an hour earlier and walk before work. In inclement weather, I can use the treadmill at my community exercise room.
- **Relevant:** This goal is relevant to me since I want to spend more time getting fit.
- **Time-Bound:** I will follow this plan for a month; at the end of that span, I will reevaluate to decide whether I will continue with this plan or modify it.

Make Mini-Habits

In his book *Mini-Habits* (2013), author Stephen Guise offers a no-fail solution to help us get motivated to make minor and major life changes: developing habits that are too small to fail. Guise suggests making your goals "stupid small" so you are bound to succeed in changing the behaviors. He uses the example of how, in his quest to jump-start a personal fitness program, he gave himself a "one push-up challenge." No matter how unmotivated he was, he managed to get in one push-up a day, and any push-ups after that he called the "bonus round." Starting small with mini-habits ends with reaping big gains in the form of lasting change. In his case, he ended up getting into shape with a regular exercise routine jump-started by his mini-goal.

Use Goals as a Tool, Not a Destination

Too often we put conditions on our happiness: "I'll be happier when I lose 10 pounds/find that special someone/get a different job." All too often we expect reaching our goals will make us happier, only to feel let down when we reach them. For example, people who achieve their target weight goal can be discouraged to find that it was not the key to happiness. Conditions for happiness will only put your happiness on hold and prevent you from making small steps toward a bigger self-care goal. Rather than just focusing on the desired results, use your goals as tools to help you move forward, but look for happiness along the way and focus on enjoying the process of getting there.

Break a Large Task into Smaller Tasks

If you have a big project, break it into small tasks. Let's say your closets are a mess—instead of thinking that all the closets need to be cleaned at once, you might take one shelf of one closet each day or devote 20 minutes each day to organizing the closets. Commit yourself to these small increments to make dents in the overall task. You might find after "breaking the ice" that you get so involved you don't want to stop!

Have Bigger-Than-Self Goals

As previously mentioned in other TIPs, in *The Upside of Stress*, Kelly McGonigal uses the idea of having bigger-than-self goals as a factor in the stress-resilient personality. These are goals outside of yourself that serve a greater purpose you find meaningful. Examples include volunteering, caretaking, parenting, pursuing your chosen vocation, working for a cause, and helping others in various forms. In short, set a goal that is focused on making the world a better place. It will make you feel more connected and proud of your contribution to something you are passionate about!

Processing the Activity

Goal setting is an important factor in personal growth. In this TIP we focused on some types of goal setting that will be motivating and ensure a sense of mastery and success. Remember, though, that the goal itself will not make you happier. What will make you happier is immersing yourself in the effort and enjoying the path toward progress. If you find goals that are relevant and offer meaning to you, you will not only enjoy the journey more, but your actions will also be a catalyst for commitment and growth.

"I will set goals for myself that are manageable, motivating, and SMART so that I can make changes in my life that are important to me."

Review, Reflect, and Renew

Theory

This final TIP in this book before the chapter self-test is a good place to have you review what you learned in this book, reflect on what was most meaningful, and renew your commitment to using tried-and-true strategies to keep on working on your mental health and wellness.

To fully master the concepts in this book, the various CBT tools and techniques need to be revisited time and time again. Handouts, worksheets, quizzes and self-tests are not meant to be a one-and-done phenomenon. Just knowing something or trying a technique once or twice will not be more than an introduction to a new way of living. Rather, CBT is centered upon the notion that tools need to be used over and over to unlearn old habits, replace them with healthier ones, and reinforce new skills. Just as with learning to play a musical instrument or getting into an exercise routine, repetition holds the key to success.

Implementing Skills

What have you learned in this book that has been the most valuable?

_____

_____

What exercises have been the most challenging?

_____

_____

What TIPs or chapters in this book have been the most meaningful for you?

_____

_____

How can you continue to practice, practice, and practice the concepts in the book?

_____

_____

What practices have you learned that you would like to incorporate in your life moving forward?

_____

_____

What did you learn about yourself from the self-tests?
_____
_____

How do you plan to use the self-tests in the future?
_____
_____

Are there reflections, thoughts, or goals you want to keep in mind?
_____
_____

How can what you learned in this book lead to a sense of motivation and renewal for you moving forward?
_____
_____

Are there other reactions or points you want to remember from working through this book?
_____
_____

Processing the Activity

Periodically review and reflect on the sections in the book that felt most relevant for you and take stock of your growth. Use the self-tests at the end of each chapter to monitor your mastery in that area and compare with the other areas. Renew your commitment to improving yourself, loving yourself, and using CBT tools to make your life meaningful, grounded, and purposeful.

"I will keep working on developing my skills and use the tools that I find most helpful to keep moving forward with practice, practice, and more practice."

TIP #110: Self-Test for a Happier You

Theory

This final self-test will focus on your wellness habits and your ability to move forward in your life with confidence, gratitude, self-love, self-care, and a sense of well-being and happiness. It will crystallize the major points in this chapter. Revisit areas that need more attention as you use CBT skills to improve all areas of your life.

Implementing Skills

In the self-test that follows, rate how true each statement is for you, from 1 to 10, to assess which areas you are doing well in and which areas need some improvement. The higher the score in each item, the higher your mastery in that area. The test is not designed to give you a one-and-done score. Your self-help journey is a continual one, and the important thing is to work to keep improving on yesterday. Making several copies of this self-test will allow you to keep retaking it to monitor your progress.

At the end of this self-test you will be prompted to calculate a total score and an average score. To get the average score, divide your total score by the number of items you responded to. For any items that are not applicable to you, just write "N/A" and subtract those items from the number you divide by when calculating your average score. As you continue taking the self-tests throughout this book, compare your average scores across the different topics. This will give you a snapshot of which areas need the most attention and which areas are the strongest.

Keep this sheet handy whenever you want some support and reminders on what tools you can use to work on the areas covered in this chapter.

Self-Test for a Happier You

Using a scale from 1 to 10, with 1 being "not true" and 10 being "very true," rate how true these statements are for you.

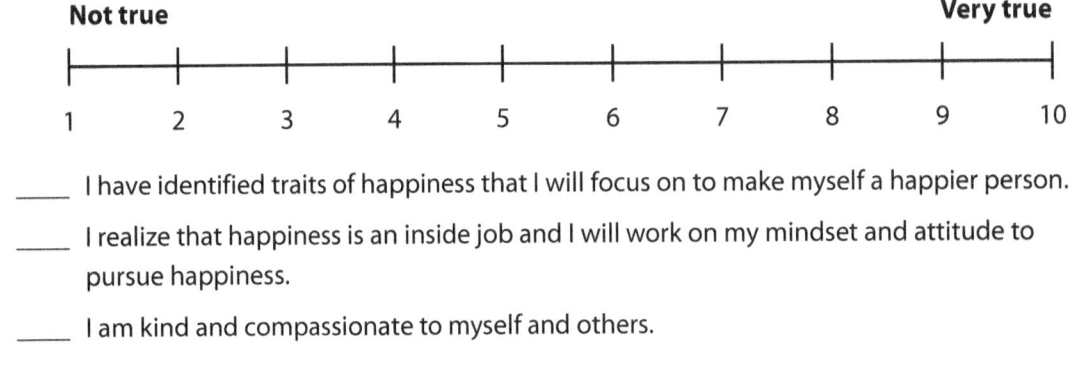

____ I have identified traits of happiness that I will focus on to make myself a happier person.

____ I realize that happiness is an inside job and I will work on my mindset and attitude to pursue happiness.

____ I am kind and compassionate to myself and others.

____ I forgive myself and others and refuse to hold on to grudges and regrets to the point where I am stuck in past hurts.

____ I will use metaphorical objects and visualizations to help me remember key concepts of wellness.

____ I have a growth mindset instead of a fixed mindset.

____ I tend to be grateful for what I have rather than feel bitterness for what I don't.

____ I have positive intentions daily that keep me motivated and optimistic.

____ I find inspirational quotes comforting and motivating and use them often to inspire me.

____ My self-care is a priority, as I know I cannot be there for others unless I am first there for myself.

____ I set behavioral goals for myself that are SMART and am able to break large goals into smaller, manageable steps.

____ I commit myself to practicing the skills I have learned, and I review and reflect on what has been most meaningful to me and what has helped me grow.

Total score: _____

Average score (*total score ÷ 12 or items answered*): _____

In the space below, process and explain your answers.

_____
_____
_____
_____
_____

If you would like further structure to process your answers to the self-test and your reactions to the chapter, here are some prompts to guide you.

My thoughts: _____
_____

My feelings: _____
_____

My self-talk: _____
_____

What I have learned: _____
_____

Additional thoughts and strategies: _____
_____
_____
_____

Processing the Activity

The purpose of this self-test is not to have a fixed score, as each time you take it the score will reflect where you are on that day. Rather, it is meant to be used as a tool to identify areas to improve on and compare with other areas of self-improvement and emotional wellness and monitor your progress over time. The higher your scores, the higher your emotional wellness IQ.

I wish you the best on your wellness journey and in incorporating CBT techniques to improve your life and the lives of those around you!

> "I will commit myself to keep growing and learning to improve
> my life and be the best version of me that I can be."

CONCLUDING REMARKS

I hope this book has helped you learn how CBT techniques can positively impact and enrich your life. Your success in mastering CBT skills depends on continued practice. The various TIPs in this book offer an array of skill-building exercises to incorporate in your life, but they need repetition to be successful. If you are a clinician or a client focusing on CBT skills, remember that much of the therapy takes place between sessions. By copying the worksheets and self-tests to fill in periodically, and keeping a log or journal of your activity, CBT skills will become a natural part of your life. If you found particular TIPs helpful, continue to revisit them periodically to reinforce your learning. Use the self-tests at the end of each chapter to track your progress and compare your average scores in each chapter to see what areas need more work.

CBT's psychoeducational focus has helped millions worldwide with its practical approach to common mental health issues. Replacing unhealthy self-talk with healthier ways of thinking shifts your mindset from negative to positive. Only with a positive mindset can we love ourselves, love others, and love our lives. CBT helps you live mindfully in the present, without rehashing and reliving moments from the past that cannot be changed or being anxious about the what-ifs of tomorrow. CBT skills help us focus on the wonders of today, changes problems into possibilities, and supports our mental health journey with a wide array of tools. In short, changing your thoughts can truly change your life.

Thank you for letting me guide you on your CBT journey.

Judith Belmont

REFERENCES

Achor, S. (2010). *The happiness advantage: The seven principles of positive psychology that fuel success and performance at work.* Crown Business.

Biegel, G. M., & Cooper, S. (2019). *The mindfulness workbook for teen self-harm: Skills to help you overcome cutting and self-harming behaviors, thoughts, and feelings.* New Harbinger.

Burns, D. D. (1999). *Feeling good: The new mood therapy.* Quill.

Burns, D. D. (1999). *The feeling good handbook* (Rev. ed.). Plume.

Burns, D. D. (2020). *Feeling great: The revolutionary new treatment for depression and anxiety.* PESI Publishing & Media.

Duckworth, A. (2016). *Grit: The power of passion and perseverance.* Scribner.

Dweck, C. S. (2007). *Mindset: The new psychology of success.* Ballantine Books.

Goldstein, E. (2015). *Uncovering happiness: Overcoming depression with mindfulness and self-compassion.* Atria.

Guise, S. (2013). *Mini-habits: Smaller habits, bigger results.* Author.

Harris, T. A. (1967). *I'm OK—you're OK: A practical guide to transactional analysis.* Avon Books.

Hayes, S. C., & Smith, S. (2005). *Get out of your mind and into your life: The new acceptance and commitment therapy.* New Harbinger.

McGonigal, K. (2015). *The upside of stress: Why stress is good for you, and how to get good at it.* Avery.

Neff, K. (2015). *Self-compassion: The proven power of being kind to yourself.* William Morrow.

ABOUT THE AUTHOR

Judith A. Belmont, MS, is the author of 11 mental health books and two therapeutic card decks focusing on providing counseling professionals, therapy clients, and self-help readers practical tips and tools for mental health and wellness. *110 TIPS and Tools for the CBT Toolbox* is the fifth book in her therapeutic TIPS series published by PESI, which also includes *150 More Group Therapy Activities and TIPS* and *86 TIPS for the Therapeutic Toolbox.*

Retired from a private therapy practice after 40 years, she now offers mental health coaching online. She has decades of experience as a motivational speaker and trainer at organizations and conferences, offering keynotes and interactive presentations on wellness topics such as communication skills, stress management, creating a positive workplace, and burnout prevention. She provides monthly webinars on workplace communication and dealing with difficult employees.

She holds an MS in clinical psychology from Hahnemann Medical College in Philadelphia and a BS in psychology from the University of Pennsylvania. She currently lives in Naples, FL, and South Jersey. Visit her at www.belmontwellness.com.